COLOR GRADING WITH MEDIA COMPOSER® AND SYMPHONY™ 6

Bryan Castle Jr.

Course Technology PTR
A part of Cengage Learning

COURSE TECHNOLOGY
CENGAGE Learning®

Australia, Brazil, Japan, Korea, Mexico, Singapore, Spain, United Kingdom, United States

COURSE TECHNOLOGY
CENGAGE Learning®

**Color Grading with Media Composer®
and Symphony™ 6**
Bryan Castle Jr.

**Publisher and General Manager,
Course Technology PTR:**
Stacy L. Hiquet

Associate Director of Marketing:
Sarah Panella

Manager of Editorial Services:
Heather Talbot

Senior Marketing Manager:
Mark Hughes

Acquisitions Editor:
Dan Gasparino

Project Editor:
Kate Shoup

Technical Reviewer:
Greg Staten

Copy Editor:
Kate Shoup

Interior Layout:
Shawn Morningstar

Cover Designer:
Mike Tanamachi

Indexer:
Valerie Perry

Proofreader:
Mike Beady

For product information and technology assistance, contact us at
Cengage Learning Customer & Sales Support, 1-800-354-9706

For permission to use material from this text or product,
submit all requests online at **cengage.com/permissions**
Further permissions questions can be emailed to
permissionrequest@cengage.com

Media Composer is a registered trademark of Avid Technology, Inc.
Symphony is a trademark of Avid Technology, Inc.
All other trademarks are the property of their respective owners.

All images © Avid Technology, Inc. unless otherwise noted.

Library of Congress Control Number: 2012945770

ISBN-13: 978-1-285-18141-7

ISBN-10: 1-285-18141-7

Course Technology, a part of Cengage Learning
20 Channel Center Street
Boston, MA 02210
USA

Cengage Learning is a leading provider of customized learning solutions with office locations around the globe, including Singapore, the United Kingdom, Australia, Mexico, Brazil, and Japan. Locate your local office at:
international.cengage.com/region

Cengage Learning products are represented in Canada by Nelson Education, Ltd.

For your lifelong learning solutions, visit **courseptr.com**.

Visit our corporate website at **cengage.com**.

This book includes material that was developed in part by the Avid Technical Publications department and the Avid Training department.

Printed in the
United States of America
1 2 3 4 5 6 7 14 13 12

Para Yulmarys, mi joya, el amor de mi vida.

Acknowledgments

Film may be the most collaborative of the arts, but publishing a book is not far behind.

From Cengage Learning, I would like to thank the publisher, Stacy Hiquet, for seeing this project through to the end. I know there were moments when we weren't sure if we'd see this day. Thanks especially to my project editor, Kate Shoup. Her work brought out the clarity of thought that was always intended, if not always written.

From Avid, I'd like to recognize the Media Composer and Symphony product managers, David Colantuoni, Doug Hansel, and Matt Fitzgerald. They were always willing to clarify the design and function of these products, taking time to answer my questions, however obscure they may have seemed. I also owe a debt of gratitude to Mary Torgersen, Sr. Manager of Curriculum and Certification, for providing me the opportunity to write an external publication. Her ongoing guidance and support is deeply appreciated.

Special thanks as well go to my collaborators, Greg Staten and Patrick Inhofer. Years ago, Greg set the foundation for this course in Avid's original curriculum, and was instrumental once again in refining it. It was a pleasure to have him participate in this project. Patrick's expertise as a full-time colorist, coupled with his own experience in teaching the color grading on various platforms, made a notable impact on this work. His contributions go well beyond his individual articles.

And finally, a personal thanks. Throughout the process of authoring this book, my wife has been an endless source of patience and support.

About the Author

Bryan Castle Jr. has worked in the post-production industry for more than 10 years as a producer, editor, trainer, and author.

Bryan started in the industry like many, working to turn his hobby and passion into a career. What started as a volunteer position at his church grew into regular production and broadcast work with the local cable station, then eventually a degree in production and broadcasting from the New England Institute of Art and Communications.

Bryan began his career freelancing as a producer and editor in the greater-Boston area in 2001. He was lured into the corporate world in 2005 to work as an instructor for Apple, then shortly thereafter joined Avid. At Avid, Bryan further developed his expertise in both broadcast and post-production workflows, providing on-site training to top broadcasters and post facilities in the U.S. and Latin America. Since 2009, Bryan has been the principal subject matter expert and author of Avid's Media Composer and Symphony training materials. Currently, Bryan works as manager of the worldwide Avid Certified Instructor program.

About the Special Contributor

Patrick Inhofer is a professional colorist working on broadcast and cable television series, independent films, documentaries, commercials, and corporate communications. He's a 23-year veteran of the New York City post-production community. Patrick takes his experience working at high-end full-service post houses and delivers those same services to low- and mid-budget productions, bringing them high-quality workflows at competitive prices.

Patrick's first experience working on Avid Media Composer was as assistant editor on HBO's *The Babysitters' Club* in 1991. His first freelance color-grading gig in 2001 was a food documentary using Avid Media Composer's Levels filter (a practice he does not recommend). Patrick founded his post-production boutique in 2002 and is currently the owner/colorist at Fini.tv, Inc. He began teaching color correction on Final Cut Pro in 2005, and in 2010 founded the software-agnostic color grading website, TaoOfColorGrading.com. He recently published the 100th edition of his free weekly email newsletter, "The Tao Colorist," which focuses on the art, craft, and business of professional color grading. Patrick is also an adjunct professor at Hofstra University, teaching digital color correction for television. Find out more at www.Fini.tv, www.TaoOfColor.com, and www.twitter.com/patinhofer.

Contents

Lesson 2
Analyzing Images with Scopes   27

Exercise 2
Analyzing Images with Scopes   61

Lesson 3
Establishing the Base Grade   65

Exercise 3
Performing Primary HSL Corrections   97

Lesson 4
Grading with Curves 99

Exercise 4
Performing Primary Grades with Curves 135

Lesson 5
Matching Shots 137

Lesson 9
Finishing the Grade   277

Exercise 9
Creating Stylized Looks   313

Appendix A
Answers to Review/Discussion Questions   317

Index   325

Introduction

Welcome to *Color Grading with Media Composer and Symphony 6*. Whether you are using this book as self-study material or taking the official course through an Avid Learning Partner, this book will teach you the skills you need to successfully perform color correction and grading on Avid editing systems.

Color grading plays an exciting and unique role in the filmmaking process. It is both highly technical and highly artistic. A well-trained colorist has tremendous control over the final look of the piece. The colorist can bring dead images to life, creating light and depth where there was none. Colorists evoke moods to reinforce the story and minimize distractions, directing the eye of the viewer to what is most important in a scene. A good one is worth his or her weight in gold.

With the availability of relatively low-cost tools, the work of color grading more than ever is being done by more than just colorists. While the high-end work will always be done by specialists, color-grading proficiency is a core skill that every post professional should have. Regardless of where you fall on the spectrum—from aspiring filmmaker, to jack-of-all-trades independent editor, to full-time colorist looking to transition to Avid—this book is for you. The lessons contained herein will give you the skills needed to perform everything from simple color corrections to creating a polished, multi-layer finished grade. Whether working on scripted dramas, documentaries, music videos, or commercial spots, you will learn the skills you need to succeed.

What You'll Find in This Book

This book is principally designed as an operational training manual. It is highly practical, rather than theoretical, in its focus. It is designed to teach you the process of color grading on Avid editing systems.

Each lesson in the book will explore a group of tools designed to accomplish a specific purpose. As you learn the tools, you will also learn fundamental concepts of color grading, specific techniques for using each tool, and how the tools fit together into an efficient, professional workflow.

In addition, each lesson contains at least one article titled "Notes from the Colorist," written by full-time colorist, Patrick Inhofer. In these articles, Patrick shares expert advice and practical tips on color theory, additional grading techniques, the role of a colorist in the post process, and more. Most lessons also include a number of sidebar notes to expound on certain points in the lesson.

Many of the sidebar notes were also written by Patrick, and are "signed" with his initials, "pi." Sidebars without his initials were written by the author.

Who This Book Is For

This book is designed for intermediate to advanced editors who are involved in the finishing stage of the post-production process. The lessons contained herein assume that the reader has the knowledge and skills taught in the companion books of the Avid Learning Series. For more information on the other titles in the Avid Learning Series, as well as Avid Certification, see the upcoming section, "Becoming Avid Certified."

How This Book Is Organized

This book is organized to enable you to effectively learn the color-grading tools of Media Composer and/or Avid Symphony. The real value of editing on Avid Symphony is for online editing and color grading. As such, it has added tools and features specific to color grading. Media Composer's toolset, while robust, is limited by comparison.

If you are working on Avid Symphony, you may proceed through the book start-to-finish. All lessons apply to the Symphony toolset.

The following lessons can be completed with Media Composer:

- Lessons 1–5
- Lessons 8–9

Note: If you are not working on Avid Symphony but would like to complete all lessons in the book, you can do so using the free, fully functional 30-day trial of Avid Symphony. For more information, visit http://www.avid.com/products/symphony.

About the Film: *Agent MX-Zero*

All the footage in this course is from a short film, *Agent MX-Zero*. The short film was written and produced by Avid Marketing. In 2010, Tom Graham of Avid marketing had the idea to work with a young, hip filmmaker to write and create "Avid's own" short film. Although unconventional, the project offered some great benefits.

As Tom put it, there were five key advantages:

■ We always need demo material to show the complex workflows between picture and sound, and it's difficult to get all of the raw files and clearances from studios (and any actors involved) to use them for any extended period.

■ The same material could be used by the Avid training department to help people learn how to edit picture and sound.

■ Avid products touch all layers of film post-production, and the workflow between them is extremely important when your money and your movie is on the line. This project was a great way to showcase how Media Composer, Pro Tools, Avid DS, ICON, C|24, and many other Avid products work together to deliver the best movie possible.

■ Owning the production gave us the chance to shoot behind-the-scenes material to help demystify the deeper production and post-production things that go into making a movie, such as Foley, field recording workflows, and more…the things you normally don't see in a "making of" piece.

■ There's no better way to relate to our customers and what they go through when making a movie than to do it ourselves!

And so, with concept approval from the marketing executives, a 12-page script, and a production plan, Tom and director Brian Thomas Barnhart set out to make something fun—not a comedy, but nothing too serious either, and not too over-the-top campy. "We wanted to make more of a tribute to the somewhat silly spy movie genre we grew up with, with 1970s retro modern look and feel," Tom recalls. "It was an incredibly fun learning experience, from script writing, to planning, to locations and permits, auditions, production, and of course, post production."

Get more insight on the process behind the project from the Avid blog, Inside Out. Read in-depth articles about the making of the film, the equipment and workflows used throughout the project, and more. To read the blog, go to http://community.avid.com/blogs/avid/archive/tags/Thomas+Graham/default.aspx.

You can see the full movie presented on YouTube, here: http://www.youtube.com/watch?v=LXzWMjNlhzI.

Companion Website Downloads

You may download the companion website files from www.courseptr.com/downloads. Please note that you will be redirected to the Cengage Learning site. There are four zip files to download for this course:

■ ACG_Projects: Contains the project files only

■ ACG_m1: Contains the media files for Lessons 1–3

■ ACG_m2: Contains the media files for Lessons 4–5

■ ACG_m3: Contains the media files for Lessons 6–9

Installation Instructions

Please follow these installation instructions exactly or you may not have access to all the project files and media associated with this course.

1. Make sure Media Composer 6.x or Symphony 6.x is installed and that you have opened the application at least once. Opening the application creates important folders that you will use during this installation.

2. Download the zip files from the aforementioned website to your desktop. As mentioned, there are four zip files to download.

3. Unzip the contents of the downloads.

4. Drag the project folder to your desktop.

5. The Avid MediaFiles folder in the folder ACG_M1 should be copied to the top level of your hard drive. If you've already used Media Composer on this system, it is possible that you have existing media folders, which you should not delete.

6. Navigate to the root level of the hard drive where you want to store the media files. This may be your internal drive, in which case navigate to C DRIVE:\ (Windows) or MACINTOSH HD (Mac). If you have a locally attached external hard drive you want to use, navigate to the root level of the external hard drive.

Note: The root level of a hard drive is also called the top level. It is the highest level in the hierarchy of folders on your computer.

7. Make sure at the top level of your hard drive that there is no existing Avid MediaFiles folder. If there is no existing Avid MediaFiles folder, drag the entire AVID MEDIAFILES folder from the desktop folder onto the top level of your hard drive. If an Avid MediaFiles folder does exist on the top level of your hard drive, double-click it to reveal the MXF folder.

8. In the desktop folder, ACG_M1, double-click the AVID MEDIAFILES folder and then double-click the MXF folder.

9. Inside the desktop MXF folder is a numbered folder, 2391. Drag the numbered folder from the desktop folder into the MXF folder on your hard drive.

10. Repeat the process for each of the other zip files, ACG_M2 and ACG_M3.

Caution: Do not rename the folder named Avid MediaFiles, nor any of its subfolders, located on the media drive. Media Composer uses the folder names to locate the media files.

System Requirements

This book assumes that you have a system configuration suitable to run Media Composer 6 or Avid Symphony 6. (This book is compatible with version 6.5 of both applications.) To verify the most recent system requirements, refer to the Avid website.

- For Media Composer, visit www.avid.com/products/media-composer and click the Tech Specs tab.

- For Symphony, visit www.avid.com/products/symphony and click the Tech Specs tab.

Becoming Avid Certified

Avid certification is a tangible, industry-recognized credential that can help you advance your career and provide measurable benefits to your employer. When you're Avid certified, you not only help to accelerate and validate your professional development, but you can also improve your productivity and project success. Avid offers programs supporting certification in dedicated focus areas including Media Composer, Sibelius, Pro Tools, Worksurface Operation, and Live Sound. To become certified in Media Composer, you must enroll in a program at an Avid Learning Partner, where you can complete additional Media Composer course-work if needed and take your certification exam. To locate an Avid Learning Partner, visit www.avid.com/training.

Note: Symphony and Media Composer have identical features and functions for all aspects of editing except color grading and tape-based mastering. The books and courses described in the next section that lead to Media Composer certification can be used to learn Avid Symphony.

Media Composer Certification

Avid offers two levels of Media Composer certification:

- Avid Media Composer User Certification
- Avid Media Composer Professional Certification

User Certification

The Avid Media Composer Certified User Exam is the first of two certification exams that allow you to become Avid certified. The two combined certifications offer an established and recognized goal for both academic users and industry professionals. The Avid Media Composer User certification requires that you display a firm grasp of the core skills, workflows, and concepts of non-linear editing on the Media Composer system.

Courses/books associated with User certification include the following:

- *Media Composer 6: Part 1–Editing Essentials* (MC101)
- *Media Composer 6: Part 2–Effects Essentials* (MC110)

These User courses can be complemented with *Color Grading with Media Composer and Symphony 6.*

Professional Certification

The Avid Media Composer Professional Certification prepares editors to competently operate a Media Composer system in a professional production environment. Professional certification requires a more advanced understanding of Media Composer, including advanced tools and workflows involved in creating professional programs.

Courses/books associated with Professional certification include the following:

- *Media Composer 6: Professional Picture and Sound Editing* (MC201)
- *Media Composer 6: Professional Effects and Compositing* (MC205)

These Professional courses can be complemented with *Color Grading with Media Composer and Symphony 6.*

For more information about Avid's certification program, please visit www.avid.com/support/training/certification.

Color-Grading Fundamentals

In this lesson, we'll begin our exploration of color grading by talking about some core fundamentals that are required for color grading using any equipment, not just that within the Avid editing system. We'll also introduce Color Correction mode for both Media Composer and Symphony.

Media Used: Avid Color Grading (MC239) project > 1_Lesson Bins folder > 1_Color Grading Overview bin > 1_Intro to Color Correction sequence

Duration: 45 minutes

GOALS

- Identify the different types of displays available for grading and what constitutes a proper display for grading
- Define the characteristics of a proper environment in which to perform color grading
- Describe the core color-grading workflow
- Explore Color Correction mode in Media Composer and Symphony

Introduction

The purpose of this book is two-fold. It will teach you the color grading tools in Avid Media Composer and Avid Symphony, and in the process, teach you the skills to use those tools effectively.

As the company slogan says, Avid systems are used to create the most watched, most listened to, and most loved media in the world. Media Composer and Symphony alike are used to edit and finish many of the films and TV shows you probably have watched yourself. Learning to use this world-class set of tools may be easier than you think. You just need to invest the time. Like all skills, you'll need to build them through repetition and persistence.

This book is predominantly operational in its focus. There is a tremendous depth of theory behind the techniques taught herein. The more you learn the technicalities of signal processing, color science, and psychology of color association, the better a colorist you can become.

What Is Color Grading?

Color grading is the process of manipulating the color, brightness, and contrast of all, or part, of a video image for corrective or creative purposes. The process is also called "color correction"; "color timing," a term that originally referred to the process applied to celluloid film; or "shading an image," a term borrowed from the process of calibrating live TV cameras.

We will use the term "color grading" throughout this book. Color correction is a very specific part of the overall color grading workflow and refers specifically to the task of fixing a problem in the image. Color grading is a more inclusive term that refers also to the creative work that colorists do.

Are You (Only) the Colorist?

The post-production industry today is more democratic in the division of labor than ever before. In some major markets, you'll find very distinct roles performed by different persons—the offline editor, the sound designer, the sound mixer, the online editor, the colorist, etc. In many other areas, one or two people perform all those tasks.

Colorists are highly specialized professionals in the post-production industry, dedicated to the task of color grading. Some colorists work exclusively as such. It is very common for an online editor to perform the duties of a colorist as part of his or her broader responsibilities. If you find that you are especially adept at seeing color, and enjoy both the technical and creative challenges of grading, you may wish to specialize your skills to become a colorist yourself. This book will do much to help you toward that goal.

The work of color grading, however, is not reserved exclusively to the online edit. Many small post houses or corporate media departments have a small staff that must do it all. Even in a larger production with clearly defined offline and online roles, it is valuable for the assistants and offline editor to know the basics of color correction. Previsualization is an important part of the offline edit process, and this can include approximating the look of a scene with basic corrections.

This brings up another important point. Professional color grading is about realizing the filmmaker's (or client's) vision. As a colorist, you'll spend your days grading other people's work. Some filmmakers will welcome your ideas as the colorist, others will have very strong ideas of their own. The opinion of the client or director is always the most important one. The same collaborative nature of filmmaking in general applies to the color suite as well.

Before You Grade

Color grading is a very precise mix of art and science. And where you grade has as much effect on the image as how you grade. A camera's "eye" sees colors however it's configured. Your "eye" sees colors based on a lifetime of experience. Your eyes also automatically correct for environmental lighting, such as incandescent lighting, and show us what our brain perceives to be balanced colors.

This is why, for example, a sheet of white paper appears to be white to our eyes in incandescent lighting even though it is actually quite yellow in that light. This automatic white balancing by your brain equally distorts your perception of colors on the screen, making color grading quite difficult! If you can't trust your eyes, how can you properly color grade a shot, let alone an entire scene?

To properly grade video or film material, the room (suite) in which you are grading must be conducive to proper color recognition. Optimally, this means your grading suite should have the following:

- A properly calibrated viewing monitor
- Lighting of the correct color temperature
- A neutral gray wall behind the monitor
- An external waveform/vectorscope

Let's discuss each one of these elements.

Properly Calibrated Viewing Monitor

The viewing monitor is the single most important tool in a grading suite, just as good audio monitors are the single most important tool in an audio mixing room.

Color grading is a visual art and science requiring you to make assessments about color, tone, brightness, contrast, and so on based on what you are seeing. Therefore, the most important tool in your suite is your monitor. Everything you see—and therefore everything you assess and correct—is displayed on this monitor. If the monitor is not properly calibrated or is of the wrong type to use for grading, everything you see will be an inaccurate representation of the shots you are trying to grade.

For example, if the monitor has a pinkish cast to it, that cast will affect what you see and your grade will be incorrect when viewed on anything but that monitor. Indeed, if you were to correct out the pink inherent in the monitor, everything you correct would end up looking much greener on any other display simply because of the monitor.

Historically, a viewing monitor in a grading suite was a professional broadcast cathode ray tube (CRT)–based monitor such as those in the Sony BVM series. These monitors cost upward of $25,000 and required daily recalibration. Not only that, but the actual CRTs had a relatively short lifespan and required retubing after a few thousand hours of use.

Nowadays, CRTs are no longer manufactured and for color critical work such as grading, so colorists are left with three options:

- Broadcast LCD, plasma, or OLED monitors
- Computer LCD monitors
- Digital cinema projectors

Let's look at each type in greater detail.

Broadcast LCD, Plasma, or OLED Monitors

This is the most commonly found type of monitor in a grading suite. These monitors tend to be quite expensive—usually costing at least $5,000 and often as much as $25,000 or more for broadcast OLED monitors. All of these monitors are designed to work with digital video signals and typically connect using SDI (serial digital interface) connections.

At a bare minimum, a broadcast monitor should be properly calibrated to SMPTE color bars so that its *setup*, *gain*, and *chroma* are properly set. But for a professional grading suite, you should also ensure that the monitor has the proper color temperature and that it has a neutral grayscale.

The recommended color temperature for a critical viewing monitor is 6,500° Kelvin, which is often referred as D65. Most consumer televisions are much bluer in tone than a D65 monitor and will not provide you with an accurate image. And don't assume that the "warm" or "cinema" modes of your consumer television produce an accurate image. Typically, they aren't D65 but are instead what the marketing departments for the manufacturers think consumers will prefer. This can cause problems in grading. For example, if the flesh tones appear too blue, but that is entirely due to the monitor's color cast, removing the blue cast caused by the monitor will result in yellow skin tones in your images. As yellow skin tones can be interpreted as jaundiced, you probably won't have a happy client!

It is also important that a monitor has a neutral grayscale. This means that the "color" of gray does not vary from black to white. Many consumer television sets shift toward green in the blacks and toward blue in the whites. If the monitor you are grading with introduces a shift that you then try to remove, you will have an undesirable result!

Computer LCD Monitors

In this age of software-only Avid Media Composer and Avid Symphony, it is possible that you will be expected (or may even want) to grade using a computer monitor. With a few exceptions, which we will discuss momentarily, this is just about the worst thing you can do! Remember, virtually all computer monitors are designed for general use and a price-sensitive market. As a result, the actual quality of your typical computer monitor varies wildly, even from the very best manufacturers and even within the same model number. This is especially true of the LCD display found in notebook computers.

There are a number of issues you'll encounter in your typical computer monitor, but most usually fail to be suitable for grading use due to three display characteristics that are more tightly controlled in broadcast monitors: gamma, gamut, and color temperature.

Gamma

Gamma is the tone response curve of a given device (the display in this case), or the way that input values, from black to white, are displayed onscreen. Most computer monitors have a target gamma of 2.2, which can be graphed as seen in Figure 1.1.

Notice that a gamma of 2.2 means that a greater percentage of the input values are displayed darker than what you might have otherwise assumed. Unfortunately, even though 2.2 may be the target gamma for a computer display, the reality is that gamma can vary wildly, especially in the less-expensive displays. This means that the tones in the shots you are grading will not be displayed correctly—for

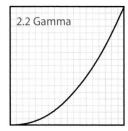

Figure 1.1
2.2 gamma.

example, the shadows may appear brighter than they would in a proper grading monitor—and you may correct for problems that don't actually exist or make a real problem look even worse.

Though a gamma of 2.2 is considered by many to be acceptable for video, the broadcast video monitors in most grading suites are calibrated to have a 2.4 gamma, which has a deeper curvature and results in even more of the input values being used to represent darker tones. Furthermore, the digital cinema standard specifies a display gamma of 2.6, which results in still more of the total signal being used for the dark tones. These three gamma curves are shown in Figure 1.2.

  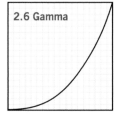

Figure 1.2
2.2, 2.4, and 2.6 gamma.

Gamut

Gamut is the range of colors that a given monitor can display. Video monitors, both high definition (HD) and standard definition (SD), have a very specific gamut. Computer monitors, on the other hand, are all over the map when it comes to gamut. The vast majority of stand-alone computer monitors and laptop displays have a much smaller gamut than a professional broadcast monitor. This means that images typically appear less saturated than they truly are, especially in the reds. Indeed, with the advent of LED backlighting, the gamut for a typical computer monitor has actually gotten smaller, not larger, and the accuracy of that gamut has suffered.

Professional computer monitors, such as those designed to be used with a high-end workstation, tend to be of higher quality, but many of those have a larger gamut than a professional broadcast monitor. This means that images on these monitors appear to be more saturated than they actually are—especially the greens and reds.

Furthermore, even if a display claims to provide the correct gamut, it may actually not display it accurately. For example, the majority of white LED-backlit displays do not have accurately positioned color primaries (the light output of the individual red, green, and blue LED sub-pixels), resulting in blues that are slightly green, greens that are slightly yellow, and reds that are more orange than red. This is an industry-wide problem with white LED displays at the time of this printing, and the severity of this problem varies from display to display.

Color Temperature and Other Issues

As mentioned, the color temperature determines the "color" of white. Whereas a professional grading monitor will have a color temperature of D65, computer monitors tend to have a much bluer color temperature—in some cases well over 10,000° Kelvin. LCD-based computer displays also typically have very poor black levels, displaying blacks at a much higher level than they should, especially when a monitor is dimmed as is typically done in a grading suite.

Finally, most mainstream computer monitors use an LCD technology that results in a very narrow viewing cone, especially vertically. As you shift your viewing position, you'll find that the blacks can actually get grayer or become plugged up, with no shadow detail. This means not only do you have to properly position the monitor relative to your head, but others in the room will see a different-looking image than you.

Computer Monitors Suitable for Grading

There are some computer monitors, however, that can be used for grading. These monitors use more sophisticated panel technology with accurately positioned color primaries and have been designed with internal lookup tables (LUTs) and color-management engines that can manage all aspects of color space and provide extremely accurate images. These monitors can also be truly calibrated, as opposed to the limited "profiling" that is available for most computer displays.

Examples of highly respected brands include Flanders Scientific displays, Eizo ColorEdge displays, and HP DreamColor displays. These monitors are more expensive than your typical display—usually over $2,000—but if you are serious about delivering properly graded video to your clients, the investment in a quality monitor is worth every penny.

Digital Cinema Projectors

If a colorist is grading for a cinema release, that person will often grade on a properly calibrated digital cinema projector so that he or she is seeing the images the way that they will be ultimately exhibited in theaters. It is possible to grade for a cinema release on a monitor, but it must be correctly calibrated for the color space defined for that film. This can be either DCI-P3 (the digital cinema standard color space) or ITU-R BT.709 (the high-definition video color space). If you are grading for a cinema release, you must coordinate with the post-production supervisor to make sure you are working within the proper color space.

Proper Lighting

Remember that the color of an object is affected by the light that illuminates it. It is critical, therefore, that the light in your suite is of the same D65 color temperature as your monitor. With the advent of compact fluorescent lighting, you can now inexpensively order D65 lighting. Certainly your big-box hardware store won't carry them, but a specialty electrical supply house should either stock them or be able to order them for you. Keep in mind, though, that fluorescent tubes will shift in color temperature as they age, so you will need to replace them every few thousand hours. (Check with the manufacturer for replacement guidelines.)

Once you have the proper color temperature lighting, you should ensure that the lighting does not directly reflect off your monitor. This will affect how you view the colors displayed and will unquestionably affect the accurate display of black. Low-wattage bulbs are recommended and will help with the reflection problem.

Proper Wall Color

Here is where you'll have to tell the interior decorator to take a hike. You don't want a richly colored wall behind your monitor! Instead, you want a neutral gray wall behind your monitor. Ideally, this wall should be softly illuminated with D65 lighting. This type of lighting is referred to as a *bias light* and is designed to create a halo of properly neutral gray around your monitor. Remember that your eyes lie. If you look at an incorrectly calibrated image in isolation, it will eventually look correct to your eyes. The bias lighting can help keep that from happening.

You can take a photographic gray card to a paint store and have them mix you a can of gray paint, but make sure that you specify that they must use a pure-white base. Many white bases are actually either warm or cool in color temperature, as they provide a better base for the paints consumers typically prefer. Figure 1.3 shows an image of a proper color-grading environment.

Figure 1.3
An Avid color grading suite.

External Video Scopes

If you are serious about color grading, you need scopes. Period. No argument or debate allowed. When you color grade, you aren't just making nice-looking images; you're also making images that meet a broadcast-delivery or film-delivery specification. This means, for broadcast delivery, that blacks can be no lower than 0 mV digital and whites typically no brighter than 700 mV digital.

There is no way you can do this with just your eyes. You need scopes to tell you the voltages in your image. Of course, you also need to know how to read them! We'll discuss some of the fundamentals of scope display interpretation later in this book.

Avid includes a set of internal scopes in the Color Correction tool, as shown in Figure 1.4. These are a good tool to learn and experiment with, but if you are going to make money color grading, you need external scopes. Internal scopes in any application are never a proper substitute.

Figure 1.4
The Avid internal scopes.

Later in this book, we will introduce the different internal scope displays along with the equivalent external scope display. We will also introduce some external-only gamut displays that can be extremely useful.

Using a Color-Grading Console

In addition to the aforementioned tools, it is strongly recommended that you use a color-grading console. This is certainly not required; indeed, colorists have done color grading with Avid Media Composer and Avid Symphony for years without one. But at the same time, those same colorists have been literally begging for a console.

One of the major changes to Media Composer 6 and Symphony 6 is that the underlying engine for the Color Correction tool was completely rewritten to support multiple simultaneous user inputs. This was necessary to support a grading console, as a colorist is likely to adjust multiple aspects simultaneously. The Avid Artist Color grading console, shown in Figure 1.5, was released alongside version 6 and is fully supported in both Media Composer and Symphony.

The biggest advantage you'll have when using the Avid Artist Color grading console is that the entire process of grading is much faster and much smoother. What is a difficult, small adjustment with the mouse becomes an easy, smooth adjustment on a trackball or wheel.

As each part of the color-correcting interface is introduced and each workflow is provided, both the relevant onscreen and Artist Color tools will be discussed.

Figure 1.5
The Avid Artist Color grading console.

Notes from the Colorist:
The Three Pillars of a Grading Room

Designing your color-correction space may seem like a daunting task, but it doesn't have to be. Here's a link to a podcast interview I did with author/colorist Alexis Van Hurkman on this exact subject: http://www.taoofcolor.com/230/alexis-van-hurkman-interview-part-3. He's done more research on this topic than anyone I know. I think you'll find it's a good listen.

—pi

Core Color-Grading Workflow

Whether you are on an Media Composer, Symphony, DaVinci, Base Light, or some other grading system, you can divide the process for color correcting into three stages. If you're a beginner, you might want to keep each stage distinct. As you become more experienced, you might work in a manner that blurs the distinctions between them. In addition, different kinds of projects will lead to different emphases among these stages and might even make some of them unnecessary.

Stage One: Set the Baseline Grade

Note: Stage one is primarily covered in Lesson 2, "Analyzing Images with
Scopes."

The first, and essential, goal of the first stage of the color-correction process is to achieve a good baseline grade for each scene. This baseline will be used as the foundation for subsequent alterations in the next stages of the process.

In some cases, you'll want to match as closely as possible what an observer standing beside the camera would have perceived when the scene was shot. In other cases, the director of photography (DP) or director will want a specific look that he or she was unable to achieve on location.

Let's take a simple yet common example of a scene of two characters that was shot as a master of both characters and an ISO of each actor. Due to the time to set up and get a successful take from each camera angle, the master was shot mid-morning, one character after lunch, and the other character late in the day, but the DP wants the entire scene to look as if it were shot during early in the morning.

The essential question is, is the desired look what was shot on location or is a different look to be created in the color-grading phase? The answer may be one or the other, but commonly the show you are grading will be a combination of the two.

The industry is moving quickly to file-based acquisition. As it does, an increasing number of productions are performing a "one light" color grading pass on set under the guidance of the director and DP. This is ideal. It enables them to make critical decisions in real time about the quality of the images being produced and make adjustments immediately. The benefit to the editors and post professionals is that they work with great-looking dailies from the start. Nonetheless, communication with the producer/director is critical at this stage to avoid costly mistakes or misunderstandings.

Here are some basic questions you can ask the director or DP:

- Were there any difficulties in the shoot, such as white-balance issues, lighting problems, or anything else that might affect the light and color of the source footage?

- Were any scenes intentionally shot in a specific way, such as scenes that were shot day-for-night?

- Did they use any specific filtration, such as an amber filter for a warm golden color? (You don't want to accidentally remove it.)

■ If you are grading an advertising spot, are there any particular colors in the shot that must be matched to a physical sample (such as the color of the car)?

To summarize, make sure you come to an agreement with the director or DP about what should be preserved and what should be changed using color-correction tools.

Previewing the Sequence

In addition to discussing the project with the producer or director, preview the sequence to get a sense of the kinds of corrections that are needed and the approach you will use to make them. When you are starting out, you might want to preview the sequence extensively and plan your corrections in advance, making note of scenes or shots that will require special attention. Or if you have more color-correcting experience, you might move back and forth frequently between making corrections and assessing the footage.

Analyzing a Shot

If you have experience as a finishing editor, you already know how to analyze shots for luma and color problems. If not, you may not have fine-tuned your luma and color sense. Here are some things to think about or discuss with the director/DP as you examine the footage for the program:

■ Is the exposure correct? In some cases, a shot will be deliberately underexposed to provide for more correction latitude during the grading session.

■ Does the image look flat? If so, is that due to a contrast or saturation problem?

■ Is there detail in the shadows and highlights? If not, you will want to correct the tonal range.

■ Is the image weighted to dark or light tones? Is that intentional or will you need to make an adjustment?

■ Are flesh tones accurate? Or do they have, for example, a pink or yellow cast? For example, in fluorescent lighting using an improperly balanced camera, flesh tones have a yellow-green cast.

■ Are there objects in the image that you know have inaccurate color? For example, you might know that an actor's hair color or the color of the sky is inaccurate.

Adjusting Individual Segments

To restore the look (as intended by the camera person), or a close approximation of it:

1. Open the tonal range (or contrast ratio) as much as reasonably possible by adjusting luma. An image with a narrow tonal range lacks contrast and detail. The human visual system (the mind's eye) generally maximizes the tonal range available in a scene. For example, in low light, we adjust to perceive a greater range of dark tones.

2. Adjust the tonal balance so that it is appropriately balanced. This is also known as adjusting the shot's gamma.

3. Improve color accuracy by removing any unintentional color casts and correcting flesh tones. Remember, though, that you don't want to remove color casts intentionally created in the shoot with gels and filters.

As mentioned, the human visual system generally compensates for color casts in order to "perceive color accurately." For example, we may perceive a person as having the same skin tonality whether under fluorescent light or daylight. It's easy to be misled; always confirm your assumptions by relying on your scopes!

Color casts can come from the following:

- Improper camera white balance
- Types of artificial lighting used
- Types of natural lighting conditions, such as bright sun or clouds

Finally, during this process, you also want to achieve good color saturation. Saturation often improves as a result of correcting the luma range, so additional saturation adjustments are made last, or sometimes not at all.

Stage Two: Achieving Shot-to-Shot Consistency

After you correct individual shots, you will move through the sequence, checking that each shot works with the adjacent shots. If not, you need to make further adjustments. If necessary, you can depart from the original look of the scene to achieve shot-to-shot consistency in your sequence, such as lightening one shot to make it match the adjacent shot.

Recall the example of the master and the two ISOs that were shot at different times of the day. As the sun travels through the sky, atmospheric conditions such as clouds cause its color temperature to change. And when the sun is very low in the sky, the angle of the sun causes the color temperature to become much warmer than it is at other times of the day.

Stage Three: Achieving a Final Look

This is where the real art of color grading comes into play. If you want a distinct stylistic look or you want to make the scene look like it was shot under different conditions than it was, you adjust your grade. As an example, you may want a scene to look like it takes place in mid-winter or mid-summer. You can also make a more dramatic adjustment—for example, applying a warm glow to the entire scene.

Color Correction Mode

Now that we'd discussed some of the fundamentals, let's take a look at Color Correction mode. We'll begin our exploration by opening one of the sequences we will work with in the lessons that follow.

Note: The following steps assume that you have downloaded and installed the projects and media that correspond with this book from the Cengage website. If you have not done so, stop here and install them before continuing. Information on installing the projects and media is provided in the front of this book.

To open the first sequence:

1. Depending on the system you are working with, launch either Media Composer or Symphony.

2. Select the **AVID COLOR GRADING (MC239)** project on the left side of the Open Project dialog box and click the **OPEN** button. The Project window opens and lists the folders and bins associated with this project. Two folders divide the Lesson and Exercise bins; there is a bin for each lesson and exercise.

3. Double-click the **1_COLOR GRADING OVERVIEW** bin in the Project window to open it.

4. In the **1_COLOR GRADING OVERVIEW** bin window, double-click the **1_INTRO TO COLOR CORRECTION** sequence. The sequence appears in the Record monitor.

To set up the system for color correction:

1. Right-click the **VIDEO QUALITY** button on the Timeline and choose **FULL QUALITY** from the pop-up menu. (See Figure 1.6.)

It is strongly recommended that you always grade in Full Quality mode. This option processes the entire signal and all image processing is done with full-frame uncompressed video. This also means that the internal and external scopes will give you a more accurate representation of the video image.

That said, although it provides the best-looking images, it does require additional processing power compared to Draft mode—which only processed 25% of the data—particularly if you are working with footage in RGB color space, such as footage shot with the RED camera.

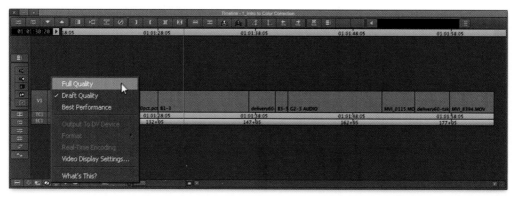

Figure 1.6
Video Quality menu.

2. If you are connected to external video hardware that supports it, right-click the **VIDEO QUALITY** button again and choose **FULL QUALITY 10-BIT** from the pop-up menu. (See Figure 1.7.)

Figure 1.7
Full Quality 10-Bit option.

This will extend the color data range, resulting in higher quality color corrections. If you are working in a software-only configuration or are using external hardware that does not support 10-bit processing, this option will not be displayed.

3. In the sequence, enable **V1** and disable all other tracks. Color correction is applied to the highest selected track in a sequence, and the clips we want to correct are on V1.

4. To enter Color Correction mode, do one of the following:

   - Click the **COLOR CORRECTION** mode button in the Timeline palette

   - Choose **TOOLSET > COLOR CORRECTION.**

Tip: You can also map the Color Correction Mode button to the keyboard from the CC tab in the Command palette.

The Avid system switches to Color Correction mode, as shown in Figure 1.8 and Figure 1.9.

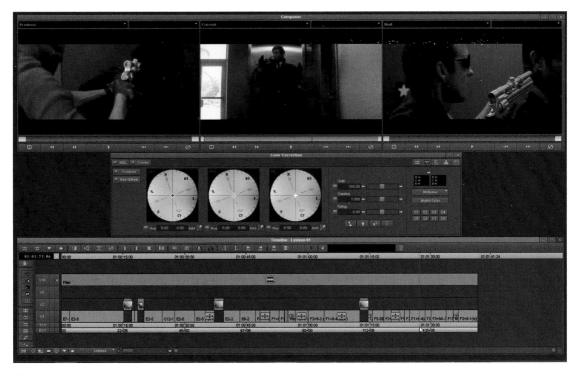

Figure 1.8
Color Correction mode in Media Composer.

Figure 1.9
Color Correction mode in Symphony.

Color Correction mode reconfigures the Avid interface into a specialized monitor configuration that includes three windows:

- The Composer window, which now displays three monitors
- The Color Correction tool
- The Timeline window, resized to accommodate the Color Correction tool

Note: Depending on your system configuration, the Timeline window may overlap the Color Correction tool. If it does, simply resize it until there is no overlap. It is strongly recommended that you work with a display resolution of 1,280×1,024 or higher when working in Color Correction mode, especially if only using a single monitor.

Let's take a look at the different parts of the Color Correction mode interface.

The Composer Window

The Composer window in Color Correction mode allows you to view material from three segments at once, so you can compare material on a shot-by-shot basis. You can also display video signal scopes by selecting them from a source menu. You will look at the options available in the source menus in the next lesson.

The bottom of each Composer monitor contains segment navigation buttons, shown in Figure 1.10. Fast Forward and Rewind move the position indicator between segments, as in Source/Record mode. Next Uncorrected and Previous Uncorrected move the position indicator between segments in the Timeline that have no corrections applied. These are convenient because you will frequently grade segments out of order. Dual Split can be used to compare the corrected and uncorrected image.

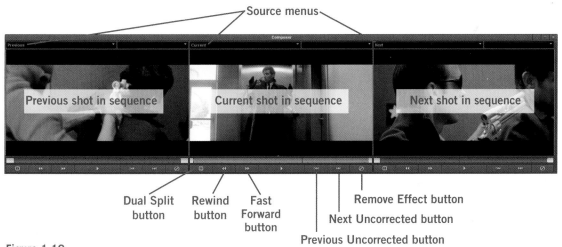

Figure 1.10
Composer window in Color Correction mode.

The Color Correction Tool

The Color Correction tool is what you use to perform a color grade. It has a different look depending on whether you are running Media Composer or Symphony. (See Figure 1.11 and Figure 1.12.) The core capabilities, however, remain the same.

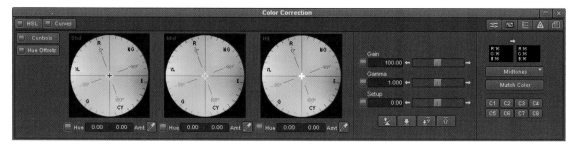

Figure 1.11
Color Correction tool in Media Composer.

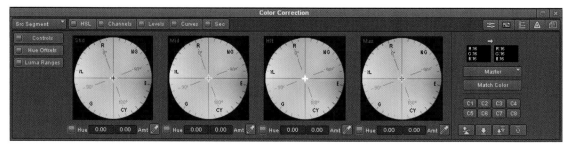

Figure 1.12
Color Correction tool in Avid Symphony.

The Color Correction tool is divided into a series of control groups: two in Media Composer and five in Symphony. These groups contain unique sets of controls that enable you to adjust the image. The available groups are as follows:

- HSL
- Channels (Symphony only)
- Levels (Symphony only)
- Curves
- Secondaries (Symphony only)

Each group may contain subdividing tabs that further break out the controls available within each group, as shown in Figure 1.11. And in Avid Symphony, those tabs can be broken down further into sub-tabs, as shown above in Figure 1.12. We will look at the capabilities of each correction group later in this book.

The Timeline

Unlike in Effect mode, it is not necessary to apply a Color Correction effect before making a correction. Instead, a color correction is applied to the selected clip when you make your first adjustment in the Color Correction tool.

These corrections are applied differently depending on whether you are using Media Composer or Symphony. In Media Composer a Color Correction effect is applied to the clip being corrected as shown in Figure 1.13. If an effect (or effect nest) is already applied to the clip being corrected, the Color Correction effect is Autonested on top of the existing effect(s).

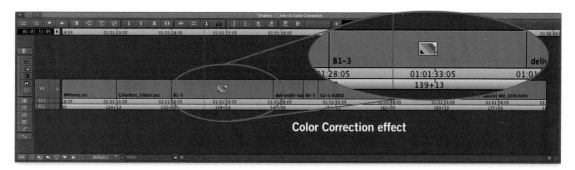

Figure 1.13
Color Correction effect applied to clip in Media Composer.

In Symphony, Color Correction effects are not applied. Instead, a correction is indicated by a colored horizontal line (green by default) that runs along the bottom of the clip, as shown in Figure 1.14.

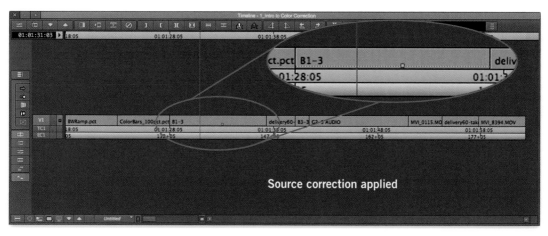

Figure 1.14
Color Correction applied to clip in Symphony.

Note that if an effect (or effect nest) is already applied to the clip being corrected in Symphony, the correction is applied *beneath* all applied effects. This is opposite of the behavior in Media Composer.

In the next lesson, we'll begin working within Color Correction mode, starting with the HSL group of corrections.

Notes from the Colorist: The 95% Solution

I have a confession to make: My business doesn't cater to Hollywood films or projects with multi-million dollar budgets. My clients are extremely price-sensitive. Most of them couldn't tell the difference between a $250 off-the-shelf computer display and a $25,000 reference monitor calibrated by a $30,000 probe. So you know what? I don't go chasing after the latest, greatest gear. I don't buy equipment priced in five and six figures.

I call it the 95% solution. I spend money where it makes sense—where it makes a visible difference in my work—but I don't spend a dollar more. Color correction can be an equipment-intensive craft. I long ago stopped trying to keep up with the Joneses. I advise the same for you. For most of us, racing after that last 5% of perfection is a fast way to the poor house.

Here's my current setup (summer 2012):

- **CPU:** 2009 MacPro. Yeah, it's getting old, and will be replaced in the next 12 months. But it still reliably runs Media Composer, Symphony, and any other app I throw at it. No need to replace it until...well, until I *need* to replace it.

- **External scopes:** Hamlet Vidscope-BX running on an HP xw4400—itself a five-year-old machine. At the time, it cost about $3,500 to put together. I'll be running that baby into the ground. That's what I like about external scopes: They should last you a decade.

- **Reference monitor:** That's where I'll spend my money. Currently, I use the $5,000 Flanders Scientific (FSI) LM-2461 LCD reference monitor. And with the rapid advances we're seeing in monitor technology, I plan to replace that monitor every two years. I'll keep my costs for this gear in the $5,000–$10,000 range because with my clients, spending more doesn't make sense. (Disclosure: FSI is a sponsor of my website and weekly newsletter—but I love their gear anyway!)

The 95% solution means you put your money where it makes a difference in your business. For me, that's the reference monitor. Just don't try to get me to spend a dollar more....

—pi

Review/Discussion Questions

1. What are the four recommendations listed for a grading suite?

2. Why is it so important to have a proper monitor for grading?

3. What are three of the problems you may encounter with a standard computer monitor if you use it for grading?

4. Does the monitor in front of you constitute a proper grading monitor? If not, what are the problems with the display that you should be aware of when grading?

5. What is the recommended color temperature for grading suite lighting?

6. Why is the color of the wall behind the grading monitor so important?

7. What are the advantages of using a color-grading console?

8. What are the three core stages of a color grade?

9. Why is it a good idea to preview a sequence prior to grading?

10. Why should you perform color grading in Full Quality mode?

11. How do you enter Color Correction mode?

12. How do color corrections appear in the Timeline in Media Composer? In Symphony?

Lesson 1 Keyboard Shortcuts

The functions in this table can be mapped to the key of your choice. For information on how to map your keyboard, see the article "Mapping User-Selectable Buttons" in the Media Composer or Symphony Help.

Lesson 1 Keyboard Shortcuts

Function	Action
Play	Play the current segment only.
Fast Forward	Move the position indicator to the next segment in the sequence.
Rewind	Move the position indicator to the previous segment in the sequence.
Next Uncorrected	Move the position indicator to the next segment in the sequence without a correction effect.
Previous Uncorrected	Move the position indicator to the previous segment in the sequence without a correction effect.
Dual Split	Activates a resizable panel over the current that reveals the uncorrected image; useful for comparison against the corrected image.

Previewing the Sequence

In this exercise you'll begin the process of grading by previewing one of the sequences you'll work with in this class.

Media Used:

Avid Color Grading (MC239) project > 2_Exercise Bins folder > Ex1_Color Grading Overview bin > Ex1_Reviewing Footage sequence

Duration:

20 to 25 minutes

GOALS

- Check for correct exposure
- Check for detail in shadows and highlights
- Check for accurate flesh tones
- Note the problems in those areas

Overview

Before we begin to learn how to use the Color Correction tool to perform a grade, let's see how good your eyes are. Your task in this exercise is to go through the entire sequence, Ex1_Reviewing Footage, looking at the clips and identifying any problems you see. Note that this sequence contains some clips that have color effects applied. The black-and-white clips are supposed to be from security cameras, while the blue-tinted clips are supposed to be of a remote location. Make notes of how you think these looks could be improved. Later in this book, we'll return to your notes and see if your analysis and opinion has changed.

As you go through the sequence, keep the following questions in mind and try to answer them for the different type of shots in the sequence:

- **Is the exposure correct?** In some cases, a shot will be deliberately underexposed to provide for more correction latitude during the grading session.

- **Does the image look flat?** If so, is that due to a contrast or saturation problem?

- **Is there detail in the shadows and highlights?** If not, you will want to correct the tonal range.

- **Is the image weighted to dark or light tones?** Is that intentional or will you need to make an adjustment?

- **Are flesh tones accurate?** Or do they have, for example, a pink or yellow cast? For example, in fluorescent lighting using an improperly balanced camera, flesh tones have a yellow-green cast.

- **Are there objects in the image that you know have inaccurate color?** For example, you might know that an actor's hair color or the color of the sky is inaccurate.

Note that it is not necessary to make notes on every shot. Instead, you should look at the different camera angles and positions and analyze those in preparation for a later grade.

Analyzing Images with Scopes

This lesson introduces the fundamentals of reading video scopes. Scopes are the essential tools that every colorist uses to grade, regardless of the application or the controls available to them. Just like a musician needs to know how to read music, every colorist needs to know how to read scopes!

Media Used: Avid Color Grading (MC239) project > 1_Lesson Bins folder > 2_Analyzing Shots bin > 2_Reading Scopes sequence

Duration: 60 minutes

GOALS

- Identify basic principles of the human visual system
- Identify the principal video scopes
- Define what portion of the video signal each scope measures
- Memorize common specification limits for video black and video white
- Recognize image elements within video scope traces
- Evaluate sequence images using each video scope
- Interpret scope readings to identify exposure and color balance problems in the images

Video Scopes, Color Science, and Speed Dating

Color grading is a unique blend of art and science. The artistic side is reflected in how you manipulate the image to evoke a mood to further the story. The scientific side is rooted in understanding the human visual system and the technicalities of video signal, compression, and image sampling.

Our biology dictates how we perceive the world. Brightness is the dominant visual stimulus. It is the contrast in brightness, the relative values of light and dark, that informs us of the objects and textures in the world around us. Color is perceived on top of those details, almost as a wash, providing additional information to our brains. You use your color perception to determine additional information about those objects. Contrast *defines* the objects; color *describes* it. What is it? A banana. What it like? It's yellow and ripe.

The combination of photoreceptors found in the human eye explains two other phenomena that we see in the world. The receptors that are used in low light don't convey much color information. As the light dims, so does your color perception. The receptors that respond to bright light are most sensitive to the colors found in skin tones—yellows and reds. As such, it only takes a moment to look at a person and decide whether they look healthy or sickly. (Of course, if good skin color was the only criteria for a good mate, speed dating could get a whole lot faster!)

Tip: Because people are more sensitive to changes in brightness than color, increasing contrast appears to sharpen an image and attracts the eye.

Not surprisingly, video systems are built on these fundamental concepts of how people perceive the world. Analog video signal is a series of voltages. Luma (light) information forms the backbone of the signal, while chroma (color) information is a subset of that. The higher the voltage, the brighter, or whiter, the pixel. The lower the voltage, the darker, or blacker the pixel. As the voltages approach either extreme, of black or white, the pixel becomes desaturated. As a result, the midtone range is where maximum saturation is possible. When you increase gamma, raising the color values for an object in your image from shadow to midtone, it not only makes it brighter, but usually increases the apparent color saturation. Digital signals, recorded as samples, behave in the same fashion. Although the signal processing is different, the underlying color science of human perception is not.

Controlling the values of luminance (brightness) and chrominance (color) within an image and matching the values of one shot to another is *the* job of the colorist.

As stated, your role is both artistic and technical. You are tasked with realizing the vision of the client or director, while ensuring that the program technically meets the delivery specifications. Video scopes are the essential tools to accomplish these goals. They enable you to objectively view component parts of the image, without being influenced by the subjective interpretations of your brain. With scopes, you're not left to guess what the difference in brightness is between shots, or in which direction you need to shift colors to match skin tones. If you can measure it, you can control it. Artistically, you may choose to "crush" the blacks, losing detail in the shadowy parts of the image, or conversely to "blow out" the highlights, losing detail in the bright parts of the image. These can be valid choices, but could easily push your signal into illegal values. Using your scopes, however, you can do it consistently while still adhering to the delivery specification.

As a final note, as critical as scopes are, remember that they are a tool, not a taskmaster. You shouldn't blindly adjust to the signal displayed on your scopes. You can't simply assume that the brightest area in the image must be video white and the darkest area must be video black.

Color as a Storytelling Tool

People have almost universal emotional associations with light and color, regardless of culture or nationality. Bright, lively, vibrant colors are associated with happiness, energy, youth, etc. Dark, dull, muted colors are associated with melancholy, death, and decay. Perhaps this is rooted in people's universal experience with the changes in the quality of sunlight as the weather changes or with the life cycle of seasons. Whatever the root cause, understanding these associations will empower you to manipulate them, using color as another powerful tool in the storytelling process.

In some productions, the use of color is a core component in the story, clearly defining place, mood, or the presence of a character. In others, it merely supports the emotional tone of the scene. This is very similar to music as a storytelling device. As you become more aware of color, you will begin to watch TV and movies with a different set of eyes. Informed observation is a valuable learning tool, and can help you quickly hone your color awareness.

On the Web

On his blog Outside-Hollywood, Isaac Botkin has an excellent analysis of the use of color in the 2001 film *Black Hawk Down*, directed by Ridley Scott. Check it out at http://www.outside-hollywood.com/2009/03/color-theory-for-cinematographers.

Types of Scopes

You can perform color correction using Avid internal software–based scopes or external scopes. Professional colorists—those who make their living from color grading—work with external scopes. These dedicated pieces of equipment are by far the most accurate way to measure video signals. External scopes can be broadly defined into two categories: hardware-based scopes and software-based scopes.

External scopes require you to have video output hardware, not a software-only configuration. This can be Avid DX hardware or an I/O box from any of the third-party companies that offer Avid-compatible products. Hardware-based scopes also require careful calibration to ensure accuracy. External scopes enable you to view details of the output signal that are recorded back to tape or sent to some other distribution mechanism in your facility. They also enable you to validate the signal quality of a particular device or to calibrate a particular device, such as your video monitor.

Note: This course concentrates on the Avid internal software–based scopes. If you have external scopes available, it is recommended that you use those instead.

Dedicated Hardware Scopes

The most respected name in hardware scopes is Tektronix. For years, Tektronix equipment has been standard in color suites. Tektronix offers a range of products, with differing capabilities. The top-of-the-line WVR8000 series includes powerful devices with a wide range of features for grading everything up to 3D stereoscopic images and digital cinema mastering in the XYZ (DCI-P3/SMPTE-431-2) color space. Their capabilities justify the premium price.

In addition to producing high-quality components, one of the reasons Tektronix has remained a leader in the industry is the company's innovative, proprietary displays such as the Arrowhead, Diamond, and Spearhead displays. These scopes display the composite luma and chroma signals so that the colorist can verify gamut compliance with just a glance. (See Figure 2.1.)

On the Web

For in-depth information on Tektronix's proprietary displays, watch the free webinar, "Color Gamut Monitoring," at http://www.tek.com/webinar/color-gamut-monitoring-webinar. It also includes excellent information on your perception of color, the graphical representation of color, and the measurement of video signals.

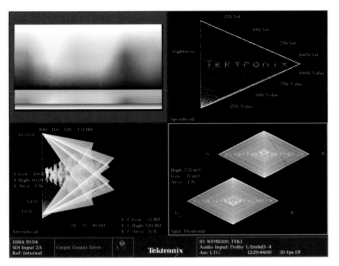

Figure 2.1
The Tektronix Arrowhead, Split Diamond, and Spearhead gamut displays.
(© Tektronix. All Rights Reserved. Reprinted with permission.)

Dedicated Software Scopes

In recent years, a number of dedicated software packages and hardware-software hybrid systems have come on the market. These applications typically require a separate computer that can be connected to the output signal from your Avid I/O hardware. (Rather than purchase a new one, many editors repurpose their old CPU.) Two excellent examples include the following:

■ **ScopeBox from Divergent Media.** ScopeBox is a software-only system that can use a wide range of input signals, including third-party cards, devices, or even FireWire. It also reads video files, such as QuickTime movies. ScopeBox can even be used to ingest media while recording. Most importantly, ScopeBox has a respectable range of highly accurate scopes and a flexible interface that makes it easy to see the scopes you need, where you want them. As a software-only package, ScopeBox has a low price point, making it a great choice for students and professionals alike.

■ **UltraScope by Blackmagic Design.** UltraScope is a hybrid system that comes in two flavors: workstation-based and laptop-based. The one you choose depends on which hardware option fits your production needs better. Because you're buying the hardware with the software, the price point is a bit higher than ScopeBox, but still very reasonable. UltraScope more closely matches the feature set of dedicated hardware scopes, including, for instance, the ability to zoom in on a region of a scope display. This is quite helpful when doing critical work.

Working with the Avid Internal Scopes

Avid's internal software–based scopes are convenient, accurate, and require no calibration. They are always available to you, even when working in a software-only configuration.

Note: One challenge of using the built-in scopes is that they do not update in real time as adjustments are made with the mouse. If you use an Avid Artist Color console, however, the internal scopes update continuously as you adjust the grade with the console, making the internal scopes much more useful.

As mentioned, Color Correction mode gives you three monitors with which to work. You can use them to compare different segments in your sequence and to display scopes to help you adjust the color and brightness of the image. To change the image or scope displayed in one of the Composer monitors, use the drop-down menu at the top of the monitor, as shown in Figure 2.2.

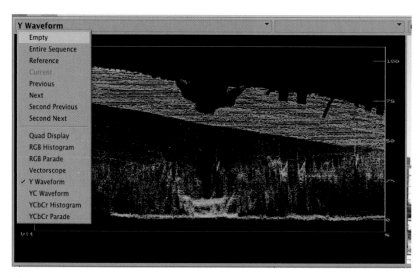

Figure 2.2
The drop-down menu in each monitor includes scope and shot-selection options.

The Avid system includes seven video scope displays. This course covers the four most useful ones and their primary functions.

For luma adjustments, you use the following scope:

■ **Y Waveform.** This enables you to adjust setup (black level), gain (white level), and gamma (midtones).

For color adjustments, you use a mix of the following scopes:

- **RGB Parade.** This enables you to balance blacks and whites, as well as adjust color cast.

- **Vectorscope.** This enables you to adjust skin color (no matter what the color of the skin) and other color casts.

- **YC Waveform.** This enables you to make sure that chroma doesn't exceed broadcast limits.

Note: For information about the other scopes, see the *Avid Media Composer and NewsCutter Effects and Color Correction Guide*.

Notes from the Colorist:
Why You Must Blindfold Your Brain When Color Correcting

It sounds counterintuitive, doesn't it? Blindfolding your brain. But vision scientists have proven that the human visual system isn't passive. What you see isn't objective reality. The raw retinal data that's sent to your brain is manipulated before it becomes the image that you see. This process happens at a very low level. It's as difficult to regulate as your heartbeat.

You don't have to take my word for it. I can prove it to you. Take a look at the optical illusion in Figure 2.3. The cool thing about optical illusions is that they reveal the inner workings of your visual system. They let you peek into processes that you can't intuit any other way. This one is one of the most important when it comes to color correction. Take notice of the center gray boxes. Which one looks brighter to you? The gray box on the left or the gray box on the right?

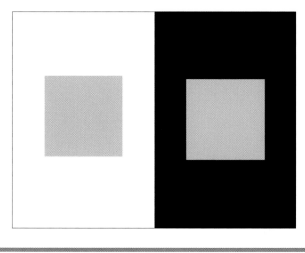

Figure 2.3
Which gray box is brighter?

Almost everyone says the gray box on the right is brighter. And if 98% of you see it that way, can you all be wrong? YES! Those two gray boxes are perfectly identical. Yet everyone who looks at it sees exactly the same thing. Seeing it any other way is like trying to stop your heart with your thoughts…only Zen masters and savants have that kind of internal control.

Vision scientists call this illusion the simultaneous contrast effect. It demonstrates that raw RGB data received at your retina is intercepted and re-interpreted. Your brain sees the gray boxes in the context of the white and black surroundings, making all sorts of assumptions about this image including that they have the same light source and they are made of different materials with different reflective properties. Only the former is true.

So how does this affect your jobs when color correcting? Almost everything you read about room setup is designed to minimize the brightness contrast effect. Replace those two gray boxes with your reference monitor, and you can see how you'll make very different color-correction choices depending on the brightness (and color) of what's behind and surrounding your monitor. This effect also describes why you need vectorscopes and waveform monitors. As I'll explain later, you use these tools to bypass your visual system.

As you read this chapter, remember this: The human visual system is active and makes all sorts of assumptions about the raw data hitting your retina. It's a fundamental truth: Your eyes mislead you. When color correcting, you must find ways around this truth. I call the act of learning how to do this "blindfolding your brain." Many parts of this book are devoted to doing just that! Journey onward….

—pi

Overview of Scope Displays

This section provides an overview of the four principal scopes identified earlier. These four are typically available in any set of scopes, both hardware and software. This lesson introduces you to each scope and its usage. You will become more familiar with them as you continue working with them through the rest of this course.

To prepare for this lesson:

1. If it's not already open, launch Media Composer or Symphony.

2. Open the project AVID COLOR GRADING (MC239).

3. Open the bin 2_EVALUATING IMAGES and load the sequence 2_READING SCOPES. This sequence includes a series of duplicate shots. The first instance of each is unaltered; the second is graded.

4. Move the position indicator to the first segment, **BWRamp**.

5. Enter **Color Correction** mode.

6. Set the left monitor to **Y Waveform**, the center monitor to **Current**, and the right monitor to **Empty**.

Understanding the Y Waveform

A waveform monitor is a visual display that shows the electronic pattern of the video signal, or *trace*, over a measurement graph, known as a *graticule*. The Y Waveform displays luma, which is the core of the video signal. You use the Y Waveform scope to analyze whether blacks and whites are too low or too high, and determine whether the image has a good balance of blacks, whites, and mid-tones. This scope is key to the first stage of the grading process: opening up the tonal range.

Tip: The Y Waveform is also useful for matching scene brightness from one shot
to another.

The Y Waveform displays all the luma information for the current video field over-laid in the waveform. (Luma is often referred to as Y.) Each left-to-right trace in the waveform represents one (horizontal) scan line. If you see a bright object on the left side of the image, you will see its peak on the left side of the waveform. (The higher the green trace, the brighter that part of the image.) A bright object on the left of the image produces the same trace on the waveform whether it is in the top-left or bottom-left area of the image. This light-dark relationship is clearly seen when you look at test patterns on the Y Waveform monitor, as shown in Figure 2.4 and Figure 2.5.

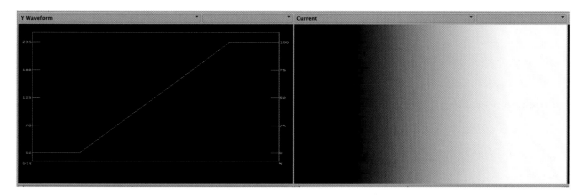

Figure 2.4
The Y Waveform monitor displaying a B/W ramp.

On the Y Waveform, the trace of the B/W ramp forms a straight line up and to the right, in the direction of the gradient, dark to bright. Now look at the Y Waveform for a set of standard color bars. Click the Fast Forward button in the center Composer window. The position indicator jumps to the first frame of the next segment in the sequence, ColorBars_100.pct. The Composer display should match the image shown in Figure 2.5.

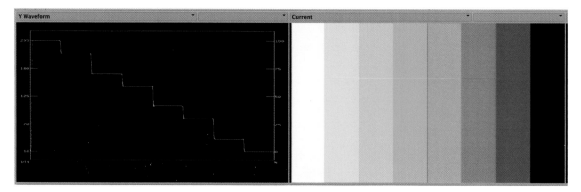

Figure 2.5
The Y Waveform displaying 100% color bars.

The Y Waveform now forms a stair-step pattern, moving down to the right. Again, the direction of the slope matches the luminance of the color bars, moving from white to black.

Luma Measurements on the Y Waveform

On the Avid internal scope, the scale on the left is a digital level scale using a 256-step (8-bit) range; 16 bits is the level for video black and 235 bits is the level for video white. The scale on the right shows the amount of white in the image as a percentage; 0% represents video black and 100% represents video white.

A reference black of 0% corresponds to a digital level of 16; an analog NTSC level of 7.5 IRE; and a PAL, HD, and digital NTSC level of 0mV (millivolts). A reference white of 100% corresponds to a digital level of 235; an analog NTSC level of 100 IRE; and a PAL, HD, and digital NTSC level of 700mV. Table 2.1 summarizes the correspondences among various types of measurements for the SMPTE REC.601/709 standard, which has been adopted as the broadcast standard internationally.

Table 2.1   Measurements of Video Black and Video White

Equivalent Measurements on the Waveform Monitor	Digital Bits	Percent	NTSC Analog Scope	NTSC Digital/ PAL/HD Scope
Video Black	16	0	7.5 IRE	0mV
Video White	235	100	100 IRE	700mV

Parts of an image can have values outside the 0%–100% range, but you should deliver a signal within this range. The digital video standard allows for *headroom* and *footroom* so that you can correct a mistake in level in the post-production process. The minimum is digital 0 or –7%, and the maximum is digital 255 or 108%. For ease of reference, throughout this book, I refer to values on the percent scale.

Shot Analysis with the Y Waveform

Let's analyze some real images on the Y Waveform. As you analyze each image, you have two goals:

■ To see how the content of the waveform corresponds to the content of the image

■ To analyze the waveform so you can determine what you will need to adjust

To continue analyzing shots with the Y Waveform:

1. Continue working with the same sequence, **2_READING SCOPES**.

2. Click the **FF** button under the center Composer monitor. The position indicator jumps to the first frame of the next shot, the uncorrected version of **ZERO_ROOFTOP1**.

3. Drag the position indicator to scrub through the shot. The camera pushes in on Agent Zero during the shot.

4. Park the position indicator in the middle of the segment. The exact frame is unimportant right now. (The reference frame used for the following figures is indicated with a marker, if you'd like to use it.) Figure 2.6 shows the image and its corresponding Y Waveform display.

Figure 2.6
The Y Waveform of Shot Zero_Rooftop1.

What does the Y Waveform tell you about the image? You are looking at it for luma—that is, for the range of darkest (or blackest) tones to brightest (or whitest).

5. Look carefully at the overall image, and the Y Waveform. As you do, consider each of the following points, and identify the elements and characteristics described, and as shown in Figure 2.7.

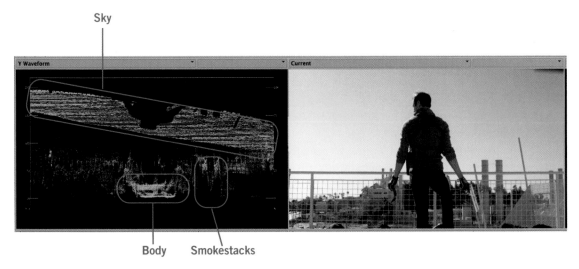

Figure 2.7
The picture elements are easily identified on this Y Waveform.

- Overall, the image has good luminance levels. The traces cover the full contrast range, with values that range from 0% to 100%. Locate the brightest and darkest values on the scope.

- One of the first things your eye will probably go to is the upside-down silhouette of Agent Zero in the center of the scope. The dark body of the actor punches a hole in the otherwise bright band that represents the background sky. Similarly, the buildings in the background can be seen punched out of the sky band. This is because the sky itself is a gradient. If it were a uniform tone, these shapes would not be visible.

- Below the silhouette are two small bands, ranging in values from 0% to 5% and 10% to 15%. These represent Agent Zero's body. His gray shirt is the upper band, his black pants the lower band. Banding occurs when there is a concentration of pixels with similar luma levels.

Recommended adjustments to the luma range based on the Y Waveform: None.

6. Click the **Next Uncorrected** button under the center Composer window. The position indicator moves to the first frame of the shot **Burlesque_2**.

7. Scrub the shot to see how it changes over time. The stage lighting changes dramatically after the first couple seconds before changing to a dark shot with minimal lighting. This will appear very different on the waveform from the previous shot, as shown in Figure 2.8.

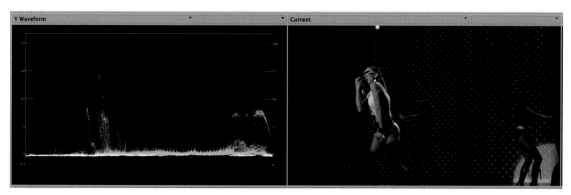

Figure 2.8
A dark shot appears very different on the Y Waveform.

8. Park the position indicator halfway into the shot.

9. Look at the Y Waveform to analyze the shot and identify the elements and characteristics described, and as shown in Figure 2.9.

Body   Curtain   Spotlight

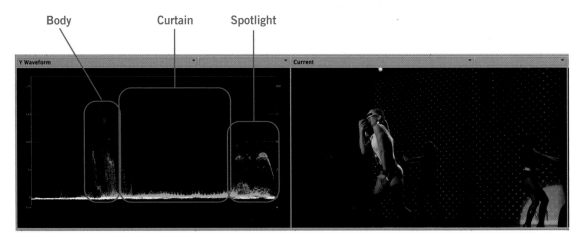

Figure 2.9
The picture elements are also easily identified on this Y Waveform.

- Overall, the image is very dark. As a result, there is a thick band of traces along the bottom of the waveform. These correspond to the black shadow areas of the background.
- The actress on the left and the spotlight on the right are the brightest points in the image, and are clearly visible in the waveform as distinct rises in the traces. However, even these bright areas only reach 50% to 75%, meaning the full tonal range is not being used.
- The "strings" of traces that look a bit like the Matrix represent the light beams and sparkles in the stage curtain.

Note: The traces in Avid's Y Waveform scope turn from green to white when they exceed the legal limits of broadcast, as shown in Figure 2.9.

Recommended adjustments to the luma range based on the Y Waveform:
Increase the tonal range by bringing up the bright tones while maintaining the dark tonalities.

10. Click the **FF** button to advance to the corrected version of the Burlesque_2 shot. The shot is vastly improved. There is a clear difference in the luma levels visible on the Y Waveform. Highlights now approach 100%. (See Figure 2.10.) Additional improvements to this shot were made in color balance and saturation. To see these, you need other scopes.

Key Concept: The Y Waveform is used to determine the corrections needed in the luma range.

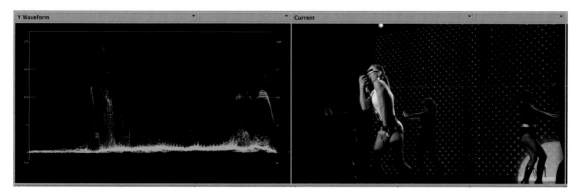

Figure 2.10
The corrected version shows an expanded luma range.

Understanding the RGB Parade

The RGB Parade is the rock star scope. If pressed to choose one scope, most colorists would universally choose the RGB Parade over any other. Simply put, no other scope is more versatile.

Note: A parade display, by definition, arranges component signals side by side.

The RGB Parade contains three panels. From left to right, these are the red, green, and blue panels. You read the content within *each panel* as you read the *entire* Y Waveform: from left to right. The value of seeing the component signals side by side is to easily compare their relative voltages. Comparing the voltages enables you to determine the color balance of blacks and whites in the image, and to check for an overall color cast. As such, this scope is key to the second part of stage 1 of the color-correction process: improving color accuracy by removing a color cast.

You also use RGB Parade to check the peaks in the RGB channels. Regardless of the delivery format, signals that exceed the delivery spec are likely to be clipped, or chopped off. This can result in degraded image quality in those regions. This is equally true for the overall composite signal as for each individual color channel.

Tip: As a rule of thumb, keep RGB levels between 0 and 700mV, even if you have to clip the signal yourself. At least you'll do it intentionally and can verify the impact on the image rather than leaving it to chance. You never want to be surprised by the results of clipping when a show is going to air or in the screening room with the director.

Because the RGB Parade can be used to determine the luma range, peak color values, the overall color balance of the image, and the color balance of individual elements within the image, it is perhaps the single most useful scope. As Patrick (pi) says, "I make my living in the RGB Parade."

Tip: After skin tones, viewers will unconsciously hone in on white objects. If they change from one shot to another or don't match the lighting of the scene, it will break their suspension of disbelief. The RGB Parade is key to being able to verify that the whites in a scene are balanced.

Shot Analysis with the RGB Parade

To begin working with the RGB Parade:

1. Continue working with the same sequence, **2_READING SCOPES**.

2. Open the **SOURCE** menu in the right Composer monitor and select **RGB PARADE**. Leave the Y Waveform in the left monitor for now.

3. Press the **HOME** key or manually move the position indicator back to the first shot in the sequence, **B/W_RAMP.PCT**.

4. Compare the waveform displays in the Y Waveform and the RGB Parade. They match, as shown in Figure 2.11.

Figure 2.11
The waveform slope matches between the two scopes.

RGB signals together create all other colors. When they are in perfect balance, the resulting color is on the gray scale, ranging from black to white depending on the given voltage.

5. Look at the RGB Parade for the B/W Ramp, as shown in Figure 2.11. This principle is what enables you to use the RGB Parade to determine the color balance of color neutral (black, white, or gray) objects. If their traces line up on all three channels, they are balanced; if they don't, they're not. It's just that simple.

Tip: **The key to using RGB Parade to determine color balance lies in being able to identify the traces for black and white objects in the scopes. If you identify them first in the Y Waveform, you can pick them out more easily on RGB Parade.**

6. Navigate to the shot **ZERO_ROOFTOP1**.

7. Take a moment to identify traces in the Y Waveform of key elements within the image, such as Zero's black pants, gray shirt, and the (presumably) gray buildings.

8. Look at the RGB Parade for this shot. Identify those same elements in the RGB Parade.

9. Compare your conclusions to the identifications revealed in Figure 2.12.

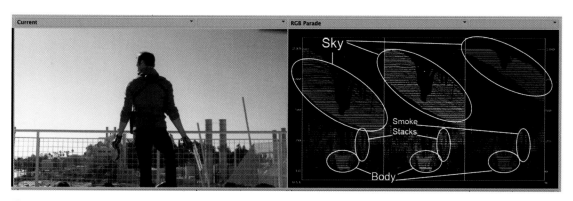

Figure 2.12
Could you identify these picture elements in the RGB Parade?

10. Carefully examine the levels of the R, G, and B traces of Zero's pants. Are they identical? You're right—they're not! The green channel is lowest, and the red channel slightly higher than blue. Therefore, because red and blue combine to create magenta, it can be said that the blacks have a slight magenta cast. Also note that the traces representing the buildings don't show the same cast. It is not uncommon to see a color cast in one portion of the luma range that is absent in others.

Recommended correction based on reading the RGB Parade: Increase green (or reduce red and blue) in the shadows to balance the blacks; make no change to the midtones or highlights.

Note: A deeper analysis, and further corrections will be made to this image in a later chapter.

11. Move the position indicator to the next segment, the corrected version of the **Zero_Rooftop1** shot.

12. Again, examine the values of the black traces, as shown in Figure 2.13. The image has been balanced, so the traces are now relatively even.

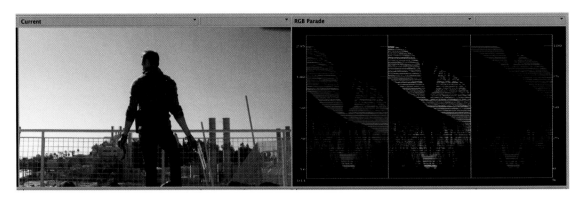

Figure 2.13
The corrected image shows balanced blacks.

Slight variations in the shape of the traces between the color channels are normal. The important thing to determine if an object is color neutral is that the trace group covers the same range of values. Blacks are balanced when the bottoms of all waveforms are equivalent. Likewise, whites are balanced when the tops of all waveforms are equivalent.

Analyze another shot before you leave the RGB Parade:

1. Continue working with the same sequence, **2_Reading Scopes**.

2. Advance the position indicator to the shot **Aerial_Cityscape1.mov**. This shot is an aerial shot taken out the door of a helicopter, showing downtown Los Angeles.

3. Look at both the Y Waveform and RGB Parade to analyze the shot and identify the elements and characteristics described, and as shown in Figure 2.14. For ease of reference, I have divided the image in Figure 2.14 into three panels.

White towers

Black towers, washed-out blacks   Sloping values indicate color cast

Figure 2.14
The Y Waveform and RGB Parade of the uncorrected Aerial_Cityscape1.mov.

- Notice the waveforms of this image are much busier. There aren't the same simple, distinctive elements seen in the previous shots.

- There is a heavy band at 80%–85% that represents the sky.

- The bright tower exiting the top of the frame is discernible in the center of the waveform, in the second panel. Likewise, the cross-shaped tower in the first panel is visible as a double peak in the waveform. Numerous groups of shadow traces along the bottom correspond to the black towers, and the shadowed side of brighter towers.

- Overall, the image has a broad luma range and bright whites. The white point (the highest trace) reaches the maximum of 100%.

- The blacks are washed out. The black point (the lowest trace) technically does reach 0%, but this is the doorframe of the helicopter. It has no relation to the scene, nor any detail to lose. If you discount that—as you would with a matte box, for instance—the black point would be too high, sitting at only 15%.

- A cursory glance at the RGB Parade tells you that the entire image is tilted toward blue. This blue cast is also visible in the image itself.

- Look at a few areas of the Parade and you can see specific patterns emerge. If you look at traces for most of the other objects in the image, you find a similar pattern: The blue trace is consistently higher than the corresponding green and red traces.

Recommended correction based on reading the Y Waveform and RBG Parade: Adjust the black level to darken the shadows. Balance the image by boosting red and reducing blue across the entire luma range.

4. Click the **FF** button to advance the position indicator to the corrected version of the **AERIAL_CITYSCAPE1.MOV** shot, shown in Figure 2.15.

5. Compare the relative position of the overall patterns within the traces.

Figure 2.15
After color correction, the trace patterns are well-balanced.

Red and green channels are nearly identical across the luma range. In the shadows, the blue channel matches the others, but the highlighted blue voltages are higher than the others. In this image, that is the natural blue haze of the atmosphere as seen on the mountains and clouds in the distance.

Key concept: The RGB Parade is used to determine the overall color balance as well as the balance within portions of the luma range.

Understanding the Vectorscope

The Vectorscope is a visual display that shows the electronic pattern of the color portion of the video signal. It does not display luma. The Vectorscope is to chroma what the Y Waveform is to luma.

The Vectorscope trace represents the blend of red, green, and blue throughout the image. It is presented on a circular graph, where the center represents no chroma and chroma increases in saturation (or intensity, or energy) as the trace moves away from the center. The Vectorscope is used to determine two things: the saturation of colors in the image and the overall color balance of an image (especially the accuracy of skin tones).

In addition to RGB Parade, this scope is key to the second part of stage one of the color-correction process.

Note: The Vectorscope, like the waveform scopes, is useful for validating the integrity of video signals. For more on this, see the Help article, "Using the Waveform and Vectorscope Information."

Hue values are mapped around the circumference of the color wheel. Moving clockwise around the wheel, the colors are red, magenta, blue, cyan, green, yellow, and then back to red. All white, black, and gray parts of the image appear at the center. In fact, if you look again at the B/W ramp on the Vectorscope, no trace whatsoever is visible. (See Figure 2.16.) (Feel free to follow along in your sequence.)

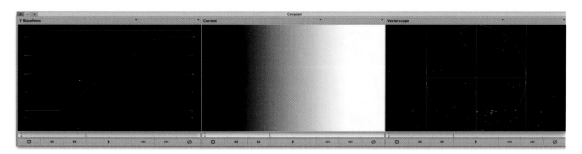

Figure 2.16
The Vectorscope, which shows color information only, is empty on a B/W image.

Saturation specifies the amount, intensity, or richness of the color; values are mapped along the radius of the wheel. The center point of the wheel represents zero saturation (neutral gray); the edge of the wheel represents maximum saturation. In other words, the farther out a trace extends, the more saturated are those colors. Figure 2.17 shows the Vectorscope reading for 100% color bars. Each color reaches the corresponding 100% vector on the scope.

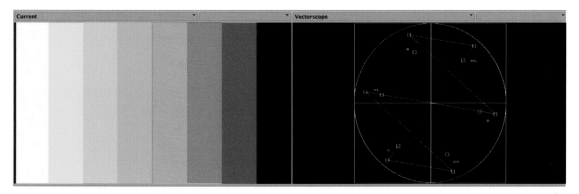

Figure 2.17
Color bars with 100% saturation form a precise pattern on the Vectorscope.

To better understand the display of the Vectorscope and how it might relate to a real image, let's look at the trace of a real video image. Figure 2.18 shows the Vectorscope trace and superimposes a color wheel on the Vectorscope display. As you can see, the color relationships between the Vectorscope and color wheel are the same. Not only does this make it easy to identify the colors represented by the trace concentrations, it also makes it easy to correct them because they match the color wheels of the Hue Offset controls in the HSL group.

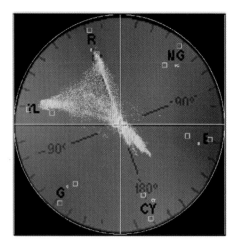

Figure 2.18
The Vectorscope matches the color orientation of a standard video color wheel.

The trace in this image shows very saturated reds and yellows, with less saturated (but still strong) blues. The Vectorscope doesn't tell you where in the image those colors are, simply that they are present. Figure 2.19 shows the video frame and a normal view of the Vectorscope.

Figure 2.19
The bold colors in the image are seen as branching arms in the Vectorscope.

The Vectorscope is relied on heavily when grading shots with faces. If you imagine a clock face on the Vectorscope, the traces of a proper skin tone, regardless of race or complexion, will line up approximately at the 11 o'clock position. Many Vectorscope displays include a dedicated line, known as the I-line, for visual guidance. Figure 2.20 shows the Vectorscope display found in ScopeBox, complete with an I-line.

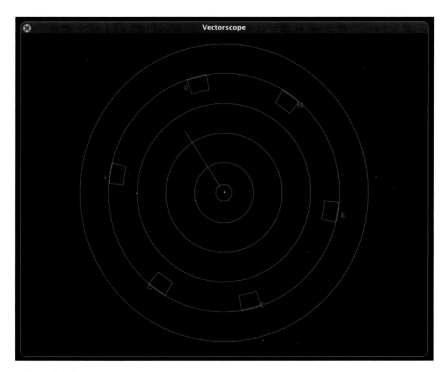

Figure 2.20
ScopeBox's Vectorscope, with I-line display.

Note: People are keenly aware of skin tones. If skin tones are not correct, viewers
        will pick up on it immediately. If the actor is in an unusual situation—in
        front of the lights of a police car, a tornado, a fire, a transporter beam,
        etc.—the viewer will excuse skin tones that look unnatural. Otherwise, it is
        the single most important tone in a scene. To get it right while portraying
        the other tones in the scene as desired, secondary color correction is often
        used. You'll learn more about this in a later chapter. For now, don't under-
        estimate its importance.

Shot Analysis with the Vectorscope

To begin working with the Vectorscope:

1. Continue working with the same sequence, **2_READING SCOPES**.

2. Using the **SOURCE** menus, change the Composer monitors to display the **RGB PARADE** on the left and the **VECTORSCOPE** on the right.

3. Move the position indicator back to the uncorrected version of the **AERIAL_CITYSCAPE1** shot and look at the Vectorscope. (See Figure 2.21.) It was already determined that there was a blue color cast to this image. This is shown on the Vectorscope as a shift in the trace blob toward the blue.

Figure 2.21
The trace is not centered. Rather, it is shifted toward blue, indicating a color cast.

4. Move the position indicator to the corrected version of the **AERIAL_CITYSCAPE1** shot. Notice how the Vectorscope changes. The trace is now centered.

5. You may wish to jump between the corrected and uncorrected versions several times, watching the Vectorscope, until the differences are clear to you.

6. Repeat the process of comparing the corrected and uncorrected versions of a shot with both **ZERO_ROOFTOP1** and **BURLESQUE_2**.

Note: The Vectorscope doesn't provide luma or gamut information, so it doesn't tell you whether your signal is within valid limits. You may be tempted to interpret what's inside the circle as a valid signal and what's outside the circle as unacceptable. Do not do this! Instead, use the YC Waveform and a gamut display for this purpose. YC Waveform is covered later in this lesson.

7. Move the position indicator to the shot **ZERO_ROOFTOP2**.

8. Look at the Vectorscope to analyze the shot. Identify the characteristics described here and shown in Figure 2.22.

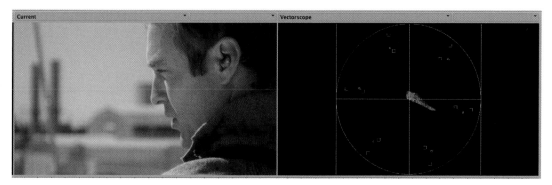

Figure 2.22
Shot Zero_Rooftop2 and its Vectorscope display.

- There is relatively low saturation in the image. The blob, or trace concentration, is compacted toward the center.
- The trace has only one significant color arm, which extends toward the blue vector. This is presumably the sky.
- Looking closer, the main trace concentration is not centered, indicating a color cast. It appears weighted toward magenta, but likely includes some blue (hidden by the valid sky tones). When you start manipulating the image, it will become clear which part of the trace is sky versus color cast.
- If you have a waveform display up, you'll notice that the image is also very flat, with a limited luma range that doesn't exceed 60% at the highlights.

Recommended correction based on reading the Vectorscope: Neutralize the blue/magenta color cast; increase saturation.

9. Move the position indicator to the corrected version of the **Zero_Rooftop2** shot. Examine the Vectorscope, as shown in Figure 2.23.

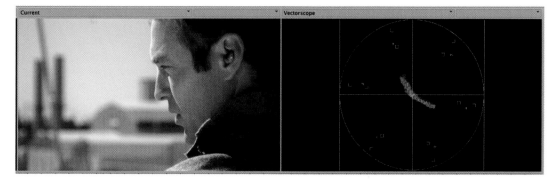

Figure 2.23
The corrected Zero_Rooftop2 and its Vectorscope display.

Analysis of the corrected image:

- The traces are now balanced, passing through the center point of the Vectorscope.

- The correction has changed the shape of the trace, giving it two distinct branches. One is a more refined branch for the blue sky; the other stretches up along the I-line. Naturally, these are the skin tones.

- It is worth mentioning that this correction did not include any adjustment to saturation levels. The colors naturally become more saturated through the correction process, as is frequently the case.

Key concept: The Vectorscope is used to determine the overall color balance of a shot, saturation levels, and proper flesh tone.

Understanding the YC Waveform

The YC Waveform displays the total composite video signal: the chroma (C) waveform laid on the luma (Y) waveform. The YC Waveform is Avid's only gamut display. This scope is useful when checking that color and luma are within safe limits, according to the delivery specification. If you are delivering to another spec, you can adjust the safe limit values the YC Waveform references in the project setting, Safe Colors. (The Safe Colors setting is covered in detail in a later chapter.)

Note: Media Composer and Symphony are configured by default to use SMPTE REC.601/709 as the Safe Colors reference standard.

Figure 2.24 shows a familiar shot, with the Y Waveform and the YC Waveform displayed. You see the luma waveform displayed on its own in the Y Waveform monitor; its trace is green. This same luma trace is visible in the YC Waveform, and it's identical in both scopes. The chroma waveform shows color difference signals for C_B (derived from the B–Y digital video signal) and C_R (derived from the R–Y digital video signal) components; its trace is cyan (blue plus green).

The left side of the YC Waveform shows a scale marked either for NTSC or PAL, depending on your project. NTSC black is 7.5 IRE (except in Japan) and NTSC white is 100 IRE. PAL black is 0mV and PAL white is 700mV. The scale on the right shows the amount of white in the image as a percentage; 0% represents black and 100% represents white. (Refer to Table 2.1 earlier in this chapter.)

Figure 2.24
Shot Zero_Rooftop1 and its Vectorscope display.

To make sure you do not have too much bright chroma (or luma plus chroma out of limit), refer to the following guidelines:

- The C (blue-green) Waveform should not exceed 110 IRE (NTSC) or 850mV (PAL). Any chroma above these numbers will be displayed as yellow.

- The C Waveform should not fall below –20 IRE (NTSC) or –200mV (PAL). Any chroma below these numbers will be displayed as white.

- Composite (chroma plus luma) video values above or below acceptable limits are indicated by a red edge on the display.

It is best to grade the image to be within spec. However, there are times when it is realized too late in the post process that an image has illegal levels. Rather than regrade the image and risk missing a deadline, you can use a Safe Color Limiter effect to clamp the levels to a specification. This is not an ideal solution by any stretch, but will get you through in a pinch.

The Safe Color Limiter is discussed in depth in a later chapter. For now, you should understand the principle behind using it. If there are gross overages in the signal, it is better to grade them out. If there are minor ones, the Safe Color Limiter is a safe choice. This is the same principle mentioned earlier about clipping. You never want to be surprised by how an image looks when it's going to air or screened by the director.

Tip: The YC Waveform is useful to evaluate the combination of chroma and luma. Don't use it to evaluate luma alone. Because the two parts of the signal are overlaid, the display is too cloudy to be useful for that purpose. Instead, stick with the Y Waveform to evaluate luma.

Shot Analysis with the YC Waveform

It is far more likely that images will exceed specification after the grading process than in their raw state. In this section, you'll analyze the graded images in the Timeline.

To begin working with the Vectorscope:

1. Continue working with the same sequence, **2_READING SCOPES**.

2. Using the **SOURCE** menus, change the Composer monitors to display the **Y WAVEFORM** on the left and the **VECTORSCOPE** on the right.

3. Advance the playhead to the corrected version of the **ZERO_ROOFTOP2** shot.

4. Analyze the YC Waveform, as shown in Figure 2.25. You read the YC Waveform much like the Y Waveform, but in this case the blue-green trace (chroma) overlays the green trace (luma). For the chroma, as with luma, you see a range of values, representing all shades of colors in the image.

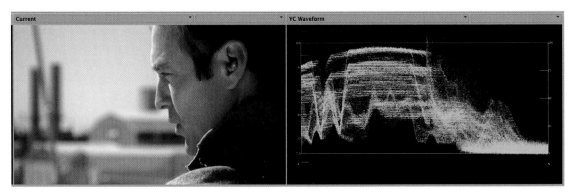

Figure 2.25
Shot Zero_Rooftop2 and its YC Waveform display.

5. Examine the top and bottom of the YC Waveform, looking at the C waveform values to see whether the chroma is too high or too low. Are there any red lines? Because there are no red lines at the top or bottom of the monitor, you know that chroma is within acceptable limits.

   Recommended correction based on reading the YC Waveform:
   No adjustment necessary.

6. Move the playhead to the corrected version of the **BURLESQUE_2** shot.

7. Analyze the YC Waveform, as shown in Figure 2.26. Remember, this shot has dramatic variations in color and lighting. It will be important to scrub through the shot to verify compliance on all frames.

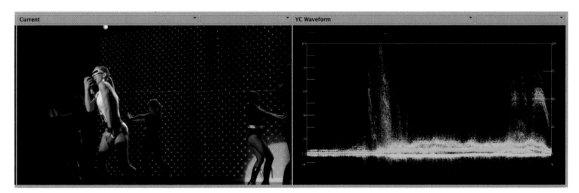

Figure 2.26
Shot Burlesque_2 and its YC Waveform display.

8. Carefully examine the top and bottom of the YC Waveform as you scrub through the shot. A number of frames show red bars at the peaks associated with the singer and the background light visible at the top of the image frame. (See Figure 2.27.)

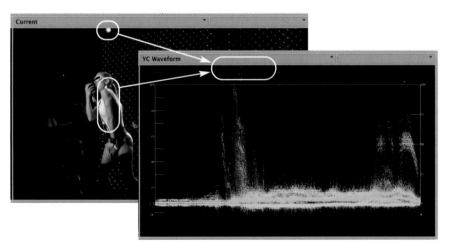

Figure 2.27
Shot Burlesque_2 has illegal chroma values.

Recommended correction based on reading the YC Waveform: Adjust the grade or apply a Safe Color Limiter to clamp the excessive signal.

Key concept: The YC Waveform is used to determine whether the composite signal is legal for the intended delivery specification.

Summary

As you have seen, each scope is a valuable and unique tool. As you grade, you will need to use each one. To grade efficiently, you must seamlessly move back and forth between the scopes, using the scope that is best at providing the information you need at that moment.

Most colorists grade with four scopes displayed at all times—another advantage of using external scopes. If you are using the Avid internal scopes, you will simply need to switch back and forth between scopes as you grade. Fortunately, the versatility of the Composer windows should enable you to find a setup that works efficiently for you. For example, if you are using a calibrated client monitor, you can use all three Composer windows for scopes, looking at the shot exclusively in the client monitor.

Tip: The Artist Color controller makes it very easy to switch scopes. Each window's Source menu is mapped to a soft knob. Turn the knob, and you scroll through the various scopes and Source menu options.

Notes From The Colorist:
How the 60-Second Rule Will Make You A Better Colorist

Earlier, I talked about blindfolding your brain. It's built on the proven premise that the human visual system is an active participant in analyzing the raw retinal data it receives. I break this concept down into two parts:

- **Part 1: Your eyes lie to you.** Or more precisely, they actively try to help you make sense of the world even if your brain has to distort the raw data to do so. The brightness contrast effect is proof of this. The two gray boxes shown earlier look different precisely because they are the same! Your brain alters your perception of them based on many factors, including the context of the entire scene, real-world physics, and a lifetime of visually interacting with the world around you. Your brain is a comparative beast and doesn't have much use for absolute values. (If this notion is driving you crazy, you're not alone! Welcome to the world of color correction.)

- **Part 2: The more you look at something, the more correct it looks.** I don't have an optical illusion that can prove this to you, but I do have another reference: *The Art and Technique of Digital Color Correction* by Steve Hullfish. It's a terrific book with a unique angle and is absolutely worth reading. For it, Hullfish interviewed more than a dozen colorists and gave them the same project to color correct. While interviewing those colorists, he noticed that they all said the same thing: They had to make their initial corrections (their primary grades) very quickly. They didn't have much time to look at an image before their eyes would fool them. After a certain amount of time, their brains take over and the images looked just fine!

The 60-Second Rule

Steve dubbed this effect the 60-second rule. And Steve is dead on. Colorists the world over will confirm that you have under a minute to do the following:

■ Judge the initial quality of an image.

■ Identify its problems.

■ Execute your solution to the problems.

■ Judge the effectiveness of your solution.

Universally, colorists agree that after 45–60 seconds, your internal white-balance takes over. Your brain auto-corrects the image for you and you can no longer trust your eyes. You need to (you guessed it) blindfold your brain.

Stretching Out Those 60 Seconds

And *that* is the point of using vectorscopes, waveforms, and histograms. These visual representations bypass your normal visual processes. They look nothing like the images you're evaluating. They're abstract representations, which engage a completely different part of your brain. By using scopes as your main evaluation tools—and only cheating a quick glance here and there—you can put those 60 seconds in your wallet and buy yourself more time. Learning to read scopes to make your initial color-correction decisions will make you a better colorist. And once you've made your initial fixes?

After the 60-Second Rule, It's All *You*

After making your initial corrections, don't forget to take the blindfold off your brain and use your eyes. The scopes may say everything looks good, but does it *actually look good*? Remember, your visual system is active—it's a comparative system. The raw values might be where you want them, but in context they may be off.

Don't be disheartened by this thought. You should be happy! I'm saying that after a certain point, you should trust your gut! You know what the world looks like. And you know what you want *this* world—the one you're color correcting—to look like.

But what if you get lost? What if you've been looking at an image too long and no longer know what to do with it? Take a note of the timecode number and move on. Come back to it later, when you can again see that shot with fresh eyes. Chances are, you'll fix it much more quickly the second time around.

My advice: Heed the 60-second rule to get to an evenly balanced image that generally feels the way you want it to feel. Once you're there, you're in control, baby! Revel in it.

—pi

Review/Discussion Questions

1. What effect does increasing contrast have on an image?

2. What happens to saturation as luminance approaches the extremes of black or white?

3. What does the Y Waveform scope display?
   a. Luma
   b. Chroma
   c. Luma + Chroma composite
   d. Saturation
   e. All of the above

4. What does the RGB Parade display?

5. How can the RGB Parade be used to determine the balance of the black point or white point?

6. How is the Vectorscope useful for correcting skin tones?

7. Look at the following figure. Which statement is true?

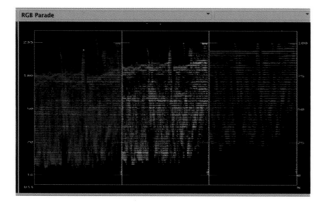

   a. The image is well balanced
   b. The image has a magenta cast
   c. The image has a red cast
   d. The image has a blue cast
   e. None of the above

8. Look at the following figure. Which statement is true?

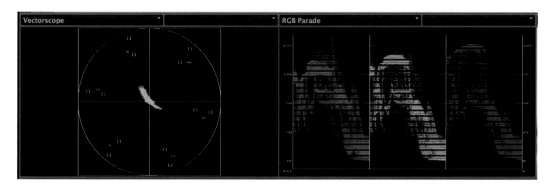

   a. The image has a broad luma range

   b. The image is balanced

   c. The image has proper skin tones

   d. The image has good saturation

   e. All of the above

9. What is the YC Waveform used for?

10. What are two ways out-of-range chroma and luma values can be corrected?

Lesson 2 Keyboard Shortcuts

The functions in this table can be mapped to the key of your choice. For information on how to map your keyboard, see the article "Mapping User-Selectable Buttons" in the Media Composer or Symphony Help.

Lesson 2 Keyboard Shortcuts	
Function	**Action**
Play	Play the current segment only.
Fast Forward	Move the position indicator to the next segment in the sequence.
Rewind	Move the position indicator to the previous segment in the sequence.
Next Uncorrected	Move the position indicator to the next segment in the sequence without a correction effect.
Previous Uncorrected	Move the position indicator to the previous segment in the sequence without a correction effect.
Dual Split	Activates a resizable panel over the current that reveals the uncorrected image; useful for comparison against the corrected image.

Analyzing Images with Scopes

In the last exercise, you made notes on your visual impressions of a shot. In this exercise, you analyze color and luminance problems using scopes. Some of the shots you analyze here, you will correct in later exercises. Don't worry, your efforts won't go to waste.

Media Used:

Avid Color Grading (MC239) project > 2_Exercise Bins folder > Ex2_Analyzing Images bin > Ex2_Analyzing Images sequence

Duration:

20 minutes

GOALS

- Use each of the internal video scopes to analyze images
- Identify image elements in the waveform scopes
- Evaluate the luma range of an image
- Identify color casts in an image
- Evaluate skin tones for color casts

Overview

Analyze each shot in the sequence visually and technically, using the broadcast monitor (if you have one) and the various scopes. Take a moment to glance at the image first; it will give you context as you look at the scopes. Remember the 60-second rule, though, and don't look too long. As you analyze the images, use each scope to answer the following questions. Write your analysis in the spaces provided below each shot listed on the next page.

- Does the luma cover the full range?

- Does the gamma need to be adjusted to set the proper mood for the shot?

- Is there detail in the shadows and highlights? Is this detail important?

- Does the black point need to be adjusted? Does the white point? If so, to what value would you set it?

- Does the image have illegal luma or chroma values?

- Does the image have a color cast? If so, what is the color of the cast? In the direction of which color would the image need to be adjusted to remove the cast?

- If there is a cast, does it cover the image equally, or is it confined to one area of the luma range?

- Are the flesh tones accurate?

Shot Notes

Use the spaces on this page to write your notes.

Agent Sierra_XCU:

Agent Sierra_typing hands CU:

Zero_helicopter flight 1:

Ext.Helicopter_landing fisheye:

Zero_Dramatic entry:

Phantom Zero_CU:

Note: If you are using this book in the classroom, plan to discuss your analysis as a group.

Establishing the Base Grade

This lesson covers the procedure for color correcting individual segments (clips) in the Timeline. This procedure corresponds to the first stage of the color-correction process, as explained in Lesson 1, "Color Grading Fundamentals." In this lesson, you use the controls in the HSL group—a versatile group that many experienced colorists will find familiar.

Media Used: Avid Color Grading (MC239) project > 1_Lesson Bins folder > 3_HSL Primary bin > 3_HSL Lesson sequence

Duration: 60 minutes

GOALS

- Understand the general workflow for making primary corrections
- Perform a base grade in HSL mode
- Correct tonal range
- Neutralize color casts with the Hue Offsets Tab > ChromaWheel controls
- Keyframe color corrections

Performing a Primary Correction

The first step in the grading process is to perform primary corrections to establish a baseline, or base grade. Your two objectives in this process are to set a consistent luma range for the shots and remove any *unwanted* color casts. This establishes a consistent foundation on which you can build a more stylized look adding secondary corrections, vignettes, etc. The controls in the HSL group are ideally suited for these tasks and are the focus of this lesson.

Frequently, there is a great deal of latitude in how you shade an image in the primary grade. Ask yourself, What is the tone, or mood, the filmmakers are trying to create here? What role does this shot, or scene, play in the overall story arc? Your discussions with the stakeholders—the director, producer, client, etc.—should drive your decision-making process here.

It is your job to bring to life the vision of the filmmakers. Setting the base grade is an important first step in that process. Remember, the goal is not to create a finished image. The goal of the primary grade should be to make the shot visually more interesting and notably closer to the final look that is desired by the stakeholders.

The HSL Group

The Hue, Saturation, Luminance (HSL) group provides controls that enable you to alter attributes in the image such as hue, saturation, gain, and gamma. These controls resemble those found in the Video Input tool and in the Color Effect, so some may be familiar to you.

The HSL group is divided into tabs:

- **Controls.** The Controls tab, shown in Figure 3.1, provides sliders to adjust various attributes of hue, saturation, and luma. The Hue and Saturation sliders are marked as such. Luma controls include Brightness, Contrast, Gain, Gamma, and Setup. To the right side of the tab are the Color Match controls for automatically adjusting hue, saturation, and luminance, based on selected input and output color values. Color Match is covered in Lesson 5, "Matching Shots."

Note: In Media Composer, the Gain, Gamma, and Setup controls are located on the Hue Offsets tab rather than the Controls tab.

- **Hue Offsets.** The Hue Offsets tab, shown in Figure 3.2 and Figure 3.3, displays Avid ChromaWheel controls to adjust the hue and saturation. Media Composer displays three color wheels—labeled Shd, Mid, and Hlt—that manipulate the shadows, midtones, and highlights, respectively. Symphony adds a fourth Mas (short for Master) wheel for adjusting the overall image.

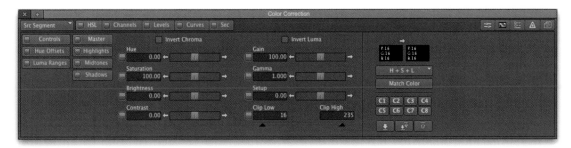

Figure 3.1
The HSL Controls tab in Symphony.

In this course, you will use the Hue Offsets tab to set black (setup), white (gain), and gamma levels.

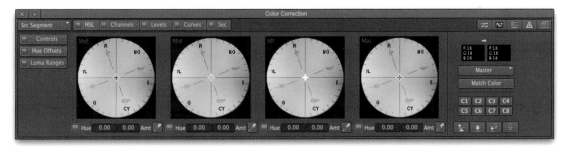

Figure 3.2
The HSL Hue Offsets tab in Symphony.

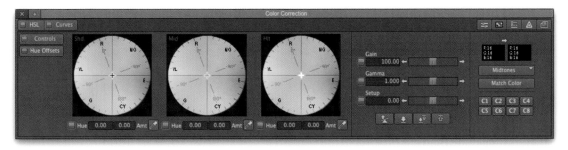

Figure 3.3
The HSL Hue Offsets tab in Media Composer.

- **Luma Ranges (Symphony only).** The Luma Ranges tab provides controls that enable you to manipulate the range of luma values that will be altered by the highlight, midtone, and shadow controls in the other HSL tabs. These tabs are discussed in greater detail in Lesson 6, "Stepping Up to Symphony." Controls and buttons for the HSL group in the Effect Editor and in the Color Correction tool are ganged together, so changes in one are immediately represented in the other. For now, you'll work exclusively in the Color Correction tool; I'll discuss the Effect Editor later.

Note: If you are working in Symphony, the default color correction relationship is Src Segment. This is a good choice for the base grade. Color correction relationships will be discussed in detail in Lesson 6.

What Is Hue Offset?

Most of us immediately understand the word hue. When we hear the word, we think color, and know that adjusting hue means shifting the colors. With video, the hue control—also known as phase control—typically rotates the hue of all colors by the same amount.

So what is hue offset, and why is it the preferred method of correcting color problems? Rather than simply rotating the hue of all colors, hue offset adjusts, or offsets, the hue in specific luma ranges, and therefore does a better job of fixing color-cast problems such as poor white balancing.

Adjusting the Controls and Hue Offsets Tabs

Let's get you familiar with the controls first; then, you'll put them to use in the next section. When it comes to making HSL adjustments, the Avid Artist Color controller shines. With it, you can grade very quickly and efficiently. Without it, the process can be slower and more deliberate. But if the boss is too cheap or the budget too tight and you're stuck grading with the mouse, no worries! Many an Avid colorist grades with only a mouse, and the results are just as good.

Making HSL Adjustments Using a Mouse

Manipulating the controls with a mouse is straightforward and intuitive. Just click and drag. Avid also built in some useful shortcuts and modifiers that make mouse-keyboard grading more efficient.

The following apply to all controls in the color correction toolset:

- Click in the slider track; the slider will jump to that location (making a dramatic adjustment in value).

- Shift-drag a slider to make finer adjustments.

- Click the arrow on either side of a slider to make single-unit adjustments.

- Click and hold the arrow to make continuous, slow adjustments.

- Click in the value text box to enter a numeric value using the keyboard.

Take a moment to experiment with manipulating the HSL controls using the mouse.

Making HSL Adjustments Using the Artist Color

Avid designers did a great job integrating the Artist Color into Symphony and Media Composer. The default mapping of the Artist Color is intuitive and ideal for a broad range of users. For now, I'll assume you're using the default settings.

As you become more experienced, you may find that you want to change the defaults. All soft knobs and function keys on the Color controller can be remapped using the EuControl software.

Tip: This section covers the full range of functions covered in this lesson. Keep the page marked for easy reference as you work through the lesson.

To make adjustments to HSL controls and hue offsets:

1. In Source/Record mode, load the sequence **3_HSL LESSON**. Using the mouse or keyboard, make sure the Record Track button for the track on which you want to make corrections is the topmost selected button in the Track Selector panel in the Timeline. (Color correction is applied to the topmost selected track in a sequence.)

2. On the Color controller, press the **F1** button to activate the Color Correction workspace.

Tip: You can color correct nested tracks by stepping into the nest.

3. To set up the Composer monitors, press the controller's **SHIFT** button, found in both the bottom-left and bottom-right corners. The OLED display changes to show the current contents of each monitor over the first three soft knobs. Rotate the left knob to change the scope or source displayed in the left monitor to the desired selection. Repeat for the right monitor. For this example, let's use Y Waveform and RGB Parade. Press the **SHIFT** button again to deactivate it after you've made your selection. Great, you're all set up! Now to make some adjustments.

4. Moving left to right on the panel, the three trackwheels are mapped to Setup, Gamma, and Gain, respectively. (See Figure 3.4.) Rotate each dial clockwise to increase the value of the corresponding parameter; make a counter-clockwise rotation to decrease it. The scopes will update in near real-time as the adjustments are made. The values are also reflected in the OLED display at the top of the controller.

Figure 3.4
The relationship of the Artist Color trackwheels to the HSL luma controls.

5. The three trackballs correspond to the same luma ranges as the trackwheels but control the Hue Offset ChromaWheels, as shown in Figure 3.4. Roll the ball in the direction of the desired hue offset; the crosshair will simultaneously move and the image will update.

6. To adjust Symphony's Mas ChromaWheel, press the **BANK 2** button, shown in Figure 3.5. With Bank 2 active, the right trackball controls the Mas ChromaWheel; the trackwheel, however, still controls gain. After making the adjustment, press the **BANK 1** button.

7. To adjust overall hue, saturation, brightness, or contrast, rotate the corresponding soft knob as labeled in the controller display. The soft knobs are touch sensitive; when you touch one, the corresponding label changes to the current value of that parameter. This is a convenient way to check a value when that parameter is not currently visible on the Avid interface.

8. To reset a parameter, such as Saturation, press and hold **SATURATION** soft knob for a full second, then release. Upon release, the value is reset.

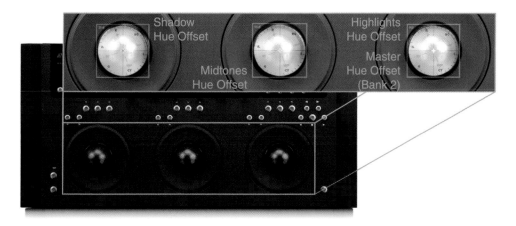

Figure 3.5
The relationship of the Artist Color trackballs to the HSL Hue Offset controls.

9. To reset the value on a trackwheel or trackball, press the **R** key just above the trackwheel. For example, to reset the Setup, press and hold **R1**. To reset the Shd Hue Offset, press and hold **R2**. A quick press of each button will toggle the corresponding parameter adjustment on and off.

10. To move between segments, press the transport buttons above the right trackwheel, as shown in Figure 3.6. The left and right buttons on the top row move the playhead to the previous and next clip, respectively. Holding down the Shift key (on the Color controller) as you click these buttons will jump you to the previous and next *uncorrected* segment. The second row of buttons function as J-K-L.

Figure 3.6
In Color Correction mode, the transport controls buttons have special functions.

11. Another way to navigate the sequence is using the trackballs. Press the **SHIFT** key to toggle Shift mode on. In Shift mode, the left and right trackballs shuttle through the entire sequence in the corresponding Composer monitor. The center trackball shuttles through the current clip. Like any shuttle transport control, the farther you roll the ball, the faster it moves the playhead. Practice this a few times before doing it in front of a client. It takes some getting used to! When finished, press **SHIFT** again to return to normal HSL controls.

12. There will still be times when you want the random access control of a mouse. The Artist Color has a built-in mouse mode, which enables you to keep your hands on the control surface rather than reaching across the desk for the mouse. To activate mouse mode, press **F5**. In mouse mode, the center trackball behaves like a standard trackball, controlling the pointer. Press **R3** to perform a left click; press **R4** to right-click.

13. Additional functions are mapped to the other function keys and soft knobs. To quickly see the current mappings, press the **EYE** button in the top-right corner of the panel. The EuControl Settings dialog box opens, as shown in Figure 3.7. Use this dialog box as a reference or to change the current settings.

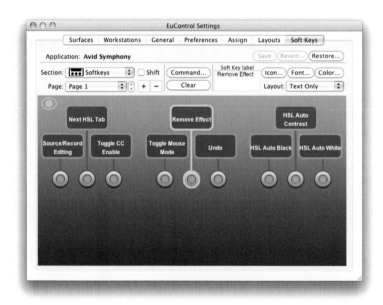

Figure 3.7
The EuControl Settings dialog box is a handy reference of controller mappings.

Now that you're familiar with the Artist controller, let's use it to perform a base grade.

Using Tonal Controls in HSL

The first step to performing a base grade is to set the tonal range for the shot. This is a simple process of deciding what the contrast will be for the shot by setting the *black point*, the darkest point in the image, to give depth to the shadowed areas, and setting the *white point*, the brightest spot in the image, to determine how bright the highlights should be. In setting the black point and white point, you define the range of brightness values between the darkest part of the image and the lightest part of the image—literally defining the *luma* range. This alone can dramatically increase the quality of the image.

The next step in setting the tonal range is to adjust midtones to control how much of the tonal range falls above and below the middle value. You use this step to adjust the relative balance of light and dark, of highlight and shadow.

Tip: Setting the midtones of the tonal range has a strong effect on the mood of the shot. Remember, midtones = mood!

Take a moment to think about a scene that is bright and cheery, dark and moody, or dreary and melancholy. Visualize each in your mind. How would you describe the relative brightness and contrast in each scene? When grading, you should be able to visualize what it is you want from the shot, and work toward that. Otherwise, you'll waste a lot of time just playing with the controls.

Identifying the Tonal Controls

Luma controls are tonal controls. In HSL, these include Setup, Gain, Gamma, Brightness, and Contrast. The first three are the professional choice the world over to manipulate the luma range.

It is possible to use Contrast and Brightness controls to adjust tonal range, but they don't give you as much control as Setup, Gain, and Gamma. Brightness and Contrast controls make uniform adjustments to the entire image, whereas Setup, Gain, and Gamma controls give you precise control over defined regions within the luma range.

Finally, there are automatic correction functions within Media Composer and Symphony, as shown in Figure 3.8. Like any automatic function, they make calculations that are indiscriminate of the content of the image. Sometimes the results are desirable, sometimes not. Avid's autocorrect functions are not discussed in this course. Please see the Help menu or the introductory books in the Avid Learning Series for more information.

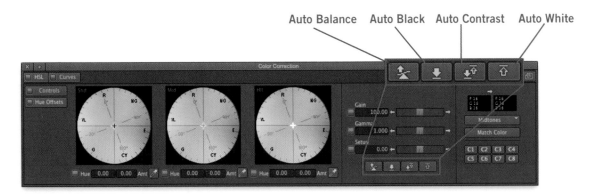

Figure 3.8
The automatic color balance and contrast controls.

Understanding Tonal Adjustments

To help you understand how Setup, Gain, and Gamma settings affect the image, you're going to start with a test pattern. I know, I know—how dry can I make it? But trust me, there are core concepts that are easier to understand by spending five minutes with a test pattern than by spending 50 minutes muddling with complex images. Using the black/white ramp pattern, you can clearly see the result of manipulating each of these parameters, including which portion of the luminance signal is being affected by each control.

Here are a few key points:

- The black point is set using the Setup control. Setup has a range of values from –255 to +255, with 0 representing an unchanged value.

- The white point is set using the Gain control. Gain has a range of values from 0 to 200, with 100 representing an unchanged value.

- The midtones are adjusted using the Gamma control. Gamma has a range of values from 0.100 to 10.000, with 1.000 representing an unchanged value.

To learn the range and limitations of the luma controls:

1. If it's not already open, open the **3_HSL PRIMARY** bin and load the **3_HSL LESSON** sequence.

2. Enter **COLOR CORRECTION** mode.

3. Set the left monitor to display **Y WAVEFORM** and the right to display **RGB PARADE**.

4. Click to activate the tabs **HSL > HUE OFFSETS** (Media Composer) or **HSL > CONTROLS** (Symphony).

5. Move the blue position indicator in the sequence to the first shot, **BWramp.pct**. Your Composer window should match the one shown in Figure 3.9.

Figure 3.9
Composer window displaying scopes and a black/white ramp pattern.

6. Using the mouse or Artist Color, raise the **Setup** value. Notice how the entire pattern in the Y Waveform scope lifts up uniformly.

7. Lower the **Setup** value. All values now lower by the same amount. This is because Setup is an additive adjustment. If the black point is lifted 10 IRE, all other values are lifted by the same amount, including even the very brightest whites!

8. Reset **Setup** to **0**. If you are using a mouse, reset the value by Option-clicking (Mac) or Alt-clicking (Windows) the **Setup** enable button.

9. Raise the **Gain** value a little at a time to approximately **150**. With each small adjustment, watch the result in the Y Waveform scope.

10. Toggle the **Gain** parameter off and on several times. If using the mouse, do so by clicking the enable button on the **Gain** parameter. Notice how the angle changes, starting at the black point itself. (See Figure 3.10.) This means all parameters from the black point up are affected. The higher the value, the greater the degree of change. Also, the black point itself doesn't move. This is because the Gain setting is a *proportional* adjustment.

Note: To use analogies, the Setup control is like an elevator platform. As it rises and falls, everything standing on it lifts and falls equally. In contrast, the Gain setting is proportional and acts like a rubber band. If you hold one end and pull on the other, the more you pull, the more everything in between gets stretched out (or compressed, if you perform the reverse operation). In fact, just like pulling a rubber band too far causes it to snap, applying too much of the Gain setting can add so much contrast it reveals defects in the image, such as sensor noise or the macroblocking in compressed media.

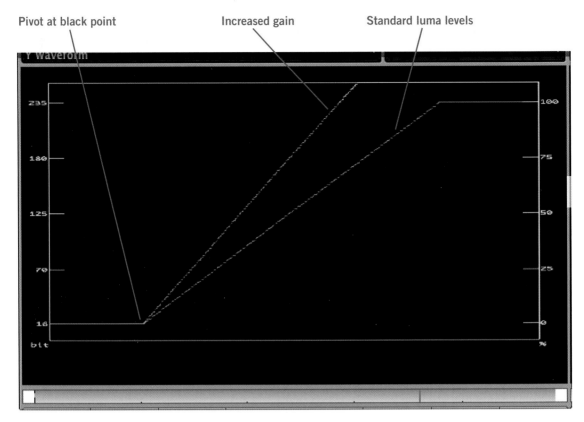

Figure 3.10
The angle changes as the Gain setting is increased.

11. Lower the **GAIN** setting back to **100** or reset the **GAIN** control.

12. Increase the **GAMMA** setting a little at a time to approximately **3.0**. With each adjustment, watch the result in the Y Waveform scope. This time, you should see the luminance line bend and deform, increasing contrast in the lower range and decreasing contrast in the upper range.

13. Reset the **GAMMA** control. As before, if working with a mouse, Option-click (Mac) or Alt-click (Windows) the **GAMMA** enable button.

14. Decrease the **GAMMA** setting a little at a time to approximately **.3**. Notice how the luma curve is almost reversed, reducing contrast in the lower range and increasing contrast in the upper range. Notice also that whether increasing or decreasing Gamma, neither the white point nor the black point moves.

Note: The Gamma control clearly bends the luminance curve of an image. In the HSL tools, you have no control over the shape of that curve. In Curves, however, you have complete control; you can make contrast adjustments within very specific portions of the luma range. More on this is Lesson 4, "Grading with Curves."

Seeing how each parameter works should help clarify a couple things. First, what portion of the luma range is affected by each control should be clear. Second, the order of operations in which you set the luma range is logical and efficient. Setup affects all values, including the black point. Once this is set, neither Gain nor Gamma will change it much. Next, Gain sets the white point. This will most dramatically affect the highlights but also affects the midtones. Finally, Gamma gives you broad control over the luma values between the black point and white point, while having a minimal impact on either.

Setting the Tonal Range Using HSL Controls

Let's take the theoretical concepts you just learned and apply them to a real image. Rather than broad bands of black and white, real images show complex trace patterns on the scopes. The skills you learned in Lesson 2, "Analyzing Images with Scopes," to identify picture elements on the scopes will be put to the test here.

Here are some points to keep in mind:

- To set the black point, identify an element in the image that should be black. The darkest shadows in an image can usually be pushed close to black.

- Consider carefully whether the image requires absolute blacks—that is, values at 0% or less. Absolute black is uncommon in nature and causes you to lose detail in those areas. Crushing the blacks, as it's called, is a popular look but you should make this choice consciously rather than out of habit.

- If the image is intentionally light, such as a beach or snow scene, you may want to avoid lowering the darkest shadows to 0%.

- To set the white point, look for a good white in the image, such as a white shirt or other object or a highlight (light area) on a face or object.

- Do not use intense reflected spots of light (known as speculars or specular highlights), such as the glint on glasses or the reflection on a motorcycle, to judge where your white point should be. Choose a more significant picture element instead. If your image has specular highlights, don't worry if they go above 100%. These points typically don't have any detail in them anyway, so they can safely be clipped.

- In general, you will adjust the Gain slider until the whitest part of the image approaches 100% on the waveform. (For most images, the whites should approach, not reach, 100%.) If the image is intentionally dark, you may not want to set the Gain control to this value.

- If the brightest element in the image is a face, 75% is generally a good target value.

To prepare for this grade:

1. If it's not already open, open the **3_HSL Primary** bin and load the **3_HSL Lesson** sequence.

2. Enter **Color Correction** mode.

3. Set the left monitor to display **Y Waveform** and the right to display **RGB Parade**.

4. Click to activate the tab **HSL > Hue Offsets** (Media Composer) or **HSL > Controls** (Symphony).

5. Scrub through the first shot, then park on a good representative frame.

6. The second shot, B3-3, is a close-up profile of Agent Zero, backlit by the sun, as shown in Figure 3.11. Take a moment to analyze it on the scopes.

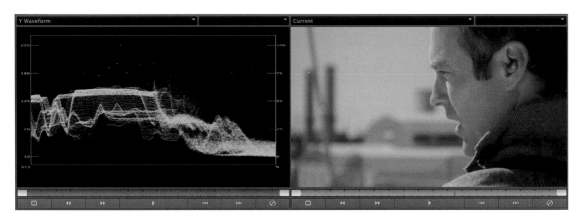

Figure 3.11
Y Waveform display of shot B3-3.

Analysis of Shot B3-3

Overall, the shot B3-3 is somewhat flat and needs more contrast. The blacks—as seen in his holster strap—are very close to where they should be. The whites, however, are not bright enough. The shot also looks blue overall, and the RGB Parade display confirms that. There is a distinctive blue push, especially in the highlights, which corresponds to the blue sky. This is natural, even in a balanced image. More importantly, all the tones are raised on the blue channel, indicating a color cast.

Setting the Luma Range on Shot B3-3

Many productions call for a conservative approach to the base grade. As a general best practice, avoid clipping any significant part of the image. For most scenes at this stage of the grading process, you want the range between your darkest value and your lightest value to be as large as possible. You should be careful not to lose detail by reducing all your very dark values to absolute black—this is called crushing the blacks—or all your very light values to bright white, which could cause clipping.

Tip: Learn to set the black point and white point primarily by looking at the scopes. The less you can look at the image during this process, the more successful you'll be at grading. (See "60-Second Rule" in "Notes from the Colorist" in Lesson 2 for the full explanation.)

To set the black point and white point on shot B3-3:

1. If necessary, set up to grade the shot as described previously, in the section "Setting the Tonal Range Using HSL Controls."

2. Using the Y Waveform scope as your reference, identify the traces on the right side of the waveform that correspond to the subject's holster strap. It is very close to 0 IRE. To ensure that you lose no detail in his hair, lift the blacks very slightly. The **SETUP** value should be approximately **3.00**.

3. Now that the black point is set, set the white point for the same segment. To begin, examine the image again. What are the most important highlights in this scene? I think they are the highlights that define his profile. Using the Y Waveform scope as your reference, raise the **GAIN** setting until the trace spike is at about 90 IRE. The Gain value will be approximately **132**. The results of this adjustment are shown in Figure 3.12.

4. If you don't like your results, readjust the level. If you want to start over, Alt-click (Windows) or Option-click (Mac) the **GAMMA** button. The slider is reset to its default value. Then try again. If you are happy with the corrections, turn your attention to the midtones!

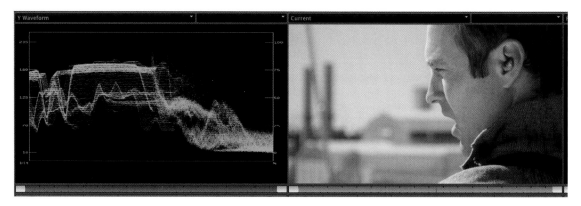

Figure 3.12
Shot B3-3, with black and white points set.

Note: If you see a solid black line at 7.5 IRE, it might represent blanking, or
for DV media the black lines at the top and bottom of the frame. (DV media
records six fewer lines than analog NTSC media.) It's okay if this solid line
falls below 7.5 IRE/0mV as you make your adjustments. This blanking can
be safely clipped with no impact to the image.

Adjusting the Gamma

When you make a Gamma control adjustment, you define how much of the overall tonal range is between black and mid-gray, and how much is between mid-gray
and white. It either lightens or darkens the overall look of the image. Large adjustments are almost always undesirable because they leave the whole image much too
dark or too light. Small Gamma control adjustments, however, can be useful for
fine-tuning the relative weight of darks and lights.

Also, because a Gamma control adjustment expands the tonal range on one side
of the midpoint and contracts it on the other, it can be useful for improving contrast and detail. For example, some images look better if you lighten the midtones,
increasing the contrast in the range between gray and white, even though you
sacrifice the contrast between gray and black. However, if the program was shot
day-for-night, you may want to darken the midtones, increasing contrast in the
range between gray and white.

Look at the image. If it has good contrast and detail and good balance between
light and dark tones, you may not need to adjust the Gamma control. Also,
because the level of gamma you choose can be so determined by context, it may
help to compare this shot to adjacent shots; you may want to lower or raise the
gamma to better match an adjacent shot.

Tip: Most shots with flesh tones, no matter what the skin color, can be improved
      by opening up (raising) the gamma. Typically, make the flesh tones a little
      higher than mid-point.

To set the gamma on shot B3-3:

1. Keep the position indicator parked on the same segment.

2. Examine the shot in the monitor. What's the mood of this shot? At the
    moment, it is too bright. There's no intrigue or danger in it. Let's give it a
    bit of an edge by darkening it, exaggerating the contrast on the subject's
    face.

3. Using the Y Waveform scope as your reference, lower the **GAMMA** setting
    until the arc of midtone traces that represent the subject's face sits at about
    40%. The Gamma value should be approximately **0.850**. This will further
    darken the shot, giving it more of a moody feel.

Tip: The process of adjusting any parameter, especially when it's a subjective
      adjustment, is a little like manually focusing a camera. You have to play with
      the adjustment, adding a little more, then a little less, until you settle in on
      the point that seems best. Don't be afraid to experiment.

4. Double-check the impact of the grade. Toggle the **CC** button. Alternatively,
    toggle the **DUAL SPLIT** button on and off if you dragged the triangle over
    the majority of the image. (See the section "Navigating Segments in the
    Monitors" in Lesson 1 for more information.) Well done! The image is
    much improved and headed in the right direction. The final result is
    shown in Figure 3.13.

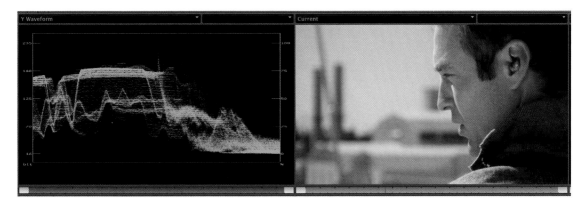

Figure 3.13
Shot B3-3, after the luma range was set.

Note: Most gamma adjustments don't affect the black and white points, but occasionally there may be some effect with extreme gamma adjustments. If necessary, readjust the Setup and Gain controls.

5. Move the playhead to the next shot, C3-1 and repeat the process of setting the luma range on this shot.

Tip: Resist the temptation to try to finalize the look now. Remember, at this point, you want to make the shot more interesting, creating a good starting point for the desired final look. Later, you can create a stylized look.

Analysis of Shot C3-1

Before beginning, scrub through the shot. Pick a good representative frame and take a moment to analyze it on the scopes. The first thing that jumps out is the extreme spike to the right of the Y Waveform scope. Looking at the image, it's clearly from the reflection on the equipment rack in the background. This is unfortunate, because it's not important to the shot.

In addition, overall, the shot is flat, lacking sufficient contrast. The blacks are slightly lifted. There are blacks throughout the image that should be at 0%, including the subject's collar, headset, and glasses, and the instrument panel with the blue lights in the background. None of these blacks sit at 0%.

The highlights are more complicated. There's the problem of the bright spot in the background. The white of the shirt, appearing in the lower-left corner, is the only real white. The other highlights are more important or more interesting, such as the instrument panels and the highlights on her glasses. The reflections on her glasses look blue to the naked eye, but that would seem appropriate for the scene because she's looking at computer monitors.

So, there's lots to be done!

Setting the Luma Range on Shot C3-1

This shot can be pushed in several directions. As you perform the primary grade, we'll discuss the options.

To set the luma range on shot C3-1:

1. If necessary, set up to grade the shot as described previously, in the section "Setting the Tonal Range Using HSL Controls."

2. Change the right monitor to display the **VECTORSCOPE** instead of the RGB Parade.

3. Using the Y Waveform scope as your reference, identify the traces to the center and left of the scope that correspond to the black band of the subject's collar and the black of the panel in the background. Lower the **SETUP** control until these traces sit at 0%. The Setup value will be somewhere around **–5.00**. As you make the adjustment, glance back to the monitor and make sure you're not losing detail in the subject's hair or the texture in her collar. If you are, back off the adjustment slightly.

4. Now that the black point is set, let's set the white point. Which are the most important highlights in this scene? I think they're the reflections on her glasses. The reflection on the equipment rack is the brightest, but not the most important. Set the white point for the glasses. Using the Y Waveform scope as your reference, raise the **GAIN** setting until the traces representing the highlight on the glasses sit at about 75%. This will cause some clipping in the metal equipment rack, but there wasn't much detail there anyway. Watch the client monitor as you make this adjustment; if you clip the highlights too much, they will lose detail and take on an electronic look. If this happens, back off the Gain setting a little. The Gain value should be approximately **145**. The result is shown in Figure 3.14.

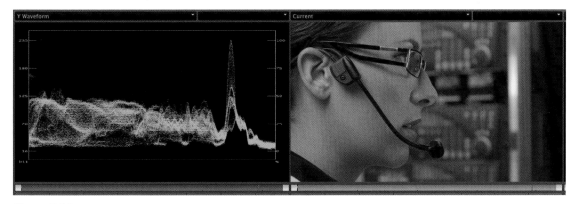

Figure 3.14
Shot C3-1, with black and white points set.

With the black point and white point set, let's turn our attention to the midtones. What's the mood of this shot? Right now, it's a little too bright to invoke the feeling of secret agent spy stuff; it's more like a friendly telecom operator. This is a tense, edgy scene. Sierra sits in the control room, playing Agent Zero's high-tech eyes in the sky as he infiltrates the bad guy's headquarters. No, a friendly telecom operator just won't do. Let's give if it a more appropriate feel.

Tip: People are especially aware of skin tones. Making a conscious choice of where to place the skin tones of the subject within the luma range is key to helping define the mood of a scene.

To adjust the midtones:

1. Using the Y Waveform scope as your reference, lower the Gamma setting until the series of wavy traces that represent the video decks in the background sit at about 15%–20%. The arc of traces representing her ear and cheek should sit no higher than 40%. This will further darken the shot, giving it more of a secret-control-room feel, as shown in Figure 3.15. It also fits better with the previous shot of Agent Zero.

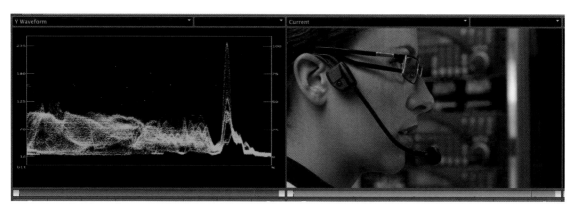

Figure 3.15
Shot C3-1, with Sierra looking properly secret-agent like.

2. Toggle the correction on and off while watching the Vectorscope. Notice how the traces seem to expand. This means there is greater saturation in the corrected image.

Tip: Always correct the luma range before adjusting color! Luma adjustments can change the saturation in the image, and therefore your perception of the colors.

Using Chroma Controls in HSL

Having set the tonal range for the shot, it's time to adjust the color. You will do this using chroma controls. In the HSL group, these are the Hue Offsets.

Understanding the ChromaWheel Controls

You use the color wheels in the Hue Offsets tab in the HSL group to correct color casts. For example, when Agent Zero's neutral gray sweater appears tinged with blue, you can use the offset adjustment to restore the correct gray color. The Hue Offsets controls enable you to adjust hue and saturation values at the same time by using color wheels and linked text boxes.

The ChromaWheel controls are based on the principles of hue offset. A hue off-set color wheel is a circular graph that represents hue and saturation values. You can use the color wheels to quickly locate the sector of the wheel that represents the color cast in the image and then adjust in the opposite direction of that color. Hue values are mapped around the circumference of the wheel, with colors in the same positions that they occupy on a vectorscope. As you move around the wheel, you shift from red to blue to green and then back to red. Hue values are measured in degrees by default. The position of red on the wheel is 0º, green is 120º, and blue is –120º; values range from –180º to 180º, as shown in Figure 3.16.

Figure 3.16
The color wheel hue values.

Saturation specifies the amount or intensity of color. Values are mapped along the radius of the wheel. The center point of the wheel represents zero saturation (neutral gray); the edge of the wheel represents maximum saturation. Saturation values are measured on a scale from 0 (zero saturation) to 100 (maximum saturation). By picking a specific point on the wheel (the position of the crosshair pointer), you select an exact combination of hue and color intensity to add to your image. You can select a gray with a slight yellow tinge near the center of the wheel, for example, or an intensely saturated blue at the outer edge.

When you use the color wheel to correct a color cast, you employ a basic principle of color theory: You can cancel out one color in an image by adding an equal amount of the opposite color (called its complementary color) on the wheel. For example, to remove a red cast, add some cyan. To remove a yellow cast, add some blue.

As a novice, you don't need to remember which colors are opposite (complementary); simply add some color from the opposite side of the wheel from the color you want to remove.

Note: Experienced colorists may find the ChromaWheel displays distracting. On Symphony, you can choose to hide them to help preserve the color fidelity of your vision. To do this, disable the Show ChromaWheel and ChromaCurve Graphs option in the Correction Mode settings > Features tab. The Hue Offsets display as simple graphic controls.

Removing a Color Cast Using Hue Offsets

To make a correction using the Hue Offsets color wheels:

1. Click the HUE OFFSETS tab.

2. If you are not working on an Artist Color, make your adjustments by doing one or more of the following:

   - Drag the crosshair pointer on the appropriate color wheel. For finer control, Shift-drag the mouse to make color wheel adjustments. As you move the pointer in the wheel, the Hue and Amount text boxes update to display numerical values for the adjustment. The more you want to increase the saturation (amount), the farther from the center of the wheel you should drag the crosshair pointer. The image updates as you drag the mouse; the Avid internal scopes don't update until you release the mouse.

   - Type values in the HUE and/or AMOUNT (saturation) text boxes for the appropriate color wheel to set the offset you want and press RETURN (Mac) or ENTER (Windows). You can also adjust hue and saturation separately by using either the Hue or Amount text box. However, to adjust either the Hue or Amount value separately, you must have some non-zero value in the other text box. Hue values range from –180º to 180º, where 0º is the position of red on the wheel. Amount values range from 0 to 100. When you change the Hue and Amount values, the pointer on the color wheel updates to represent the adjustment.

3. Fine-tune your adjustments until you are satisfied with the result. Remember that you can make adjustments on more than one color wheel, and turn them on and off individually to assess their affect on the image.

Neutralizing an Overall Color Cast (Symphony Only)

Professional colorists generally neutralize shadows, midtones, and highlights rather than using Symphony's Mas control. The Master Hue Offset color wheel is more commonly used to create an intentional color cast as part of a look rather than to correct one. However, if the entire image has an obvious color cast, you might want to correct that first, before making any other color-cast adjustments. You do that by making a single adjustment on the Master Hue Offset color wheel. For example, if the image is too blue, make the correction by moving the crosshair pointer away from blue.

To neutralize the color cast:

1. On the Artist Color, press the **BANK 2** button.

2. Rotate the right trackball to adjust the Master color wheel, moving in the opposite direction from the color(s) that has the high red, green, or blue value. (You can also use the mouse to drag the crosshair.)

3. To increase the intensity of the color adjustment, move the crosshair pointer farther from the center of the wheel.

Neutralizing the Black Point on Shot B3-3

To neutralize an image, begin by neutralizing black and white points. Black and white are easily identifiable colors that should have nearly identical values for red, green, and blue. When you neutralize the black, you want to achieve a true black—not, for example, a bluish black or reddish black.

Don't forget to adjust luma before you neutralize color casts. As discussed, adjustments to luma can have an impact on the saturation and therefore on your perception of the colors in the image.

Finally, as with setting the luma range, you must learn to neutralize a shot primarily looking at the scopes. Remember the 60-second rule; steal small glances as needed, but the less you can look at the image during this process, the more successful you'll be at grading. (See the section "Notes from the Colorist" in Lesson 2 for the full explanation.)

To neutralize the black:

1. If it's not already open, open the **3_HSL PRIMARY** bin and load the **3_HSL LESSON** sequence.

2. Enter **COLOR CORRECTION** mode.

3. Choose **HSL > HUE OFFSETS**.

4. Display the **RGB PARADE** scope in the left monitor and the **VECTORSCOPE** in the right monitor.

5. Move the position indicator to the second segment, **B3-3**. The image has already been corrected for luma.

6. Locate a shadow or an object in the image that you feel should be neutral black and find that area in each of the three panels of the RGB Parade scope. This is an easy task here: the gun strap on Zero's shoulder. Is it in the same position on all three panels? If not, you have to correct the color cast. Again, this example is easy to see. As shown in Figure 3.17, the red channel is lower than the green channel, and the blue channel is notably higher than both.

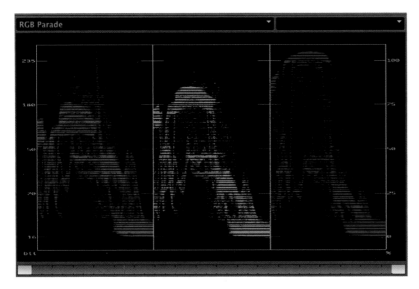

Figure 3.17
RGB Parade display of shot B3-3.

7. Neutralize the blue cast by rolling the left trackball (Artist Color) or Shift-dragging the crosshair pointer in the **SHD** (shadow) color wheel, moving directly toward yellow (opposite blue). Watch the RGB Parade scope as you do this.

8. Adjust the angle of your movement up to increase the red or down to increase the green. Stop when the traces on all three channels are balanced for the blacks. The result of your adjustment should look similar to Figure 3.18.

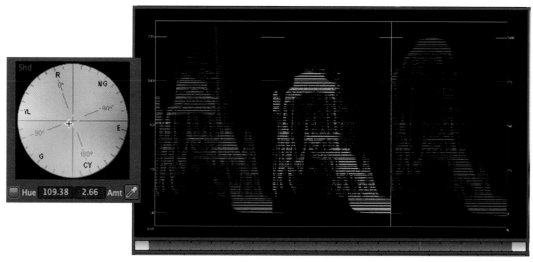

Figure 3.18
The Shd Hue Offsets neutralizing black and resulting RGB Parade display.

Getting RGB Information Using the Color Match Control

When neutralizing a color cast, you may find yourself wondering, are the blacks true black? Do they still have a color cast? Even using the scopes, there are moments when it is difficult to identify the point. If the problem is subtle, it may be difficult to detect with the naked eye. And of course, the longer you stare at it, the less likely you will be able to see the problem as your eye adapts to the colors. Thankfully, there's an easy way to know for sure.

The Color Match tool holds the key. The Color Match tool is displayed to the right of both the HSL and Curves tabs, as shown in Figure 3.19. It is covered in detail in Lesson 6; for now, let's just get what you need out of it.

Figure 3.19
The Color Match controls.

Tip: You can use the Color Match eyedropper to precisely measure RGB values. When new to grading or looking at a complex image, this can be very helpful to determine the exact luma and chroma.

The RGB swatch in the Color Match area displays the RGB values of a selected point in the image. This control can be useful for detecting a subtle color cast. For example, Figure 3.20 shows the Color Match controls with an active sample in the left RGB swatch. This was taken from the shadow area of Agent Zero's back in shot B3-3, before we neutralized the black. The sample indicates how far its RGB values depart from a true black. The values are R:25, G:24, B:36. Being a very dark gray, we expect the values in the low 20s, but the blue channel is 11–12 points higher than green or red, indicating a blue cast. You should remove a little blue to achieve a more neutral shadow tone. If you wanted this area in the image to be exactly reference black (R:16, G:16, B:16), you know that you also need to adjust the black point slightly to lower the RGB values.

To use the Color Match controls to measure tonal values:

1. Click either the **HSL** or **CURVES** tab within the color correction toolset.

2. Click the **COLOR CORRECTION SETTINGS** button in the Color Correction tool, as shown in Figure 3.20. The Color Correction Mode Settings dialog box opens.

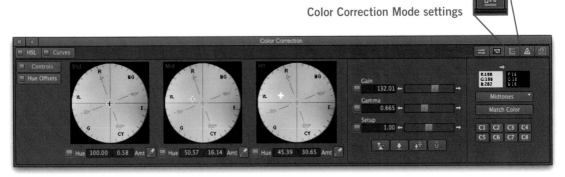

Figure 3.20
You can open the Color Correction Mode Settings dialog box from the Color Correction tool.

3. Select **EYEDROPPER 3×3 AVERAGING**. When you select this option, the system calculates the color value to pick by averaging the values of a 3×3 sample of pixels centered on the eyedropper's position. This is useful because it compensates for shifts in color value from one pixel to another. If you don't activate this option, the system selects the color value of the exact pixel at the eyedropper's position.

4. Click **OK**.

5. Display the RGB values of a good black. To do so, move the pointer over the input (left) color swatch; the pointer changes to an eyedropper. Holding down the mouse button, drag the eyedropper to an area in your image that has a good black or shadow. The input color swatch updates as you move the cursor in the image, displaying the RGB values. Release the mouse button to complete the selection. The input color appears in the input color swatch. In a good black area, the RGB numbers will be relatively low. If the RGB values are unequal in value, you need to correct the shadow.

Neutralizing the White Point and the Gamma on Shot B3-3

After neutralizing the black point, neutralize the white point. Follow the same procedure as for the black point, but adjust the Hlt (highlight) wheel instead of the Shd (shadows) wheel. Do not expect the white point to have the same color cast as the black point! Frequently, the color cast will vary throughout the luma range. This is especially true in mixed lighting situations.

If you want a selected area in the image to be exactly reference white, use the RGB swatch in the Color Match area to display the RGB values for that area. For true white, the R, G, and B values should be at or near 235. Figure 3.21 shows the RGB Parade and Hlt wheel for the corrected white.

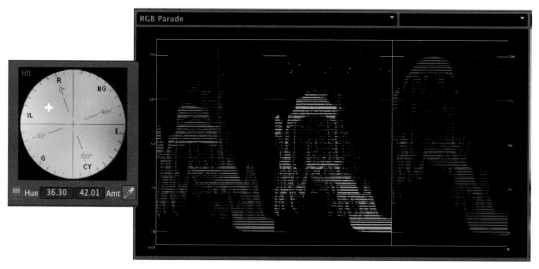

Figure 3.21
The Hlt Hue Offset neutralizing white and resulting RGB Parade display.

Neutralizing the Gamma on Shot B3-3

Adjusting the gamma is where you make the greatest changes to the scene's color temperature. You want to choose an object or area that should be neutral gray, or nearly so, for neutralizing the gamma. In some images, however, you might not have any gray at all. In that case, you will almost certainly have some other area where even a small departure from neutral color is noticeable. If your shot includes people, you will primarily be concerned with getting the flesh tones right.

To neutralize the midtones in this shot:

1. Display the **RGB PARADE**.

2. Follow the same procedure as for the black point, but adjust the **MID** wheel instead of the Shd wheel.

3. As you make your adjustments, seek to balance the midtone traces that correspond to the white and gray rooftops in the middle background. (See Figure 3.22.) Pay careful attention to Agent Zero's skin tone as you do. Back off any adjustment that negatively affects the tone of his skin.

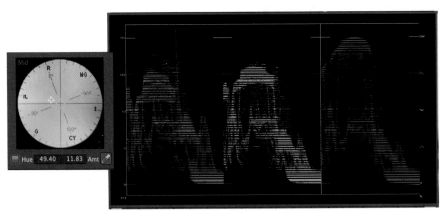

Figure 3.22
The Mid Hue Offset neutralizing midtones, and resulting RGB Parade display.

Tip: Any time your image includes flesh tone, grade for the skin. Non-human objects always take second place. Skin doesn't always have to look healthy and well-lit, but it is always the priority.

Using the Vectorscope to Correct a Color Cast

The Vectorscope can also be used to neutralize color casts. This method takes more practice, but can be quite effective. Many colorists will use this in conjunction with the RGB Parade. The Vectorscope shows color information only, not luma.

Neutral tones sit in the dead center of the scope. (Remember, the black/white ramp pattern didn't even appear on the Vectorscope.) Neutralizing a color cast in the Vectorscope is a process of moving the traces toward the center.

To remove a color cast using the Vectorscope:

1. Option-click (Mac) or Alt-click (Windows) the enable button of each color wheel to reset the hue offsets on shot B3-3. (On Symphony, you can reset the enable button of the entire Hue Offsets tab.)

2. To use the Vectorscope to correct the black point, first identify where the shadow areas fall in the Vectorscope. Drag the crosshair pointer in the Shd color wheel in broad circles. As you do, watch how the traces move. There should be a blob that moved the most with the shadow adjustment. These are the shadow traces.

3. To neutralize the color cast, drag the same crosshair pointer so the blob is at the dead center of the wheel. This area is, as you know, color neutral.

4. Repeat this procedure for the highlights and midtones, if necessary. Shot B3-3, uncorrected and corrected, with the corresponding Vectorscope readouts, is shown in Figure 3.23.

Tip: On an image like this one with dominant flesh tones, remember the I-line is an ideal reference tool for balancing flesh tones. Although not present on the internal scopes, it is available on most external scopes.

Uncorrected

Corrected

Figure 3.23
B3-3 image and Vectorscope, uncorrected and corrected.

There is no doubt, the image looks dramatically better. Notice, too, that the colors have much greater saturation (as seen by the extension of the traces on the Vectorscope). Through the process, you never used the Saturation control to boost the colors. Always save Saturation adjustments for last.

Review/Discussion Questions

1. What do the letters HSL stand for?

2. Which are the principal tonal controls in the HSL group? On which tab are they found?

3. Which are the chroma controls in the HSL group? On which tab are they found?

4. What is the recommended workflow for setting the luma range?

5. Define "black point" and "white point."

6. Which parameter adjustment most strongly affects the mood of the shot?

7. How would a blue color cast appear in the shadows of the RGB Parade?

8. How would you correct a blue cast in the shadows?

9. How can you get precise RGB values for an item in the image?

10. At which step in the process should you adjust saturation?

Lesson 3 Keyboard Shortcuts

Key	Result
Shift-drag (a control slider)	Fine control of the adjustment
Shift-drag (a Hue Offset crosspoint)	Fine control of the adjustment
Alt-click (Windows) or Option-click (Mac) a parameter	Reset the parameter to its default value enable button
Alt-click (Windows) or Option-click (Mac) a control tab enable button	Reset the value of all parameters in the tab to their defaults
Alt-click (Windows) or Option-click (Mac) HSL group tab enable button	Reset the entire HSL group to default values

Performing Primary HSL Corrections

Now it is time for you to apply what you've learned. Use the HSL controls to perform a primary grade on each shot in the full scene from which the examples were taken. As you work through the scene, you may find that you are performing the same types of corrections on similar shots. This is good practice, and it's realistic. Later in the course, you'll learn about tools and techniques to reduce some grading redundancy; for now, repetition is the best thing for you!

Media Used:

Avid Color Grading (MC239) project > Ex2_Exercise Bins folder > Ex3_HSL Exercise bin > 3_HSL_PrimaryGrade sequence

Duration:

60 minutes

GOALS

- Perform primary HSL corrections on a full scene
- Use Gain, Gamma, and Setup controls to set a good luma range on each shot
- Reference the appropriate scope and remove any unwanted color casts

Overview

You don't need step-by-step instructions to complete this exercise. You know what to do. If you get stuck on a procedure, flip back to check the step-by-step directions in the lesson.

The following is a list of tips that will help guide you as you work. In addition to these tips, markers have been added to certain shots in the sequence with additional tips or information to guide you in grading them.

- Remember, this is a primary grade only. Don't try to really finish the look on each shot. Stick with the process you just learned.

- Follow the 60-second rule; grade as much as you can from the scopes. This will keep your eye sharp and help you get fast.

- Try to work quickly. Professional colorists have about three to five minutes per shot. This exercise has 24 segments, but only six new shots. You should be able to finish the sequence.

- On the control room shots that include blue and green screens, disregard the screens and just grade the scene. We'll discuss grading for composites later in the course.

Grading with Curves

This lesson presents the other Media Composer color-correction group: Curves. Curves is a powerful primary grading tool set. When used for simple primary grades, there is often no difference between using HSL and Curves. When used in conjunction with HSL, Curves enables you to perform some secondary corrections. As you practice using the Color Correction tool, you will decide which group you prefer to use to make which kind of adjustment.

Media Used: Avid Color Grading (MC239) project > 1_Lesson Bins folder > 4_Curves Primary bin > 4_Curves Corrections Lesson sequence

Duration: 60 minutes

GOALS

- Identify the differences between HSL controls and Curves
- Identify the order of processing for Curves adjustments
- Identify the recommended order for performing Curves adjustments
- Understand the relationship between chroma and luma in Curves
- Adjust the tonal range using Curves
- Neutralize color casts with Curves
- Perform fine color and contrast adjustments using Curves

Identifying the Curves Controls

The Curves group enables you to control color and luma voltages by placing control points on curve graphs and then adjust those points. A *curve graph* is one that maps the relationship of input values (the values of the unchanged image, on the horizontal axis) to output values (the values of the adjusted image, on the vertical axis). The input is what's being fed to the color corrector; the output is the adjustment to the signal made by the color corrector. Before any adjustments are made, you see a straight diagonal. That is, the input values equal the output values.

Note: You may be familiar with curves controls from other applications, such as Photoshop. Curves graphs work similarly in most applications.

Figure 4.1 shows the Curves tab in the default setup, with callouts identifying the controls. As you can see, the Curves group displays four curve graphs, called ChromaCurve graphs, one for each primary component signal (red, green, and blue) and a master curve for brightness and contrast adjustments.

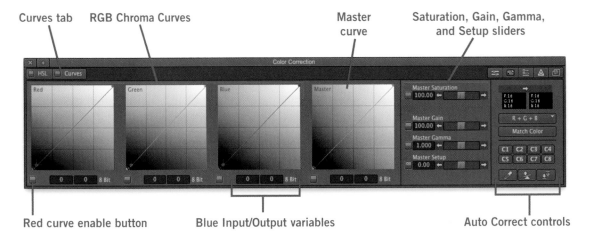

Figure 4.1
The Curves group.

By default, each ChromaCurve graph has a control point at the upper and lower extremes for the black point and white point. These can be manipulated along with other points you add to the curve. Each ChromaCurve graph displays a gradient and a background grid that subdivides the grid into quarters (on both axes). These are designed to guide you in placing the control points and making adjustments.

Adding new points is as easy as clicking the curve where there is no point already. To delete a point, click the point to activate it and, keeping the mouse over it, press the Delete key on your keyboard.

Exploring Curves Adjustments

The Curves group works in the RGB color space. RGB signals embed chroma and luma information in each of the three component color signals. When all three are in perfect balance, the result is neutral gray. When you adjust color in a curve, you are affecting voltage. This is unlike HSL in which chroma adjustments can be made with little to no impact on luma.

Note: Even if media in your project was recorded in the YC_BC_R color space, Media Composer and Symphony perform a 12-bit conversion to RGB for Curves adjustments through the Color Correction effect for real-time play-out. This maximizes the color information available in the original image and ensures adjustments are processed at the highest quality. When the media is rendered, the changes are recorded back to the file as YC_BC_R.

The default curve (before any adjustments have been made) is an ascending 45° straight line because input and output voltages are the same across the entire range. Let's explore how those curves—and the corresponding input and output values—change as you manipulate them.

To prepare for these Curves adjustments:

1. If it's not open already, open the **AVID COLOR GRADING** project.

2. Open the **4_CURVES PRIMARY** bin and load the **4_CURVES CORRECTIONS LESSON** sequence.

3. Move the position indicator to the midpoint of the first shot, **BWRAMP.PICT**.

4. Enter **COLOR CORRECTION** mode. Set the left scope to **Y WAVEFORM**, the center to **CURRENT**, and the right to **RGB PARADE**, as shown in Figure 4.2.

Figure 4.2
Proper setup to explore the Curves controls.

The Master Curve

The master curve is shown as gray but is actually red plus green plus blue. Any changes you make in the master curve apply uniformly to all three color channels and therefore appear to affect the brightness of the image.

To experiment with the master curve:

1. Move the mouse pointer over the white-point control point. The mouse pointer becomes a finger when over the point.

2. Drag the control point to the left along the top edge. This is similar to increasing the Gain setting. Similar to a Gain adjustment, the black point on the graph remains anchored, while the angle of the trace line in the scope increases. (Skeptical? Use the master Gain control to the right of the master curve to repeat the adjustment. The results are identical.)

Key Concept: The sharper the angle of the curve, the higher the contrast.

3. Delete the effect.

4. Make a black-point adjustment. To do so, drag the black control point on the master curve from the lower-left corner toward the right. The shadows darken.

    But wait a minute! Did you see that? The shadows darkened, but the white point didn't move. That's very *unlike* a Setup control adjustment! In Curves, a black-point adjustment on the curve is less like a Setup adjustment (which lowers or lifts all values equally) and more like an inverse Gain adjustment.

    Remember, Gain affects the highlights most strongly while the black point stays locked in place. As a result, the contrast changes. On the master curve, adjusting the black control point affects the shadow areas most strongly while the white point stays locked in place because of the upper control point. Again, the contrast changes. (You'll explore this technique of using control points to lock the curve in place later in this lesson.)

5. Delete the effect.

6. Make a midtone adjustment. To begin, click the master curve about three-quarters of the way up. A control point appears where you clicked.

7. Drag the control point diagonally up and to the left. The master curve bends as you move the control point farther from the default 45° line.

Notice how the midtones brighten and the trace on the Y Waveform scope displays an identical curve to the one you created in the graph, as shown in Figure 4.3. In addition, the RGB Parade scope indicates that the adjustment has affected all three channels.

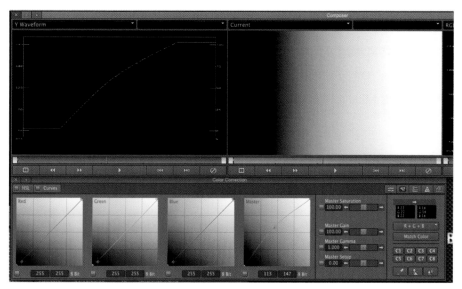

Figure 4.3
A midtone adjustment on the master curve is like a gamma adjustment.

The result of this adjustment is two-fold. First, you increase brightness throughout the image but mostly in the highlights. This creates more contrast in the lower three-quarters of the image. Second, because you are really amplifying all three color channels simultaneously, it increases chroma saturation. You will see this more clearly on the footage.

In review, when working in the Curves, whenever you drag the line up and/or to the left, you increase, or amplify, output voltage. Whenever you drag the line down, you decrease, or lower, output voltage. Here is the rule to remember:

Up/Left = Brighter (Positive Values)

Down/Right = Darker (Negative Values)

Note: Each ChromaCurve graph in the Curves tab enables you to add and manipulate up to 16 control points. Using more than six or eight points, however, can be counterproductive as the effect becomes overcomplicated.

Using Avid Artist Color to Adjust the Curves Graphs

Using the controls on the Artist Color control surface, you can add control points on the graphs and then use the trackballs to adjust the red, green, and blue point graphs.

Note: For more information on all the controls available on your Artist Color control surface, see "Controller Application Sets" in the Media Composer or Symphony Help file.

To make Curves adjustments with the Artist Color:

1. Move the position indicator to the segment in the Timeline you want to correct. You also can use the navigation controls on the Artist Color control surface to move the position indicator in the Timeline.

2. If your Artist Color control surface does not display the Curves group functions, press the **Nav** button; the soft knobs will display the names of the tabs displayed in the Color Correction tool. Press the **Curves** soft knob to activate the Curves group.

3. The LED displays list the functions for the track wheels and trackballs (top row) and the soft knobs (bottom row). Turn the appropriate soft knob to adjust the color saturation, brightness, or correction type of your segment. As you turn the knob, the LED display updates the value of the parameter. These values also display in the Color Correction tool.

Tip: The soft knobs are touch sensitive. The faster you turn the knob, the more dramatic the adjustment. The slower the turn, the more precise the adjustment.

Similar to the Symphony HSL mapping for the trackballs and track wheels, the three wheel/ball sets correspond to the three colors, as shown in Figure 4.4. The right-most set changes from Blue to Master when the Bank 2 button is activated.

4. To make an adjustment, you must either activate an existing control point or create a new one. Point selection is made with the track wheels. Rotate the track wheel corresponding to the curve you wish to adjust. As you turn the track wheel, a ghosted point will slide along the curve and the LED display identifies the value position of the point. When the ghost point approaches an existing point, it will snap to the existing point, thereby activating it.

Figure 4.4
The relationship of the Artist Controls to the ChromaCurve graphs.

To create a new control point on a ChromaCurve graph, place the ghost point at the desired position on the curve, then press the corresponding left RESET button to create the point: R1 for red, R3 for green, R5 for blue.

5. With a point selected, turn the appropriate trackball to adjust the offset of that point. The change is reflected on the corresponding graph, and visible in the image and on the scopes in real time.

6. To see the impact of a curve adjustment, toggle the ChromaCurve graph on/off using the corresponding right RESET button: R2 for red, R3 for green, R5 for blue.

7. To see your segment with and without all color corrections, press the **F3** (TOGGLE COLOR CORRECTION EFFECT [ON/OFF]) button.

Exploring R, G, and B Curve Adjustments

The ChromaCurve graphs display the primary color and its complement. This is a distinct method of indicating the same color relationships displayed on the color wheel, which present the complementary colors directly opposite the primary color. (See Figure 4.5.)

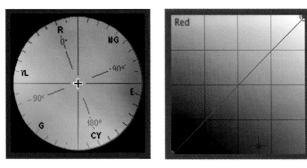

Figure 4.5
Red versus cyan, displayed on a color wheel and a curve graph.

To explore RGB adjustments:

1. If it's not loaded already, load the **4_Curves Corrections** sequence in the **4_Curves Primary** bin in the **Avid Color Grading** project.

2. Move the position indicator to the first shot, **BWRamp.pct**.

   The principles demonstrated in the preceding section apply to each color channel, giving you Gain-, Gamma-, and Setup-like controls for each color channel using control points. As you drag your control points off the center line, however, the color shifts toward the primary or secondary color.

3. On the red curve, drag the upper control point to the left, along the top of the graph. Stop about midway. The adjustment and its results are shown in Figure 4.6.

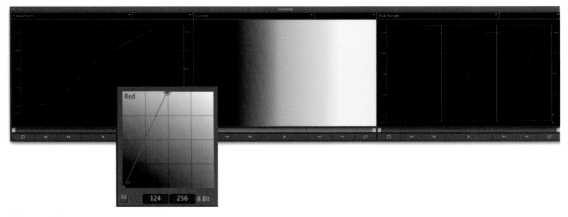

Figure 4.6
A red channel Gain adjustment.

4. Look at each of the scopes. The adjustment has created a strong red cast on the ramp image. In addition, the RGB Parade shows that the red channel has been dramatically lifted all the way to the blacks, but as expected, there's no change to the green or blue channels. Notice, too, the Y Waveform also shows a gamma-like change, bumping out at about 75%.

Key Concept: RGB channel adjustments in Curves affect the luma signal. Unlike HSL, in Curves, the luma and chroma signals are mixed.

5. Click the same control point again to activate it. A circle appears around the active point. (One point can be active per graph.)

6. Click the red channel **INPUT** text box and type **256**. Then press the **TAB** key to jump to the **OUTPUT** box, type **128**, and press **RETURN** (Mac) or **ENTER** (Windows). The control point jumps to the midpoint of the right edge of the graph. (You could have also dragged it there, but typing in values is so much more impressive to clients.)

   This adjustment has created an equally strong shift in colors on the ramp —this time to cyan. You didn't add cyan, you removed red (no cyan voltage exists); but the result is the same. With regard to the color shift, it is as if you increased both green and blue voltages.

Key Concept: You can achieve a hue shift in two ways: Either manipulate the corresponding primary channel or manipulate the other two primary channels. For example, to shift toward yellow, either decrease blue or increase both red and green equally.

7. Option-click (Mac) or Alt-click (Windows) the **CURVES** enable button to reset the effect.

8. Repeat steps 3–5 on the green and blue curves. As you do, take special note of the degree to which the Y Waveform scope responds to the different channel adjustments.

9. Click the center of the green curve to add a control point.

10. Add another control point to the green curve at the 75% mark. Drag this point diagonally up and to the left, bending the upper portion of the curve, as shown in Figure 4.7.

Figure 4.7
Control points limit the green adjustment to the highlights only.

11. Look at the **BWRamp** image. Notice that the green cast is limited to the highlight range, having minimal effect on values below 50%. The center control point acts as an anchor, restricting the curve values below it.

Key Concept: **You can limit the tonal range of an adjustment by using additional control points as anchors.**

That's it! You now know the mechanics of working with Curves. In the next section, you'll practice using these to grade images, moving from mechanic toward artist. Before you move on, let's recap the key concepts to be learned here:

■ RGB channel adjustments in Curves affect the luma signal as well as the chroma signal. Unlike HSL, Curves processes its adjustments in the RGB color space, in which the luma and chroma signals are mixed. The master curve appears to affect only the luma signal because it makes equal adjustments to the R, G, and B channels.

■ Luma is not represented evenly between the RGB channels. The green channel contains approximately 60% of the total luma, red about 30%, and blue about 10%. Because green is the core of luma, any adjustments to the green channel will have a greater effect on luma than adjustments made to the red and blue channels. That means you will want to be careful with the green curve. By working in the middle of the green curve, you can tweak the adjustment without overdriving the luma values. You will see this in action as you grade shots. Unlike working in HSL, when grading in Curves, you can intentionally adjust luma range as you fix a color cast. (This may require you to occasionally adjust your black or white point after you set them initially because of changes made to the chroma channels.)

■ You can limit the tonal range of an adjustment by using additional control points as anchors. This technique can be applied to the master curve to adjust luma or contrast in a specific tonal range. It can also be used with individual color-channel curves to fix a color cast in the midtones, shadows, or highlights.

Order of Processing

The color-correction tools can be manipulated in any order, and all adjustments made to an image are displayed cumulatively. You can freely move between tabs and make the adjustment using the tool that is best suited for the job. That said, it is helpful to understand the order in which your Avid system processes color adjustments because it may influence the order in which you choose to make adjustments.

Any HSL adjustments made to an image are processed before Curves adjustments. Individual RGB curves are processed before the master curve. As a result, it's generally a good idea to make HSL adjustments before Curves (which include the master Gain, Gamma, and Setup controls) and adjust the RGB curves before the master curve. This order follows the system's order of processing and will give you the most predictable results. If you choose to make corrections in a different order, make sure you are not undoing the impact of one adjustment by introducing another further upstream.

Making Adjustments Using Curves Versus HSL Controls

As mentioned, you can freely move between tabs and make the adjustment using the tool that is best suited for the job. So, which do you use when?

One advantage of Curves adjustments is that you can make quite complex color and luma adjustments without having to use many controls. In contrast, in the previous lesson, you learned how to adjust luma and neutralize color using the HSL Controls sliders and Hue Offset wheels. You manipulated several tabs to accomplish what you can do in a single tab using the Curves group.

Because you can make many adjustments in a single Color Correction tab, you might grow to prefer the Curves tool to make all of your adjustments, from correcting luma and chroma levels (primarily in the master curve), to adjusting color casts, to creating a final treatment. However, at least while you are learning, we recommend the following division:

HSL group:

- ■ Use the Setup, Gain, and Gamma sliders to set the tonal range for the shot.
- ■ Use Hue Offsets to correct color casts with minimal impact on luma.

Curves group:

As you will see, the ability to create and move multiple control points gives you tremendous control in making your adjustments. Instead of a single gamma adjustment, for example, you can adjust only the low gamma or high gamma.

Use Curves to:

■ Adjust the luma for only the red, green, or blue channel.

■ Clip the signal or limit the color gamut to allowable levels.

■ Change the look or treatment of a scene.

Later in the course, you will learn how to use Curves to create several commonly used treatments, such as day for night and sepia.

Performing a Primary Grade Using Curves

In this section, you will learn to grade with curves, moving from simple to more complex primary grades. Since you already know the mechanics, the directions will be presented as generic tasks. Perform them using the mouse, keyboard, or Artist Color control surface, depending on your hardware setup and comfort.

If you are working with external scopes and a client monitor, real-time adjustments are possible and will make the grade go much more quickly. If not, make small repeated adjustments, checking the internal Avid scopes after each adjustment.

Input and output values will be noted where appropriate. For example, after making an adjustment to the green curve, the control point may have an associated Input value of 138 and an Output value of 159; this would be noted as (G: 138, 159).

Performing a Basic Grade

Let's start with a relatively simple shot. As you'll see, it has some basic luma and chroma problems, and will be a great way to get started grading in Curves.

To perform a simple primary grade in Curves:

1. If it's not loaded already, load the **4_CURVES CORRECTIONS** sequence in the **4_CURVES PRIMARY** bin in the **AVID COLOR GRADING** project.

2. If you're not in it already, enter **COLOR CORRECTION** mode. Set the left scope to **Y WAVEFORM**, the center to **CURRENT**, and the right to **RGB PARADE**.

3. Click the **NEXT UNCORRECTED** button under the center scope to move the position indicator to the second shot, **G2-3(A)**.

The first frame is rather dramatic, especially in the scopes where you can see the outline of the dancers in the traces. Red is the dominant color, with blue and green having only very low levels in the shadows.

4. Press the **SPACE BAR** to play the shot. The lighting in the shot quickly changes to dim colored lights on the background of the stage and a white spotlight on the singer.

Tip: Always play, or scrub through, the shot before you start grading. It's a common rookie mistake to grade the first frame, only to realize later there's a dramatic change in the shot. (Some experienced colorists are reluctant to admit they still make this mistake once in a while too!)

5. Move the position indicator to the marker about two-thirds of the way into the shot. Alternatively, choose your own representative frame in the shot to grade.

6. Take a moment to analyze the shot, shown in Figure 4.8.

Figure 4.8
The uncorrected shot G2-3(a) and scopes.

Here's a quick analysis of the shot:

- The shot is dark, with areas of high contrast. This is expected, because it's a theatrical stage production, but overall it is too dark. The blacks are clipped, and only the reflective dots on the background curtain reach 100%.

- There is a blue cast to the image, especially in the subject's white costume and in the pool of light from the spotlight.

- Additional issues may become evident as you begin to grade and expand the luma range.

7. In the master curve, raise the black point straight up the vertical axis until you can see into the blacks in the image. You are looking for additional detail to appear in the shadowed areas. (This is especially visible on a client monitor.) There is some detail in the folds of the curtain and in the outline of the background dancers' legs; you want to keep that detail in the shot.

8. Lower the control point to set the black point for the image. Bring the lowest traces in the Y Waveform scope down to just barely touch the 0% mark. You should still be able to see the outline of the background dancers' legs (**M: 6, 0**).

9. Set the white point. To do so, drag the upper control point in the master curve to the left until the traces representing the singer's glasses and costume reach 100% (**M: 198, 256**). In a later step, you will clip the specular high-lights that exceed 100%; for now, it is more important to make her pop.

Key Concept: You increased contrast on the shot by increasing the angle of the curve. This technique can be used on the master curve, on individual chroma curves, or within a region of a curve.

10. Check the black point again. If it has lifted, adjust the control point again, as needed (**M: 2, 0**).

11. Toggle the **Dual Split** button a couple times to refresh your eye and see the impact of the changes to far.

12. Finish the luma range with a midtone adjustment. On the master curve, add a point approximately two-thirds of the way up the curve. Move it up and to the left to raise the brighter midtones—the range in which the singer sits (**M: 113, 182**).

The image is already looking better, but the blue cast is now especially clear, visible in the traces of the subject's costume and the spotlight (see Figure 4.9). As you know, blue is directly opposite the warm skin tones of yellow and red on the color wheel. That means the blue cast is neutralizing the natural color of her skin. You need to fix that next.

Tip: When correcting a color cast, you'll achieve the best results if you adjust the strongest and weakest channels to the level of the middle channel (speaking in terms of values). Trying to raise the weakest channel up to the level of the strongest will usually result in a noisy image.

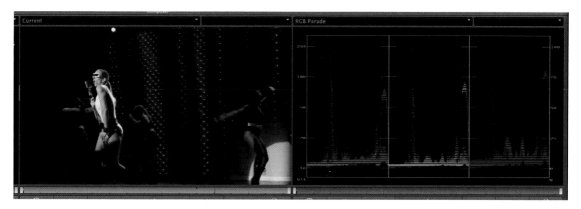

Figure 4.9
The blue cast is clearly visible in the RGB Parade scope.

13. On the blue curve, drag the upper control point down on the vertical axis, lowering gain on the blue channel until the costume and spotlight traces reach the level of those in the green channel on the RGB Parade scope (**B: 256, 195**).

14. On the red curve, drag the upper control point horizontally to the left, raising the red gain until the same traces on the red channel match the values on the green and blue channels in the RGB Parade scope (**R: 200, 256**).

15. Examine the red channel in the RGB Parade scope and the black areas of the image. The strong red gain adjustment you just made has lifted the blacks in the red channel, giving them a red cast (see Figure 4.10). You need to fix that.

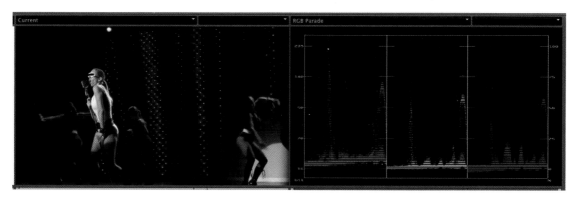

Figure 4.10
The red gain adjustment has fixed one problem but created another.

16. On the red curve, add a control point about one-fourth of the way up. Move it down and to the right until the shadows of the red channel are balanced with the blue and green (**R: 69, 69**). This new control point is essentially an anchor point, restoring the original balance in the shadows by limiting the gain adjustment to the midtones and highlights. Figure 4.11 shows this adjustment on the curve.

Figure 4.11
The red curve adjustment to fix the red cast in the shadows.

Nice job! It's looking great so far. The subject just lacks some warmth. Resist the temptation to warm the image by automatically adding red or reducing blue. Instead, try increasing what's already in the image and see that result first. Often, it's a more natural look.

17. Increase the **MASTER SATURATION** until the colors really pop, at approximately **140**. Beautiful!

18. Play the clip to admire your handiwork. The red wall at the beginning is definitely clipped, but that can be addressed with a secondary adjustment (Symphony) or color limiter effect later. The rest of the shot looks fantastic. Nicely done! The primary grade is complete. See Figure 4.12 for a before and after comparison.

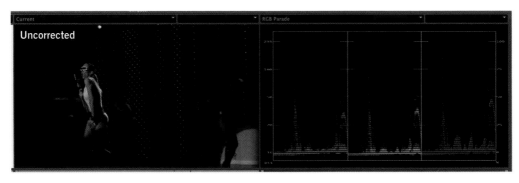

Figure 4.12a
Before...

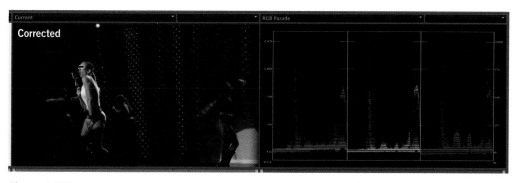

Figure 4.12b
... after. What a difference!

The Epic S-Curve

If you read enough books, blogs, and articles about color grading, you'll see lots of talk about S-curves. Some of this talk raises the S-curve to epic proportions.

Figure 4.13 show a typical S-curve. Looking at it, you can see how it gets its name: it resembles an S. In Avid, it's usually applied to the master curve, which affects all three color channels evenly. It's designed to thicken blacks and compress the highlights.

Figure 4.13
S-curves compress the shadows and highlights.

The S-curve mimics the non-linear response curve of film. Film tends to have a nice roll-off in both highlights and shadows; that's what the S-curve is trying to reproduce. When it's working well, your black levels build up or thicken as you push shadows near 0 IRE. And then, if you push hard enough, the shadows will finally start dropping below 0 IRE and clip out. This is also true for the highlights. A nice-looking S-curve often requires a very soft touch. When people talk of wanting a film look, the S-curve is often where they begin. (See Figure 4.14.)

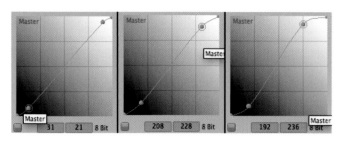

Figure 4.14
Three different intensities of S-curves from left to right: light, medium, heavy.

I have on my system a few saved S-curve color effects of different intensities. When I start a new project or scene, I'll often take a quick moment (and I do mean a moment) to see if any of those S-curves make good starting points. First impressions can be deceiving when applying the effect, so I'll immediately switch to the HSL Offsets to lift or drop the shadows and see how the image interacts underneath the S-curve. Depending on the camera and how the DP shot the footage, an S-curve can either look really really good or be really really unmanageable.

As mythic as the S-curve is, it's not appropriate for all jobs. But I find once I start using it on a scene I'll want to keep using it for the entire scene to make it easier to match shots.

Correcting a Color Cast Automatically

All the color-grading tools in Media Composer and Symphony excel at certain tasks. As you gain more experience, you'll learn to recognize problems in the image and instinctively know which tool to use to address it. Two tasks at which Curves excels are fixing color casts and working with extreme exposure problems.

In the previous section, you corrected color casts manually. Already you've seen the ease of use in performing these corrections. In this section, you will use a combination of manual adjustments and user-directed automated tools to achieve the grade very quickly. As with any automatic function, there are distinct limitations to the usefulness of automatic corrections. It should go without saying that they'll never create a polished, finished grade. But when used appropriately—with attention and discretion—they can help speed the process of establishing the base grade.

To remove a color cast using Curves:

1. If it's not loaded already, load the **4_CURVES CORRECTIONS** sequence in the **4_CURVES PRIMARY** bin in the **AVID COLOR GRADING** project.

2. Use the transport controls to move to the next shot in the sequence: **MVI_0105.MOV**.

3. If necessary, set left scope to **Y WAVEFORM** and the right to **RGB PARADE**.

4. Drag the position indicator through the shot. Using the scopes, analyze the shot and identify image elements in the traces. The uncorrected shot and scopes are shown in Figure 4.15.

Figure 4.15
The uncorrected helicopter shot with scopes.

Here's a quick analysis of the shot:

- The shot has a very high contrast range, with deep blacks and bright whites. Unfortunately, the area of interest—inside the helicopter—is very dark and rather flat.

- The whites are clipped neatly at 100%. This is a classic clipping problem characteristic of DV and D-SLR footage. (This is D-SLR footage.) Any detail clipped in camera will be permanently lost.

- The DP obviously exposed this shot for the highlights, so there is only a small amount of detail lost in the clouds. The landscape outside the helicopter has plenty of detail—most of which would have been lost had the DP exposed for the subject.

- The shot exhibits a classic blue cast throughout the entire range, characteristic of an incorrect white balance. Even with the proper white balance, this blue cast is very common in the shadows of day-lit scenes, which is how this shot was filmed.

- The image has low color saturation (as confirmed in the Vectorscope).

5. Having identified the image elements in the Y Waveform and RGB Parade scopes, adjust the scopes to a better working setup. Set the left scope to **RGB Parade** and the right to **Vectorscope**.

6. For efficiency, click the **Auto Balance** button in the lower-right corner of the color-correction window. (Auto Balance is the middle of the three Auto Correct buttons; the icon is the same as the one you used in the HSL group.) There is an immediate change. The black and white points on each of the ChromaCurve graphs jump to new locations, and the blue cast is very slightly improved.

7. Click the **Auto Contrast** button, the right-most Auto Correct button. This action makes no apparent change on this image. In the master curve, you see the black and white points have moved inward from the corners, but the input and output values are identical. This is not always the result, but rather the result based on the calculations made on this image.

Note: **The recommended order of operations when using the auto-correction controls in Curves is Auto Balance first, then Auto Contrast. This is based on the order of processing of the adjustments in the curves.**

8. The area of interest is still quite dark, so let's rectify that. Add a control point to the master curve at approximately 40%. Drag the control point up and to the left to increase the voltage. Continue until the traces that represent Agent Zero's arm sit at about 50% (**M: 75, 116**). If the Auto Contrast adjustment had not limited the adjustments to the legal range of 16–235, this adjustment would have lifted the blacks and blown out the whites. The image is starting to look much better, as shown in Figure 4.16.

Figure 4.16
Luma corrections have improved the shot.

Tip: You can use the same technique of locking the input and output values
    to safe limits of 16–235 when grading manually. Simply Shift-drag the
    white-point control down to 235 and the black-point control up to 16
    (or type the value in the Input and Output boxes). The angle of the curve
    will be maintained but the output will be limited to broadcast-safe levels.

9. Toggle the correction and note the change on the scopes and in the image.
   There is still a strong blue cast that was not resolved by the Auto Balance
   function. You'll address that with the Remove Color Cast tool, shown in
   Figure 4.17. Using Remove Color Cast is like performing a manual white
   balance on a camera. It enables you to tell the system what should be white,
   black, or gray. In Curves, you simply identify a tone on the gray scale. The
   system automatically identifies the luma values and corrects accordingly.

Figure 4.17
The Remove Color Cast button.

Remove Color Cast button

10. Click the **REMOVE COLOR CAST** button. The button appears highlighted
    to indicate it is active.

11. Move your cursor to an area of the image that should be a neutral (grayscale)
    tone. The bright portion of the seat back in the lower-left corner of the
    frame will make an ideal sample point. Click it. Note that there is an
    immediate improvement to the image. Control points are added to each
    ChromaCurve graph in the lower midtone range. Their position is deter-
    mined by the calculation required to bring the sample point to neutral gray.

12. Toggle the correction and note the change on the scopes and in the image.
    The finished grade is shown in Figure 4.18.

Figure 4.18
The finished primary grade.

Super Sampling

Media Composer and Symphony have several correction tools that enable you to sample colors from the image. The accuracy of these luma and chroma values is critical to getting the best results from the system. While it might seem that even a blind monkey could do it, there is some skill in choosing a good sample point. When sampling, keep these tips in mind for best results:

- For color cast removal, look for gray tones. If no black is available, very deep shadows are a good substitute. If no gray is available, use a white object in shadow. If no white is available, a bright gray will work.

- Never sample a specular highlight, such as the reflection on a metallic object. (The sun glinting off a car is not a good white sample.)

- Sample an object or a portion of an object that is lit by the dominant light source in the scene.

> ■ For color matching (covered in Lesson 6, "Stepping Up to Symphony"), sample a flat tone that accurately represents the majority of the object to be matched. Watch out for ridges and wrinkles in clothing—or skin—that would have strong luma or chroma variations.
>
> ■ Always work with 3×3 Averaging enabled to avoid erratic results from the variation of individual pixels.

There are three key points in this section of the lesson:

- Curves can be used to easily increase or decrease contrast. The sharper the angle of a curve, the greater the contrast.

- It is very easy to correct a color cast in Curves. It seldom requires more than a couple control points in conjunction with black-point or white-point adjustments on each chroma channel.

- Curves controls can be used to legalize signals that are too high. Rather than applying a broadcast-safe effect, this is the preferred method of dealing with the problem because it keeps you in control of the clipping. Further adjustments can be made to preserve the image quality.

Grading a Sequence in Curves

Learning how to approach the grade on an individual shot is a foundational concept and is the first step in learning color grading. In this section, you will discover techniques for approaching a sequence of shots as you continue practicing with Curves. The shots in this section require a more nuanced approach.

Grading the First Shot

It's tempting to grade these in order, starting with the close-up beauty shot of the actress, but you may find that starting with her is troublesome. The challenge is that you can often grade these types of close-ups so beautifully, the following shots pale in comparison.

Instead, start with a wider shot that includes all, or most, of the principal characters in the scene. In this example, it's the four-shot. Avoid establishing shots as these are generally too wide. Grade this shot to its maximum potential, then grade the others to match. Doing so will create a more cohesive scene. Note that matching shots is covered in greater detail in the next lesson. This section will serve as a primer for the next lesson.

To establish a reference shot:

1. Continue working on the same sequence. If it's not loaded already, load the **4_CURVES CORRECTIONS** sequence in the **4_CURVES PRIMARY** bin in the **AVID COLOR GRADING** project. If not already set up, set the left Composer monitor to RGB Parade and the right to Vectorscope.

2. Following the shot you just graded is a series of three shots, in order, from a scene in the film. Using the transport controls, review each of the three shots. In order, they are a close-up of the villain's mistress, Kitty. (K3+5–1), the reverse close-up of Agent Zero (L1+2–2), and a wide shot of the card table from Agent Zero's point of view (U2+5A–1). The latter, which is a good choice to start grading the scene, is shown in Figure 4.19.

Figure 4.19
The wide shot is a good choice to start grading the scene.

3. Move the position indicator to the third shot in the series, the wide shot.

4. Play the shot and look for a representative frame.

5. Move the position indicator to the marker or choose your own representative frame to grade.

Tip: Whenever possible, when choosing a representative frame to grade, opt for one in which the character's eyes can be seen. The eyes of the character will be the focus of the audience.

6. Take a moment to analyze the shot.

    Here's a quick analysis of the shot:

    *   The shot has good blacks and fairly good contrast. It's just a bit dark and flat, causing the characters to get lost against the background.
    *   There are problematic shadows in the eyes of the mistress, Kitty.
    *   The white jacket, frame right, is clearly a bright spot, but shouldn't be the focus of the audience's attention.

The shot and its corresponding scopes are shown in Figure 4.20.

Figure 4.20
Analyze the uncorrected wide shot.

7. Because the black point is good, move straight to setting the white point and making gamma adjustments. Create a point on the master curve at approximately the 75% guides. Raise the point until the jacket traces just touch 100% (**M: 172, 202**).

8. Notice there is still a shadow under Kitty's eyes. To address this, lift the lower midtones. Set a control point about one-third up the master curve and lift it slightly (**M: 74, 100**).

9. These changes have lifted the blacks slightly, but the overall contrast ratio in the shot feels good now. Because adjusting the black point on the master curve will change the contrast, use Setup instead. Lower the **MASTER SETUP** control until the black point is reset at 0%. The corrections to this point are shown in Figure 4.21.

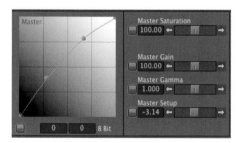

Figure 4.21
The luma range corrections.

10. Toggle the overall correction or the **DUAL SPLIT** button to compare the results of the luma range adjustments with the uncorrected shot.

11. Not bad at all. In fact, at this point, the scopes themselves show a full contrast with no significant color cast. (See Figure 4.22.) That means, however, that they can't tell you what to do next. Finish the grade using your eyes, looking at the tones of the image in your client monitor.

Figure 4.22
If the scopes look good, they can't tell you what to do next.

Tip: As much as you should rely on the scopes to inform you, ultimately it's about
how the shot *looks*. Use your eyes as the final gauge!

12. The skin tones still feel a bit dead. To rectify this, try increasing the **Master
Saturation** control approximately **120–140** points. Consider the result.

13. The increased saturation is most notable in the red wall in the background,
and the holographic blue box. These only distract the viewer's eye from
the subjects in the scene. Instead, you can add warmth to the shot with a
midtone adjustment to the red curve. First, reset the **Master Saturation**
control to **100**.

Note: The Master Saturation slider in Curves and the Saturation slider found in
the HSL group are one in the same. When you adjust one, the other will
show the same adjustment. Likewise, Master Gain, Master Gamma, and
Master Setup are connected to HSL controls.

14. Add a control point in the lower third of the red curve. Move it up and to
the left a small amount to increase the voltage (**R: 92, 108**).

Notice that the back wall is responding strongly to the adjustment. The
problem is that the wall and subjects' face tones share much of the same
tonal range. Ultimately, you'll need to address this with a secondary
adjustment, covered later for both Media Composer and Symphony, but
there's more you can do now.

15. Shift-drag the red midtone control point upward. The point slides down
the curve, changing its position—and therefore the portion of the luma
range it affects—while maintaining the same magnitude of adjustment.
Play with the position of the point until you see the greatest benefit to the
faces and the least impact on the back wall (**R: 154, 170**). See Figure 4.23.

Figure 4.23
The red curve adjustment.

16. Finally, you need to address the yellow tinge of Turk's white jacket. Drag the upper blue control point to the left, boosting the blue gain. Watch your external monitor and waveforms until the corresponding traces in the blue channel are even with those in red and green.

    Well done! The shot looks good for a primary grade. Now use it as a reference to guide your grade of the other two shots.

17. Set the right Composer monitor to **REFERENCE**. The current shot appears in the right monitor, to be displayed next to the shot you will grade next: the close-up of Kitty.

Grading the Second Shot

Approaching the primary grade on a secondary shot in the sequence is not very different from how you might approach it in isolation. The difference is that you are not only concerned with resolving issues in the shot. As you grade, you want to grade *toward* the principal reference shot.

What do I mean by grading toward another shot? As you already know, there are many subjective decisions to be made in the grading process. How contrasty should this shot be? Where do you place the skin tones in the luma range? Do you burn out the highlights or tone them down? When grading to a reference shot, many of these are answered by looking at what was established in the reference shot.

By now, you are familiar with the standard order of adjustments: black point, white point, midtones, then color cast. In these grades, you'll start to take a more fluid approach, as professional colorists do.

To grade the second shot in the sequence:

1. Use the transport controls to navigate back to the shot **K3+5-1**.

2. Review the shot. Then place the position indicator on the marker or choose your own representative frame to grade. The uncorrected shot is shown in Figure 4.24.

Figure 4.24
The uncorrected close-up of Kitty.

3. Take a moment to identify picture elements in the scopes and analyze the shot. Be sure to change scopes in the left monitor as needed.

   Here's a quick analysis of the shot:

   - The Y Waveform scope indicates that the shot is very dark and flat. The black point is fine, but the brightest highlights don't exceed 40%.
   - There is a color cast to the image. The RGB Parade scope reveals that the blue channel is quite low through the midtones and shadows, creating a warm cast throughout.

4. On the master curve, move the white control point to the left to boost the highlights. There is no real white in the shot to cue from, so increase the highlights until the traces of her face are at about 75% (**M: 149, 256**).

5. On the RGB Parade scope, you see that the gain adjustment lifted the blacks, and that the blacks have a color cast. You will correct the cast later. For now, lock in the black point at **0%**: Type **16** in both the **INPUT** and **OUTPUT** boxes and press **ENTER** (**M: 16, 16**).

6. The shot is improving, but the faces are still dark, dull. Address that with a midtone adjustment. Add a midtone control point on the master curve and raise the value by approximately **10**, noting the difference in the Input box from when you add the point to when you release it.

7. Shift-drag the midtone point along the curve. Your goal is to brighten the face and light the eyes, but to avoid losing any depth in her face by brightening the shadows too much (**M: 16, 138**).

Tip: Don't be afraid to experiment. Often, making an adjustment is like manually focusing a camera or tuning an old radio. You have to play with the adjustment, pushing it too far in either direction until you settle in to where it looks just right.

8. Compare the blacks in the subject's hair and the shadows around her eyes to the reference image. You may wish to nudge the black point slightly. To do so, click in the black point's **INPUT** box of the black point and press the **UP ARROW** or **DOWN ARROW** key on the keyboard. The numbers change sequentially and the scopes update simultaneously to show the adjusted value (**M: 17, 16**). As usual, the image is coming to life now that you've set the luma range.

9. Look at the subject's face in the client monitor. Notice that it seems to have a yellow/green cast to it (presumably the light reflecting off the card table). Similarly, the concentration of traces in the Vectorscope, which would be skin tone, is pushed toward yellow, as shown in Figure 4.25.

Figure 4.25
The close-up shot of Kitty with the luma range set; a yellow/green cast exists on the skin tones.

Tip: You can very quickly toggle between the current and reference images to compare them on your external monitor. Alternately click on each image in the Composer window to change the active image.

10. Start on the green channel. Create a control point at about 60%, corresponding to the range of her face. Adjust it *slightly* downward toward magenta (**G: 146, 143**).

11. Her skin is improving, but still looks a bit too warm when compared to the reference. Cool it with a blue adjustment. Create a control point on the blue curve, also at about 60%. Slightly increase the blue value (**B: 129, 146**).

12. Toggle the **BLUE CURVE** enable button a couple times to see the impact of this adjustment. Also, toggle between the Reference and Current views on the client monitor for a quick comparison. Nice work. The grade looks good, and very close to the reference, as shown in Figure 4.26.

Figure 4.26
The corrected close-up of Kitty.

Grading the Third Shot

The final shot will be the most challenging. It has to fit with the scene, but Agent Zero isn't in the reference shot, so there's no direct reference. Not to worry. Trust the techniques you've learned so far, and go through it one step at a time.

To grade the final shot in the sequence:

1. Use the transport controls to navigate to shot **L1+2-2**.

2. Review the shot, then place the position indicator on the marker or choose your own representative frame to grade. The uncorrected shot is shown in Figure 4.27.

Figure 4.27
The uncorrected Zero shot.

3. Take a moment to identify picture elements in the scopes and analyze the shot. Be sure to change scopes in the left monitor as needed.

   Here's a quick analysis of the shot:

   - The Y Waveform indicates that the shot is dark and flat. The black point is fine, but the bright highlight on the subject's forehead sits at only 50%.
   - The rotating geometric light in the background ranges up 100%, meaning you will have to either clip it or grade around it.
   - There is a similar warm color cast in the image to the one seen on Kitty's close-up. The RGB Parade scope reveals that the blue channel is low through the midtones and shadows, creating a warm cast throughout.

4. On the master curve, set the black point using the Input and Output controls. Type **16** in both the **INPUT** and **OUTPUT** boxes and press **RETURN** (Mac) or **ENTER** (Windows) (**M: 16, 16**). This will lock in the black point as a good starting point. You can fine-tune it later if needed.

5. To set the white point, Shift-drag the master white control point down to **235**. Then move it left until there is a good amount of contrast in the Y Waveform scope, placing the subject's face at about 40% (**M: 152, 235**). By limiting the value to 235, you clip any of the background highlights that would have blown out from the gain adjustment.

6. Looking at Agent Zero, his face seems just a little dark. Add a control point to the master curve at about 50%, corresponding to the values of his face, and raise it slightly. You want to brighten the face without losing its depth.

7. As you make your adjustment, watch the client monitor. Toggle to the reference image or the close-up of Kitty as needed. You may also fine-tune the adjustment with the arrow keys, nudging the Input value. As with the close-up of Kitty, watch for the light in his eyes.

8. He looks good, but you need to make his face pop a little more, like the others. To do this, you need to add more contrast to his face. You'll do this by darkening the shadows a bit further. Activate the master black control point. Nudge the **INPUT** values up to darken the shadows, watching those on his face and under his neck. As the shadows darken, the highlights on his face will seem to brighten and draw the eye. Stop when you've reached a good balance that approximates the relative contrast on the other two shots (**M: 21, 16**). Looking good! The adjustments you've made really make the subject's face pop, as shown in Figure 4.28.

Figure 4.28
Good contrast sharpens the image and draws the viewer's eye to the subject's face.

Tip: As colorist your job is to ensure the audience knows where they should be looking, and contrast adjustments help you achieve that goal. Contrast does two things. First, it adds apparent sharpness to the shot. Second, contrast helps draw the eyes of the viewer. As you increase the slope on a curve, you're enhancing one area with contrast but you're also de-emphasizing other areas that get flattened by that curve.

9. Address the slight green/yellow tint using the same technique as on Kitty's close-up. Make a slight midtone adjustment to the green curve, pushing it toward magenta, and a slight midtone adjustment to blue, boosting it in the midtones (**G: 143, 140**; **B: 139, 151**).

10. Good work! The base grade is complete. Compare the corrected and uncorrected images, shown in Figure 4.29. Also compare the corrected image with the other images in the sequence.

Figure 4.29
The corrected and uncorrected versions.

Notes from the Colorist: Which Control First?

As you get further into this book, more color-correction choices are opening up to you. At some point you'll set the book aside and start working on paying gigs. It won't be long before you reach to make an adjustment, hesitate, and ask, Which control should I touch first?

It just so happens I've got some thoughts on this. They differ from the disciplined approach you've learned here, but you know what they say: You have to know the rules before you can break them. I'll share my reasoning and you can decide for yourself which approach works best for you.

Shadow/Gamma/Gain Sliders Versus Master Curve

My first action is to always start adjusting contrast and gamma before working with color. But you have two places to perform this correction:

■   Shadow/Gamma/Gain sliders

■   Master curve

I prefer starting with the master curve. Why?

■   **Better shadow control:** Avid's Setup slider has enormous overlap into the midtone regions—much more than in other color grading apps I've used. On Media Composer, I make better and faster luminance adjustments by jumping straight to the master curve. And since I can add additional points on a curve, I can limit my shadow corrections to just the region I desire.

■   **The mythical S-curve:** If I'm going to be using S-curves on a scene, I like to apply those early in the correction process. Often, it's the first correction I make. Remember, the Shadow/Gamma/Gain sliders are processed *before* the master curve. If my S-curve is making the blacks too crunchy or the highlights too washed out, I can use the sliders to bring back that detail from underneath the S-curve.

■   **Quick access to RGB curves:** I *love* the individual RGB curves for repairing specific problems such as bad white balance or a weak color channel. The RGB curves usually give me better results than the HSL Offsets when repairing the image. Using RGB curves, those repairs can be very specific. Because my first step is to set contrast and I generally use the master curve for that initial adjustment, the RGB curves are just waiting for me when I'm ready to deal with color issues, increasing my overall speed.

Deciding Between HSL Offset and Curves

If your initial fixes are being done in the Curves palette, when do you switch to the HSL Offsets? If you follow my workflow, you switch to the HSLs when you're finished making your primary adjustments in the Curves. In other words, you're splitting our tasks in the different palettes. Curves are being used to make initial contrast and color repairs, after which you switch to HSLs for additional adjustments—maybe to add mood or warm up or cool down the image.

The other reason to use HSLs is if you want to remove or add a color that's between the RGB primaries, like yellow (which sits between red and green). If you wanted to add some yellow into the image (say, to improve skin tones), it's much easier to do that in an HSL color wheel (you just simply drag toward yellow) than to manipulate two RGB curves. In other words, pushing and pulling in the HSL Offset is the equivalent of manipulating two or all three of the RGB curves—simultaneously. For those types of tasks, the HSL Offsets excel.

Limitations of Curves

As you gain experience color correcting in Avid, I fully expect you'll discover Curves is extremely powerful, and many of you will use it as your main color-correction tool. I just want to offer a word of caution: For most general color-correction tasks, having more than four points on your curve (not including the end points) can be very counter-productive. If you're not careful, posterization can occur, which will destroy all the good work you've done. I'm not saying don't do it. I'm saying, be very careful when you see yourself writing really complicated curves. When that happens, put on your eagle eyes and look for problems you may be introducing.

—pi

Review/Discussion Questions

1. True/false: The master curve affects only the luma signal, independent of the color channels.

2. What effect does increasing contrast have on the image?

3. How can you increase contrast across the entire image using Curves?

4. How can you increase the contrast within a portion of the luma range?

5. What is the order of processing for Curves adjustments?

6. Which adjustments are processed first, HSL or Curves?

7. You have been grading a shot exclusively with Curves, but you notice that the HSL tab is activated. Why would the system show HSL as active?

    a. You adjusted saturation.

    b. You have too many points on a Curve.

    c. You used the eyedropper to remove a color cast.

    d. You used the Auto Contrast to set the luma range.

8. What is the value of adding points to a ChromaCurve, besides the point that is being adjusted?

    a. It's better to have extras.

    b. The extra points improve real-time performance.

    c. The extra points limit the adjustment to a given luma range.

    d. There is no value in adding extra points.

9. When choosing a representative frame to grade, which characteristic(s) of the frame is desirable? (Choose all that apply.)

    a. The actor's eyes can be seen.

    b. All the actors in the scene are visible.

    c. The lighting and setup is indicative of the shot at large.

    d. It is the first frame of the shot.

    e. It is the middle frame of the shot.

10. Name one way you can make more precise adjustments to a Curves point.

11. Which setting should you enable to improve the accuracy and predictability of color sampling?

12. When correcting a strong color cast, what is the recommended approach for balancing the three channels?

13. In Curves, what effect does a chroma adjustment have on luma, if any?

   a. No effect; they are processed separately.

   b. Minimal effect; it can be disregarded when grading.

   c. Moderate effect; it varies by color channel.

   d. Strong effect; every chroma adjustment causes a notable shift in brightness.

Lesson 4 Keyboard Shortcuts

Key	Result
Shift-drag (a curve control point)	Slide the control point along the curve, maintaining the Input/Output ratio
Alt-click (Windows) or Option-click (Mac) ChromaCurve	Reset the curve to its default values enable button
Alt-click (Windows) or Option-click (Mac) Curves tab	Reset the Curves group to its default values enable button

Performing Primary Grades with Curves

This is a lengthy exercise designed to reinforce the concepts learned in this lesson through repetition.

Media Used:

Avid Color Grading (MC239) project > 2_Exercise Bins folder > Ex4_Curves Exercise bin > Ex4_Curves_Helicopter Montage sequence, Ex4_Poker Game sequence

Duration:

60 minutes

GOALS

- Grade two scenes using curves
- Perform primary grades with consistent results
- Develop familiarity and speed with the Curves controls

Overview

This lesson requires you to grade numerous similar shots using Curves. The repetition will help you develop the habits of thought and muscle memory so you can start to get into a rhythm. After you crack the code on the first few shots in each sequence, you should be able to move quickly through the rest.

The exercise provides you with two sequences to grade—the first one easier, and the second more advanced:

- The first sequence, 4_Curves Ex_Helicopter Montage, is a series of helicopter shots used in the movie title sequence. There are contrast issues as well as a strong color cast on all shots. If you choose to use the auto-correction tools, including Remove Color Cast, limit yourself to correcting only a few shots with that method. Correct the remainder using manual adjustments.

- The second sequence, 4_Curves Ex_Card Game, includes the series of three shots from the end of the lesson. These shots require more subtle adjustments. As you work through this sequence, you may wish to combine HSL and Curves adjustments. Remember, HSL adjustments are processed before Curves; therefore, it is recommended that you perform the adjustments in that order.

Matching Shots

One of the critical requirements of grading is to match one shot to another, especially within a scene. Depending on how production went, the shots in a scene may contain images that were recorded minutes, hours, or days apart. Variations in lighting and color may range from subtle to quite distinct, yet the viewer is expected to believe that the events playing out are happening at the same time. It's the job of the colorist to construct that reality.

Media Used: Avid Color Grading (MC239) project > 1_Lesson Bins folder > 5_Matching Shots bin > 5_Matching Shots_Hallway sequence, 5_Matching Shots_Desert sequence

Duration: 60 minutes

GOALS

- Identify methods of shot matching
- Identify Avid's Color Match controls
- Identify strategies for grading a shot-matching scene
- Use color matching to create shot-to-shot consistency
- Understand the difference in matching colors with, and without, NaturalMatch
- Use NaturalMatch to grade a scene.
- Save and reuse temporary color templates
- Save and reuse permanent color templates
- Create an efficient workflow for grading large volumes of footage based on common sources

Methods of Shot Matching

In the introductory lessons, you learned that shot matching can be considered a secondary workflow step to be performed after the primary grade. As a novice, it is helpful to think of it this way. More commonly, however, it is performed at the same time as the primary grade.

There are three methods for matching shots when working in Avid:

- Correction templates

- Auto-matching tools

- Manually, by eye matching

Of the three, manual eye matching—looking at one shot and grading another to match it—is going to give you the best result. Your expert eyes, standing in for those of the viewers, are the best reference and final authority. If you want the gold standard, manually grade every shot.

But for the rest of us who live in the real world of tight deadlines and unexpected delays, a shortcut that helps us meet those deadlines can be a life-saver! The trick is to learn where you can safely shortcut without compromising the integrity of your work or the quality of the final product. In this lesson, you will learn to use all three of these methods—and more importantly, *when* to use them.

Using the Color Match Controls

Each Color Correction group includes the Color Match controls, shown in Figure 5.1. The Color Match controls enable you to quickly make a correction by selecting input and output colors from your images or from your system's Color dialog box. For example, if you want to match the blue sky tone in one image with that in another, you can use the Color Match control to pick the two colors and automate the color adjustment.

Figure 5.1
Media Composer's Color Match controls, in Curves.

When you use the Color Match control, the system replaces the input color value with the output color value and adjusts all the other color values in the image proportionally. For example, if you replace the color of the sky with a darker blue, the blue is altered across the entire image. If the darker blue is more saturated, the blue tones throughout the image become more saturated. After performing this operation, the controls in the active correction group are updated to reflect the change.

The options presented in the Match Type pop-up menu are contextual to each group. For instance, in HSL, the match options include Shadows, Midtones, and Highlights; in Curves, the match options are Master and R+G+B. Symphony adds to these options extensively. Color Match is also available in channels, levels, and secondaries, and the parameters available to match are presented individually or in combination, based on the group, as shown in Figure 5.2.

Figure 5.2
Additional match parameters available in Symphony.

This lesson focuses on the options available in Media Composer. The principles apply directly to Symphony. For full details of the various match controls in Symphony, search for "Match Type Options" in the Avid Symphony Help.

Note: You can access the Edit Review and Play Loop buttons from the Play tab of the Command palette or from the keyboard if you map it to a keyboard location.

Succeeding with Color Match Controls

When it comes to using Color Match controls, there seems to be two camps. There are the colorists who see automated color matching as a waste of time, and those that see it as a useful shortcut when time is tight. I fall into the latter. Used properly, it can quickly get you most of the way there—almost like a custom template created on the fly. You will probably need to make some minor adjustments after the match, but you still come out ahead. Understanding how best to use Color Match will ensure that you get predictable, useful results.

First, you'll experience best results if the shots are already close to each other. For example, you might use this adjustment for a multi-cam shoot; the cameras are shooting the same subject but the color may be slightly different between the two angles.

Tip: For color-critical productions, such as fashion shows, interior-design pieces, etc., you may need to match a color to a Pantone color or other such reference. Using Color Match, you can reference any color pickers available in the OS.

You will find Color Match less useful where the original footage was shot in different locations, on different cameras, or with widely varying exposures. As with any automatic function, there are limitations to its capabilities and you should set your expectations accordingly. But, Color Match can be another great tool in your toolbox—perfect for the right occasion.

Second, pick the right shot as the reference. The more significant the differences between images, the more important it is to consider how easily it is for the system to calculate the adjustments. If trying to match shots that have more significant differences in exposure or balance, use the shot with the least latitude as the reference. Grade it manually for best results, then match the others to it. This is the much like the technique used in the last section of Lesson 4, "Grading with Curves." When approaching the scene, the first shot you graded was the one that was going to make the best reference image for the scene. That is, it was the shot that would give you the best chance of creating a consistent look when grading the others toward it. The same applies here.

Finally, you can greatly improve your results if you exert some manual control by limiting the scope of the match. Consider the type of adjustments that need to be made to the image. Doing so gives you the best of both worlds—your informed control over the correction, coupled with the speed of an automated process.

Tip: Color Match requires you to sample the image using the eyedropper. The same best practices for sampling apply here as to removing a color cast. Need a reminder? See the "Super Sampling" sidebar in the section "Correcting a Color Cast Automatically" in Lesson 4.

Grading a Scene Using Color Match Controls

In this section, you will grade a scene primarily using the Color Match controls. You can know how to use a tool only if you know its strengths and its limitations.

To make a correction by using the Color Match control:

1. If you have not already done so, open the project titled AVID COLOR GRADING and the 5_MATCHING SHOTS bin.

2. Load the sequence 5_MATCHING SHOTS_DESERT. Move the position indicator through the sequence to review the footage. Markers in the sequence indicate the reference frames used for the screenshots throughout this lesson.

   The Timeline contains a series of surrealistic shots taken from a hallucinogenic dream sequence at the end of the film. The lesson sequence includes jump cuts from the film that add to the feeling of disorientation in the scene. Although they are from the same master clip, Media Composer sees it as a separate shot in the Timeline. As you can see in Figure 5.3, there are a few shots that are going to present a real challenge!

Figure 5.3
Three shots that must be matched. A challenge indeed!

   There are two shots that are quite dark and flat, R9-7 and R9-2. These will have to be pushed quite far to get a reasonable image, which also means they'll have the least amount of additional latitude for color matching. Compare those to shot R12-3, which is already well-balanced with good contrast. R12-3 will have plenty of latitude for matching.

3. Using the techniques from Lesson 3, "Establishing the Base Grade," and Lesson 4, "Grading with Curves," perform a primary grade on shot **R9-7**. Figure 5.4 shows the image before and after grading.

Note: An effect template of the primary grade shown in Figure 5.4 is included in your bin, named "R9-7—Lesson Grade." To use the template from this grade, drag the effect icon to the segment in the Timeline. How to create templates like this one will be covered later in this chapter.

Figure 5.4
Shot R9-7, before and after a primary grade. This will be the reference image.

4. Set **R9-7** as a your reference image. To do so, position the position indicator on the frame you want to use in the Current monitor. Then do one of the following:

   - In the Current monitor, right-click the image and choose **Reference Current**.

   - In the right monitor, open the monitor menu and choose **Reference**.

   This frame is now displayed in the Reference monitor.

5. Move the position indicator to the first segment, **R12-3**. Review the shot, then park the position indicator on a good representative frame.

6. If it is not active already, click the **Curves** tab.

   For many Avid colorists, Curves is the preferred toolset for color matching, due to its one-click convenience and the availability of the NaturalMatch option, covered later in this lesson.

Tip: HSL color matching can be very effective for subtle adjustments within a limited range, such as the highlights only. Curves color matching is better for creating an adjustment of the overall color tones in an image.

7. Look at the right side of the Curves group window to identify the Color Match panel. It contains auto-correct buttons at the bottom and Color Match controls at the top. (See Figure 5.5.)

Figure 5.5
The Color Match panel in Media Composer's Curves group.

The Color Match controls include an Input color swatch, an Output color swatch, a Match Type pop-up, and the Match Color button. The color swatches are used to identify the colors to be matched:

● Input color is the one you want to *adjust.*

● Output color is the *reference* or *replacement.*

When in doubt, look at the arrow. (See Figure 5.6.) It's like a little One Way sign telling you which direction the system is processing—"from this, to that." The color on the left will be matched to the one on the right.

Figure 5.6
The "One Way" arrow indicates the direction of the matching operation.

8. To select the input color (the one you want to change), move the pointer over the left (**INPUT**) color swatch. When it changes to an eyedropper, drag it to one of the lighter areas in the background sand (in the Current monitor) and release the mouse. The color appears in the input color swatch, and the RGB values are displayed.

9. To select the output color (the reference color), drag the cursor from the right (**OUTPUT**) color swatch to a similarly bright portion of the background sand in the Reference monitor.

Tip: **Double-click the Output color swatch to open the Select Color dialog box from your computer's OS. This is useful for choosing an ideal replacement color, such as a completely neutral gray, or a color-critical reference, such as a Pantone color. You can also use it to create and store custom colors.**

10. Click the **MATCH TYPE** pop-up menu to open it. This menu enables you to specify the type of match to be performed. The options available in the Match Type menu correspond to the controls in the active correction group (i.e., HSL, Curves, Levels, etc.).

11. Choose **R+G+B**. Figure 5.7 shows the Color Match setup.

Figure 5.7
The Color Match controls, ready to match.

12. Click the **MATCH COLOR** button to make the correction. The system adjusts the current segment and adjusts the group controls—red, green, and blue curves in this case—to reflect the adjustment. Figure 5.8 shows the result of the match.

Figure 5.8
The results of the RGB Curves match.

13. Enable, then examine, the **RGB PARADE**, shown in Figure 5.9. The black traces for the subject's shirt are well balanced. The landscape midtones show a yellow (red+green) color. The highlights are also strongly blue, which is right for the sky. The only minor issue is with the green channel: It's a little too strong in the sky traces, as shown in Figure 5.9. More importantly, looking at the client monitor, this slight green cast can be seen in the highlights of the subject's face and hair.

Figure 5.9
The RGB Parade shows too much green in the highlights.

14. To neutralize the green in the highlights, click the green control point at approximately 75%. Then click the green channel **OUTPUT** box and press the **DOWN ARROW** key until the green sky traces fall in line with those in the red channel.

Note: Remember, if you are working with the keyboard/mouse and internal scopes only, the scopes only update when you release the key. Make your adjustment in small increments.

15. The shot is depicting afternoon in the desert. With sun reflecting off the sand, however, the shadows on the subject's face feel too dark. Brighten them by adding a point on the master curve at about **25%**. Raise it slightly—just enough to brighten the area under the subject's eyes.

16. Increase the **SATURATION** setting to bring a bit more color to the subject's face—to approximately **120**. Even a super secret agent gets hot in the desert! Figure 5.10 shows the results.

Figure 5.10
The finished, primary grade of shot R12-3.

17. Practice on one more shot before moving on. Repeat the process, matching the first segment, **R5-SER**, to the reference shot, **R9-7**. Nicely done. Using Color Match, you were able to get an accurate grade quickly.

Understanding NaturalMatch

In many situations, when you are correcting on a shot-to-shot basis, color matching is complicated by differences in lighting between one shot and another. In this situation, the exact RGB match created by standard color matching can cause problems, either technical or perceptual. The technical problem is that the correction affects the entire image and not just the object you selected, so the adjustment can have an undesirable affect on other parts of the image. Perceptually, there are times when precise matches between input and output can result in *visual* mismatches. How?

Don't forget: Simultaneous contrast effects can cause objects with identical RGB values to appear very different. Our perception is influenced by our past experiences telling us, "Ah, this object is in shadow and if it looks that way while in shadow its properties must be different than in full sunlight." Put another way: Our brains reinterpret our retinal data to force our perceptions to align with past experiences. This is why the same object from one shot to another may not match precisely. If the new shot is from an angle showing us an object in a different context (say, the shadow side), you may need to adjust your grade to get a perceptual (or natural) match.

In the Curves group, the Color Match control includes the NaturalMatch feature. NaturalMatch enables you to replace the hue values in an image without affecting saturation and luma values. This does not produce the *exact* match that the standard color match does and, at times, can address both the technical and perceptual challenge of exact matching.

NaturalMatch is particularly useful for adjusting skin tone, even when the reference image shows a significant difference in lighting. For example, you might want to match the skin tone in shot A, which is in shadow, with that in shot B, which is well lit. NaturalMatch replaces the hue of shot A while preserving its original luma value and adjusting its saturation value in relation to the other values in the image. This feature works best when you can use a good version of the same person's skin tone for the match.

Using NaturalMatch

In this section, you will use various color-matching options to see the differences in, and potential advantages of, using NaturalMatch. For this section, you'll use a different scene from the film.

To make a correction using NaturalMatch:

1. If you have not already done so, open the project **Avid Color Grading** and the bin **5_Matching Shots**.

2. Load the sequence **5_Matching Shots_Hallway**. Move the position indicator through the sequence to review the footage. Markers in the sequence indicate the reference frames used for the screenshots throughout this lesson.

   The scene takes place in a dimly lit hall, with mixed practical lights. After neutralizing the bad-guy security detail, Agent Zero intercepts Gemini, recovers the nuclear launch key, and takes Gemini hostage as insurance while he goes to meet the boss, Mysterion.

3. As a starting shot to grade in the scene, move the position indicator to **F1+8-4**, marked with a locator. This shot includes both characters and some challenging backlighting; their skin tones are ashen. This shot will require a manual grade.

4. Using the techniques taught in Lessons 3 and 4, perform a primary grade on **F1+8-4**, then set the right monitor to **Reference**. Figure 5.11 shows the before and after of your primary grade.

Figure 5.11
The primary grade of shot F1+8-4.

Note: An effect template of the primary grade shown in Figure 5.11 is included in your bin, named "F1+8-4—Lesson Grade." To use the template from this grade, drag the effect icon to the segment in the Timeline. How to create templates like this one will be covered later in this chapter.

5. Move the position indicator to the first shot in the sequence, **F2+9-2**, and park on a frame toward the end of the clip that reveals Zero with gun drawn, lit from behind by the exterior light.

6. Click the **Curves** tab.

7. In the Color Match controls, open the **Match Type** menu and, if it is not already selected, choose **R+G+B**.

8. If necessary, reopen the **Match Type** menu; this time, however, choose **NaturalMatch**.

   When this command is selected, all the RGB match types in the Curves group use the NaturalMatch feature when making a correction and match types appear in the Color Match control with the following extension: (Nat).

9. Click the **Input** color swatch; then drag the eyedropper to the shadowed portion of Zero's right forearm in the Current monitor. Avoid the bright highlight running along the top of the arm.

10. Click the **Output** color swatch; then drag the eyedropper to the shadowed portion of Zero's right forearm in the Reference monitor. The Color Match values should approximate those seen in Figure 5.12.

Figure 5.12
The match controls are set up, ready to match Zero's forearm.

11. Click the **Match Color** button. The match is performed. There is a clear shift in color values. Points have been added to each of the color channels around 25%. Because NaturalMatch doesn't adjust luma, the image is still dark, as expected.

12. Adjust the master curve to set the luma range. Figure 5.13 shows the images and corrections after the match and luma adjustments.

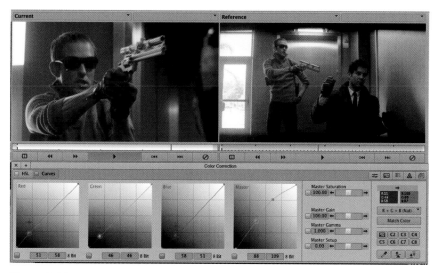

Figure 5.13
After the NaturalMatch and master-curve adjustment.

13. Examine the image in the scopes and your external monitor. If necessary, fine-tune the color in the **Hue Offsets** tab (HSL group) or adjust the Curves. If you are adjusting skin tone, use the **Midtones** wheel in the Hue Offsets tab.

Understanding the Crosshair When Using Color Match in the Curves Group

When you use Color Match in the Curves tab, a crosshair appears in the ChromaCurve graph (not on the curve itself) to mark the intersection of the input value (the existing image) and the output value (what you want to change the existing image to). Figure 5.14 shows the crosshair before you click the Match Color button.

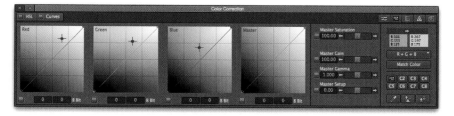

Figure 5.14
The crosshairs identify the location of matching color values.

When you click the Match Color button, the system adds a new control point and updates the curve to reflect the color match. The Input and Output values are also updated. The curve updates in one of the following ways:

- If you are not using NaturalMatch and the curve was not previously adjusted, the new control point appears at the location of the crosshair. The adjustment is made exactly.

- If you are using NaturalMatch, the system makes a more complex calculation to reflect the input saturation and luma values. The new control point does not appear at the location of the crosshair. That's because the system adjusts hue with minimal effect on luma.

- If the curve was previously adjusted, the system takes the earlier curve adjustments into account. The system adds a new control point at the location of the crosshair only if the position is *not* near the position of an existing point.

Working with Color Correction Effect Templates

It should go without saying that Avid's Color Correction tools do not cause any permanent change to clips in bins or to their associated media files. Naturally, if you make a color adjustment to a clip in one sequence in Media Composer, that adjustment does not apply to the same clip in a different sequence. By saving the grade from one segment as a color-correction template, however, you can reuse it on another.

Templates are the very definition of working smarter, not harder. By creating a template from one grade and applying it to another segment, you can immediately achieve a consistent look if the lighting and exposure are identical between shots. If there are slight variations, you only have to make minor adjustments to tweak the grade after applying the template.

The ability to move quickly through many shots has an added benefit: It keeps your (mental) eye fresh. If you spend too much time looking at each image, it will fatigue your eyes and skew your color perception, making it more likely to have the grade "drift" over time. That is, the grades late in the session will be different from those done earlier. (A carefully controlled grading environment is a great help in minimizing this effect.) So, learn this now: Templates are good! Use them. Love them.

The Avid color-grading tools offer you two types of templates:

- **Temporary templates.** Temporary templates are retained only during the current edit session. The data is lost when you quit Media Composer or Symphony. They are stored in the correction buckets, labeled C1–C8 in the Color Match panel. This gives you up to eight templates that can be saved and instantly recalled as you move through the sequence.

- **Permanent templates.** Permanent templates are saved with the project, like any other saved effect template. These are stored in a bin.

You'll start with temporary templates.

To start working with templates:

1. Reopen the sequence from the first section on this lesson, **5_MATCHING SHOTS_DESERT**.

2. Scrub through the first two segments. Look at their names. Both are labeled **R12-3**; clearly, they are from the same master clip. The edit between them is a jump cut that makes the subject's head turn faster than real time. You've seen this elsewhere in this sequence. Because the first segment is graded and the second is not (see Figure 5.15), you can use a template to quickly apply the grade to the uncorrected segment. Without a template, you would either have to grade the second segment independently or alter the edit; neither option is desirable.

Figure 5.15
A simple primary grade on the first shot, R12-3.

3. Move the position indicator to the first segment, **R12-3**. You will create the template from the grade already in place on this segment.

4. With the position indicator still over the first shot, **R12-3**, Option-click (Mac) or Alt-click (Windows) the **C1** correction bucket. A color correction effect symbol appears on the button, indicating that the template has been saved.

If the bucket that already contained a template, you will overwrite the previous template with the new settings. To empty a bucket, Option-click (Mac) or Alt-click (Windows) it when the position indicator is parked over a segment with no correction applied.

Note: The buttons CG1–CG4 and PG1–PG4 on the Artist Color controller are premapped to correction buckets 1–4. Use the corresponding CG (copy grade) button to load the template, and PG (paste grade) to apply it. To access buckets 5–8, press the Shift button on the controller.

5. Move the position indicator to the second segment, **R12-3**; then click the saved effect in the **C1** bucket. The effect is applied and the change is immediately seen in the image and the scopes. (That was easy!)

6. Move to the graded segment of **R5-SER**.

7. Repeat the process to save the correction template to a bucket, then apply the correction to the ungraded segment of **R5-SER**.

Tip: Another use of the correction buckets is when you're experimenting with a grade, trying a couple different looks. You can save the first in one bucket, the second in another. Quickly compare them by alternately applying each. For fastest grading, you can also map the Color Correction buckets from the CC tab in the Command palette to keys on the keyboard.

Saving Color Correction Effect Templates to a Bin

Saving templates to a bin is the way to save them for longer than the current session. This is the method used to build the library mentioned earlier. It is also useful for sequence-specific grades when you foresee the grading process taking longer than a single session, or that you will share the template with another editor. In either case, you will want to save the template to a bin.

In the current project, you know there are other master clips that match each of these shots, which you'll grade later. Let's be sure to save the work you've done now by creating some templates.

To save a Color Correction effect template to a bin:

1. If it's not already loaded, open the sequence **5_MATCHING SHOTS_DESERT**.

2. In the Project window, create a bin to hold your color corrections. Name it **CORRECTION TEMPLATES**.

3. With the position indicator over **R9-7**, drag the **COLOR CORRECTION** effect icon from the toolbar to the bin.

Notes from the Colorist: Working Faster Using a Color Correction Library

Speed. Colorists are always looking for small ways to get through more shots in less time without compromising the quality of their work. One method almost all colorists use is to build a library of common color-correction tasks to be applied on any shot in any project at any time.

In Avid, this means having a personal bin of common corrections that you can import into a project. You'll then have your personal library ready and waiting. But how do you build this library? Easy: Pay attention to tasks you do over and over again. One of my favorites that most colorist's can relate to is one I call "auto green tinge removal." It's designed to remove the green color cast introduced by automotive glass. There's barely a project I do where I don't use this saved correction as a starting point.

The key to saving off these corrections is removing all other adjustments you made that are shot-specific, then saving the correction. This keeps the correction clean so it performs only the specific action you've named it. For each of these corrections, I usually have multiple intensities, depending on how much of it I want to apply.

For some ideas, here are the names of a few other fixing corrections I have in my library, what they do, and the intensities I have saved:

- **Indoor Daylight Balance Fix (Light/Medium/Heavy):** Fixes the blue cast of daylight white balance with a scene lit by incandescent bulbs.

- **Incandescent Balance Fix (Light/Medium/Heavy):** Fixes the orange cast of incandescent bulbs when shooting in daylight.

- **Contrast (Light/Medium/Heavy):** A master curve adjustment with the endpoints moved toward the middle.

- **S-Curve (Light, Normal, Thick, Heavy):** Four different flavors of the S-curve.

Usually I have to make a slight tweak after applying these. And sometimes, they just don't work, and I have to throw them away completely. Overall, however, they speed up my work-flow considerably.

—pi

4. The template is named for the clip being adjusted, as shown in Figure 5.16. If you like, rename the effect.

Figure 5.16
The saved correction template, named after the clip.

5. For greater speed and efficiency, you can map the Save Correction button to a key on the keyboard. To do that now, choose **TOOLS > COMMAND PALETTE** and click the **CC** tab. Also open the Keyboard settings from the Settings tab of the Project window.

6. Drag the **SAVE CORRECTION** button to the key of your choice on the keyboard map, such as **F5**.

7. Press this key whenever you want to save a Color Correction effect to a bin. The correction will be saved to the active bin.

Finally, it is also possible to save a correction effect from a bucket to a bin. You might do this if you are in the middle of grading and are leaving for the day. You can save the bucket to a bin and reload the bucket the next day.

To save a Color Correction effect from a bucket to a bin:

1. Drag the **COLOR CORRECTION** effect icon from the bucket to the **CORRECTION TEMPLATES** bin.

   The template is named **CORRECTION #**, named after the correction bucket from which it was created, as shown in Figure 5.17.

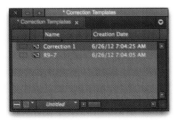

Figure 5.17
The saved correction template, named after the bucket.

2. Rename the correction template if you wish. However, if you leave the original names, then it is really easy to reload the buckets when you restart the session.

Using Color Correction Effect Templates

Once you create an effect template, you can then apply it to a segment by dragging the template from the bucket, bin, or Effect Palette to the segment of your choice. You can also use effect templates to apply an effect to multiple clips in a sequence. Like adding any other effect, this can also be done in any other editing mode.

The concept of saving an effect as a template is one with which you are most likely familiar. You can save other effect templates and apply them in a similar fashion. With color grading, however, there are some tricks to working with templates that can make your workflow very efficient.

Applying a Correction Template to a Single Segment

The easiest, albeit the slowest, way to apply an effect template is to simply drag it to a segment.

To apply a Color Correction effect template to a single segment:

1. If it's not already loaded, open the sequence **5_MATCHING SHOTS_DESERT**.

2. Move the position indicator to the segment **R9-2**. This image has the same chroma and luma problems as shot R9-7. You can use the template to fix this shot.

3. From the **CORRECTION TEMPLATES** bin, drag your effect template, **R9-7**, to the segment **R9-2**.

   The effect is applied, and the grade is seen in the current monitor. You can make additional minor adjustments as needed, but the template has you off to a great start.

Assigning a Template to a Correction Bucket

Working out of the correction buckets is faster than working out of the Effect Palette. If you will be using a correction repeatedly during the current session, assign it to a bucket for fastest use.

The only minor disadvantage to working out of the buckets is that you have to remember which template is in which bucket, because you can't see the names. No doubt you can devise some easy memory tricks to help you remember which is which.

For example, with this sequence, the shots can be classified into three categories, in terms of how much correction is required. You might put the three templates in Bucket 1, Bucket 2, and Bucket 3, in order of the severity of adjustment. Bucket 1, requiring the least amount of adjustment, would hold the template for the good-looking shots, such as R12-3. Bucket 3, requiring the greatest amount of adjustment, would hold the template for shots like R9-2.

Tip: When assigning templates to correction buckets, think of an easy way to remember which is which before mapping them.

To assign a correction template to a correction bucket:

1. Activate **COLOR CORRECTION** mode, if it is not already active.

2. Choose **TOOLS > EFFECT PALETTE** or press **COMMAND+8** (Mac) or **CTRL+8** (Windows).

3. In the Effect Palette, scroll to the bottom of the effect categories in the left column. Any open bins containing effect templates appear below the line, near the bottom of the list.

4. Select **CORRECTION TEMPLATES.** Your saved effect templates appear on the right, as shown in Figure 5.18.

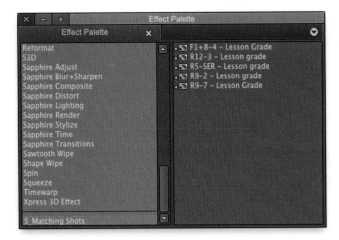

Figure 5.18
Templates in the bin appear below the line in the Effect Palette.

5. Drag the template **R12-3** to the **CORRECTION 1** bucket. The icon appears, indicating that the template is loaded.

6. Repeat step 5, loading the other correction buckets with your saved templates.

   If you are working on an Avid Artist controller, there are dedicated keys that correspond to the correction buckets. If not, the real speed advantages of this workflow are only realized by mapping the correction buckets to a key on your keyboard. Try that now.

7. Click the **SETTINGS** tab in the Project window and open the **KEYBOARD** setting.

8. Choose **TOOLS > COMMAND PALETTE** or press **COMMAND+3** (Mac) or **CTRL+3** (Windows).

9. In the Command Palette, select the CC tab. Verify that the **BUTTON TO BUTTON REASSIGNMENT** option button is selected.

10. Holding down the **SHIFT** key (to reveal the shifted keyboard), drag the **CC** buttons to the numbers **1–8** on the keyboard.

   Now you can apply each template using the shifted number keys. You will come to recognize the added speed this gives you in grading as you work through the exercise at the end of this lesson.

Using Symphony's Automatic Effect Templates

If you are working in Symphony, the system automatically creates templates for you of the most recent color corrections you made in the Effect Palette. You can quickly apply any one of these templates to the current segment in the sequence by dragging it or simply by highlighting it in the Effect Palette and pressing Return (Mac) or Enter (Windows).

The effect categories list contains bins with saved effects and color-corrected sequences that have been loaded in the Record monitor that session and stored in an open bin. When you select a color-corrected sequence on the left side of the Effect Palette, a list of templates for the most recent corrections appears in the right side. Each template is named using either the clip name of the segment on which it was originally made or, if you made a comment on that segment, the text of the comment.

The templates are listed in order of creation, with the most recently created template at the top of the list. The most recently created template is always numbered 1. The list is limited to the 16 most recent corrections. After 16 templates, the system will remove the oldest template from the list when you make a new correction.

Selectively Applying Template Adjustments

It is possible to selectively use only certain adjustments from an effect template. For example, you could have a template in your bin that represents the correction of a shot that had a color cast similar to the rest of the clips from the same camera. In that template, the color cast was removed with HSL, and an additional look was created using Curves. The HSL adjustment can be applied to remove the color cast from the other shots, without applying the Curves adjustment.

To selectively apply corrections from a Color Correction template:

1. Click the tab to which you want to apply the template and drag the effect icon to anywhere in the tab.

   The settings from the effect template are applied only to the controls in that tabbed group.

2. If you applied template settings to a subdividing tab (for example, the Controls tab in the HSL group), enable the group tab (for example, the HSL tab) to update the image in the monitor.

Workflow for Using Source-Based Templates

You will frequently find that master clips from the same tape or camera card need a similar correction. Symphony includes special features, covered in detail in Lesson 6, "Stepping Up to Symphony," that enable you to grade a shot and have the system automatically apply those corrections to other clips from the same source. This is a powerful and time-saving feature.

Are you editing and grading on Media Composer and not Symphony? No worries! I'll still show you how to get it done. In Media Composer, this is the perfect use of templates. By saving and identifying templates from a given source, it follows that you could save time by applying that template as a base grade to all other master clips from the same source as a starting point, then tweak the grade as needed.

The following workflow is designed to speed that process by leveraging editing shortcuts to identify shots by Source.

To find shots by source:

1. From the bin **5_MATCHING SHOTS**, reopen the sequence **5_MATCHING SHOTS_HALLWAY**.

2. Choose **COLOR CORRECTION** mode.

3. Move the position indicator to **F1+8-4**, the shot you manually graded.

4. Drag the effect icon to the **CORRECTION TEMPLATES** bin to save the template.

5. Enable **SOURCE/RECORD** editing mode.

6. In the Project window, create a new bin. Name it **SOURCE CORRECTIONS**.

7. Drag the sequence to the **SOURCE CORRECTIONS** bin. It is important to place the sequence to be graded in a bin by itself.

8. In the sequence bin, choose **Fast Menu > Bin Display**. Select the **Show Reference Clips** check box, as shown in Figure 5.19. This displays all the master clips linked to the sequence.

Figure 5.19
Enable the Show Reference Clips check box to reveal all the clips in a sequence.

9. With the position indicator still over F1+8-4, Alt-click the **Find Bin** button. The source master clip will be highlighted in the bin.

10. To locate other clips from the same source, sort the bin by tape (or, in some cases, by source path).

11. Select all the clips from the tape **VT101**. Right-click the color chip for any one of the selected clips; select the bright yellow color.

12. In the Timeline, choose **Fast Menu > Clip Color**. In the Clip Color dialog box, select the **Source** check box and deselect all the others except Offline, as shown in Figure 5.20.

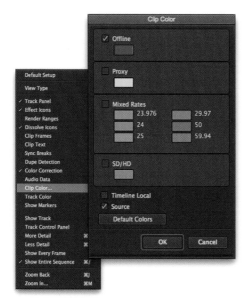

Figure 5.20
Enable source colors in the Timeline.

13. Click **OK**. The segments from tape VT101 are now highlighted yellow in
     the Timeline, as shown in Figure 5.21. (You may wish to save this Timeline
     view as "Source Colors.")

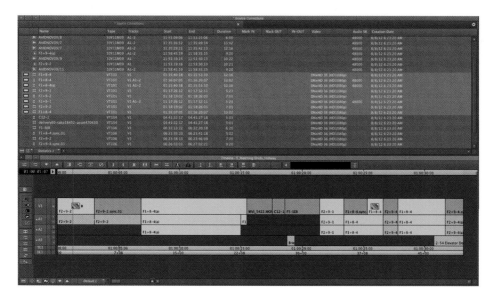

Figure 5.21
Source Colors in the Timeline reveal clips from the same tape.

14. Using a SmartTool segment mode, Shift-click the yellow clips to select them. Double-click the template of choice in the Effect Palette.

    The effect template is applied to each clip.

15. When finished, clear the clip color from the clip(s) and repeat with the next tape, or source, and its corresponding template effect.

Notes from the Colorist: Shot Matching: That's Our Job!

I said this in an earlier chapter and I'll say it again: I make my living matching shots. It often seems like we're getting paid to fix color-balance issues or create a look or perform some magic tricks like day for night. But as far as I'm concerned, my ability to do any of those tasks is meaningless if I can't get my shots to match! The truth is, most audiences will accept off-color skin tones if those skin tones are consistent across the entire scene. Their visual system will adjust the image accordingly—if it doesn't have to keep readjusting every time we cut to a new shot.

If you want to be known for your color-correction skills, then you have to master the mundane art of shot matching. I've found three good guidelines that help me when I'm deep in shot-matching mode.

#1: Black is Black; Keep It That Way

Black, by definition, is the absence of light. With no light, there is no color. Therefore, black is colorless. Your shots won't match if the black levels keep jumping up and down or if its tint keeps bouncing around. If you can keep your blacks and deep shadows (the shadows in the bottom 15% of the image) neutral of tint, you're halfway home to matching your shots together.

An added bonus of keeping your blacks, black? It helps "sell" aggressive color grades with extreme color casts. The moment color starts creeping in the deep shadows the audience starts getting distracted by the color correction. So…don't distract the audience. I consider black management to be a colorist's top priority. It's a foundational task. If you have a solid foundation, you can do almost anything else you want with the image—including having a heavy color cast in the highlights.

The challenge with controlling your blacks is that very small tweaks can have a really big impact. And it's not always obvious that the problem you're having matching shots is a problem with black balance. When I'm having trouble shot matching, I stop, look at my blacks, start moving them around a bit to refresh my eyes, and then re-neutralize the black balance. Then I'll move to the next shot and repeat that action. Often, that solves my problem and I can move on.

#2: Check the Average Highlights and Keep Them Consistent

By "average highlights," I mean ignore the specular highlights (glints of metal objects or highly reflective surfaces) and watch where you're setting the preponderance of your highlights. Make the decision about where you're going to place them—and then keep it consistent across the range of shots you want to match. This can be difficult in shots where one angle is heavily backlit but the others aren't. Still, this is a good rule of thumb.

#3: Midtone Gamma Sets a Consistent Mood

The overall brightness or darkness of a scene isn't really set by where the shadow and high-lights are set. It's set by the gamma. Comedies have their midtones set much higher than moody dramas. But within both genres, they'll each have scenes that are brighter or darker depending on the mood of the moment. And the midtone gamma helps set that mood.

When you're working the gamma controls think about the emotion you're trying to convey and let that control help you set it. And once it's set, keep your midtones in that range throughout the scene. This is one of the keys to shot matching.

Did You Notice How Little We Talked About Color?

The only time I've mentioned color is when talking about controlling your blacks—and that was to tell you there shouldn't be any color. It is counterintuitive, but shot matching is much less about matching color than it is about brightness (or luminance values). The human eye is exponentially more sensitive to changes in brightness than in color. And I mean this literally; humans have far more cells dedicated to detecting brightness. This explains why, when shot matching, color inconsistencies are less worrisome than brightness inconsistencies.

If you want to improve your shot matching, control where you place your overall gamma and your average highlights. And remember: Neutral blacks (and deep shadows) are the foundation for the rest of your image and a key component in shot matching. Control your blacks and almost anything goes when setting the color and luminance values of your image.

—pi

Review/Discussion Questions

1. What are the three methods of matching shots?

2. What are two reasons that color matching may produce unacceptable results?

3. Which is an effective strategy for using automatic color-matching controls?
   a. Manually grade the first shot in the sequence and color match the rest in order.
   b. Manually grade the best-looking shot and color match the rest to it.
   c. Manually grade the widest shot and color match the closer shots to it.
   d. Manually grade the shots with the least latitude and match shots with more latitude to it.

4. Which color should be sampled with the Input color swatch: the reference color or the color to be corrected?

5. Is the Input color swatch on the left or right?

6. Which setting should be enabled to ensure the best results in sampling colors?
   a. Eyedropper 3×3 Averaging
   b. Show Eyedropper Info
   c. Eyedropper picks from anywhere in the application
   d. None of the above

7. How can you access the OS color palette for color matching?

8. In which color-correction group is NaturalMatch available as a color-matching option?

9. How is the correction made by NaturalMatch different from a standard color-match correction?

10. What is the difference between saving a correction template to a bin versus saving it in a correction bucket?

Lesson 5 Keyboard Shortcuts

The functions in this table can be mapped to the key of your choice. For information on how to map your keyboard, see the article "Mapping User-Selectable Buttons" in the Media Composer or Symphony Help.

Lesson 5   Keyboard Shortcuts

Command	Result
Edit Review	Plays the current segment, plus user-defined pre- and post-roll
Play Loop	Plays the entire sequence, beginning from the current location of the position indicator
Double-click the Color Match	Opens the OS color picker output swatch
Save Correction (SC)	Saves the current correction as a template in the active bin
C1–C8 buttons	Applies the correction template from the corresponding correction bucket to the current segments
Option-click (Mac)/ Alt-click (Windows) with buttons C1–C8	Saves the current correction as a template to the corresponding correction bucket
Cmd+8 (Mac)/Ctrl+8 (Windows)	Opens the Effect Editor
Option-click (Mac)/ Alt-click (Windows) Find Bin	Opens the bin and highlights the master clip for the segment currently under the position indicator (not available in Color Correction mode)

Shot Matching

It is one thing to match a couple shots in a lesson demo. It is another to do it repeatedly on a sequence. This exercise is designed to give you the practice needed to develop a rhythm and comfort level with the process of shot matching.

Media Used:

Avid Color Grading (MC239) project > 2_Exercise Bins folder > Ex5_Matching Shots bin > Ex5_Matching Shots_Hallway sequence, Ex5_Matching Shots_Desert sequence

Duration:

60 minutes

GOALS

- Accurately match shots within a sequence
- Use Color Match, including NaturalMatch, to match shots
- Save and apply correction effect templates

Part 1: Matching Shots on Full Sequences

In this exercise, you will grade the full scenes from which the lesson examples were taken: the desert and the hallway. The hallway scene is easier to grade; it is recommended that you start with this one.

Grade each scene in a unified approach, using the full complement of techniques you have learned to this point. This includes both HSL and Curves corrections, color matching in HSL and Curves, correction templates, and buckets.

To begin the exercise:

1. Open the project AVID COLOR GRADING (239), and the bin EX5_MATCHING SHOTS.

2. Load the sequence EX5_MATCHING SHOTS_HALLWAY.

3. Using the techniques taught in this lesson, grade the sequence, carefully matching shots.

4. When finished, move on to grade the sequence EX5_MATCHING SHOTS_DESERT.

(Optional) Part 2:
The Ugly Side of Color Match

Got extra time? Try this one.

The lesson walked you through a good workflow and strategy for color matching the desert scenes. But to know a tool is to know its limitations as well. Let's break the rules and see what you get.

1. Reload the lesson sequence, 5_MATCHING SHOTS_DESERT.

2. Use Color Match to match the same shots you used in the lesson, but in the reverse order. The results will be very different.

3. Grade the first segment in the sequence, R12-3, and set it as the reference.

4. Match the other shots to it to see the subpar results, particularly in those shots that are very dark.

5. Spend some time exploring the extensive tweaking and experimentation that is required when trying to match them this way, and you'll quickly see why some colorists abandon the tool entirely.

Stepping Up to Symphony

When it comes to color grading, Avid Symphony represents a significant upgrade over Avid Media Composer. This lesson will introduce you to the added features and benefits of working on Avid Symphony.

Media Used: Avid Color Grading (MC239) project > 1_Lesson Bins folder > 6_Symphony Tools bin > 6_Symphony Channels sequence, 6_Symphony Levels_Rooftop sequence, 6_Symphony Lesson_Hallway sequence

Duration: 60 minutes

GOALS

- Identify the additional Symphony tools
- Explain color-correction relationships
- Leverage color-correction relationships to speed up the grading process
- Set tonal range and balance using the Levels group
- Repair damaged and deficient signals using the Channels group

The Added Power of Advanced Tools

Ask the average Media Composer editor about the difference between Media Composer and Symphony, and you'll like get a one-word answer: secondaries. But the Secondary group is only one of the advanced color grading tools that are available in Symphony that are not offered with Media Composer. Symphony also adds advanced primary correction tools, including a Levels group, a Channels group, and Luma Range controls to the HSL group. Even more important than the added tools is the enhanced workflow made possible by Symphony's relationship-based corrections.

When considering which grading application to use for a production (or to invest in for business), many users look to the marketing materials that describe the latest features. If you do that, you might be concerned to find that there are other grading applications on the market with tools that Symphony doesn't offer. But look past the marketing hype and ask the real questions:

- What's the complete grading workflow for that application?

- Does that application offer the quality I need for my productions?

When you get down to the answers to these questions, you'll see why Symphony is a dominant player in the market and has the reputation it does. There's no doubt that the quality of Symphony grades are top notch. The image quality of *Project Runway, The Oprah Winfrey Show, Dr. Phil*, PBS' *American Masters*, and many more —all finished on Avid Symphony—prove it.

But ask a Symphony colorist why he or she uses it, and that person will tell you it's the speed of the workflow. Simply put, you get from the offline edit to a finished, top-quality grade more quickly on Avid Symphony. Because Symphony offers a robust set of grading tools *inside* the editing environment, there's no round-tripping to another application, no lengthy transcodes to a secondary codec, and full access to the editorial toolset to accommodate final revisions without breaking the grade. The one-two punch comes in with Symphony's color-correction relationships. As you'll learn, these enable the online editor to work on the grade even as the offline editor is still working on the story. For reality TV, cable documentaries, prime-time episodics, and more, this speed is critical to their success. All together, it's a package that's hard to beat.

In this lesson, you'll explore the added tools and functionality you get when you step up to grading on Symphony over Media Composer.

Identifying Symphony's Advanced Tools

The Color Correction tool has five groups: HSL, Levels, Curves, Channels, and Secondary color correction. This section provides an overview of those groups of added controls that are unique to Symphony. Because there is no difference between the Curves group in Media Composer and that in Symphony, it has been omitted from this discussion.

HSL Controls

Symphony adds the following features to the HSL group:

- A subdivided Controls tab with dedicated Master, Highlights, Midtones, and Shadows controls

- A fourth ChromaWheel, Master, on the Hue Offsets tab

- Luma Ranges controls to define the luminance values attributed to highlights, midtones, and shadows

In Symphony, the HSL group contains three subdividing tabs (as opposed to Media Composer's two): Controls, Hue Offsets, and Luma Ranges. The Controls tab is further subdivided by four tabs: Master, Highlights, Midtones, and Shadows.

As you know, the HSL (Hue, Saturation, Luma) group works in the YUV color space, where luma and chroma are separate elements in the signal. This enables you to change one part of the signal without significantly affecting the other. You have used HSL for such adjustments as setting the tonal range and adjusting saturation for the entire image.

The Controls tab in Media Composer, which you have worked with, matches closely to the Master tab in Symphony. The other tabs (Highlights, Midtones, and Shadows) contain the same parameter controls, but apply only to that portion of the luma range. Figure 6.1 shows controls in the HSL group's Controls > Midtones tab.

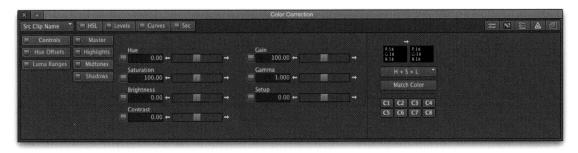

Figure 6.1
The Symphony Color Correction tool, displaying HSL controls for the midtones.

The addition of range-specific controls means that you can make more precise adjustments, such as desaturating only the highlights or shifting the shadow hue without affecting the midtones.

The inclusion of Setup, Gamma, and Gain settings on each of these tabs also means that you can affect nine distinct regions of the total luma range rather than only three. Adjusting the Gain slider on the Midtones tab, for example, would affect the brightest tones within the midtone range. This is very detailed control!

Notes from the Colorist:
Symphony's HSL Controls Tab: FCP Switchers Take Note

If you're coming from Final Cut Studio, one of the big things you're missing in Media Composer is the individual contrast controls for the Shadow, Mids, and Highlight wheels. Symphony not only gives those controls back to you, it adds full Setup, Gamma, and Gain controls for *each* of the tonal ranges. And if you're switching from FCP's Color Corrector Three-Way filter, Symphony's HSL Controls tab also adds saturation controls for each of the three tonal ranges. If you decide you need to desaturate your shadows, this is the perfect place to do it!

—pi

HSL Luma Ranges

HSL controls affect different regions of the luma range by subdividing the image into shadows, midtones, and highlights. In most applications, the way in which the system analyzes the image and assigns tonal values to one of the three regions is hard-coded into the software and cannot be changed by the user. In Symphony, however, you have the ability to alter the definition of these ranges through the Luma Ranges controls. In other words, if you want to change what portion of the image is considered a shadow versus a midtone, you can dial that in here. It's powerful stuff.

Three tabs subdivide the Luma Ranges tab, one for each of the three luminance ranges: Highlights, Midtones, and Shadows. A graph illustrates the selection curve that defines each of the luminance ranges, with all three curves always visible. The curve for the currently selected range—for example, Midtones—is displayed with a white line, while the lines representing the other luma ranges are displayed in gray, as shown in Figure 6.2.

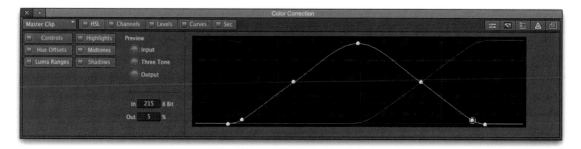

Figure 6.2
The Luma Ranges controls, with the Midtones curve active.

The types of corrections performed with the Luma Ranges controls are very precise. Some colorists perform their HSL corrections with default luma range values and use this tool to address only specific problematic areas. As such, performing HSL correction with the Luma Ranges controls becomes more like a secondary correction than a primary one. You will explore this tool in depth in Lesson 7, "Performing Secondary Corrections in Symphony." Even if you're pressed for time, using the Luma Ranges can give you a quick visual reference. Alternatively, if you recognize the image is heavily weighted to the shadows, for instance, it may be worth the extra time to adjust the luma ranges.

Tip: In Lesson 5, "Matching Shots," you learned that you can save corrections as templates and apply them in whole or in part, to other images. Use this technique to "borrow" the luma range adjustments from another image by dragging the template to the Luma Ranges tab. You may also want to create templates with specific luma range adjustments—i.e., Compressed Shadows and Midtones, Expanded Midtones, etc.

Levels Group

The main purpose of the Levels group is to rebalance the color or luma range. The Levels group enables you to define the white point, gray point, and black point of video material. You can do this for the master channel (red, green, and blue combined) or for each of the color channels, providing a great deal of control over the amount of contrast and detail that is visible in the video image. In addition, the controls in the Composite and Luma tabs are useful for maintaining overall signal levels to the gamut specifications.

Tip: If you are familiar with adjusting image levels in Photoshop, you will find this group relatively easy to learn and use.

Six tabs subdivide the Levels group, each corresponding to different aspects of the video signal:

- **Composite.** Use the settings in this tab to adjust high and low points for the composite signal to ensure that your sequence remains within legal composite limits.

- **Luma.** Use the settings in this tab to adjust levels based on luminance values only. The settings in this tab are also used to ensure gamut compliance.

- **Red.** Use the settings in this tab to adjust levels for the red channel only.

- **Green.** Use the settings in this tab to adjust levels for the green channel only.

- **Blue.** Use the settings in this tab to adjust levels for the blue channel only.

- **Master.** Use the settings in this tab to adjust levels for all three color channels.

Figure 6.3 shows the Levels group in its default configuration.

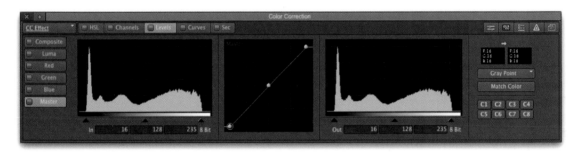

Figure 6.3
The Levels group, showing the Master histogram.

Each tab contains an input histogram, an output histogram, and curve graph. You are familiar with curve graphs, but histograms may be new. A *histogram* is a graph of the color values of all the pixels in an image. Luminance values are plotted on the horizontal axis of the graph; the number of pixels is plotted on the vertical axis. For example, if an image contains 120 pixels of luma value 30, then a bar 120 units high appears at the 30 point along the horizontal axis.

Tip: Histograms give you a quick view of where the concentrations of values lie within the image. For example, if an image is mostly dark, its histogram is humped at the low end.

In Lesson 3, "Establishing the Base Grade," and Lesson 4, "Grading with Curves," you used the HSL and Curves groups to perform these operations. Levels can be used as an alternative. The advantage of using the Levels group to perform these operations is that it preserves the use of HSL and Curves for other functions. For example, if you are making a single grading pass at the footage, one approach would be to set the tonal range and perform an overall balance in Levels, balance a color cast in the highlights using HSL, then stylize the overall look in Curves. You will work with the Levels group in depth in this lesson.

Curves Graph in Curves Tab Versus Levels Tab

The Curves graphs in the Curves tab have certain similarities to those in the Levels tab:

■ In the Curves tab, you can add up to 16 points per tab, while in Levels you are limited to the two or three points that are provided. In the Curves tab, you can make detailed adjustments to many different subdivisions of the brightness range. In Levels, the singular point is similar to a Gamma control.

■ Both graphs enable you to control the master channel or an individual color channel.

■ Holding down the Shift key while you manipulate a control point will lock the degree of deviation but slide the point along the curve.

■ As in the other groups, you can use the Input and Output text boxes and the Color Match control.

Channels Group

The Channels group (see Figure 6.4) is perhaps the least understood of Symphony's color correction groups. While the Channels group does have some creative applications, it is first and foremost a corrective tool. For those who understand it, the Channels group provides the magic that saves images from the cutting room floor. How? Simply put, the Channels controls enable you to redefine each output color channel (red, green, and blue) by blending different input color components in various proportions. Poorly exposed images frequently are deficient in one particular color channel. The Channels group enables you to identify and repair it by borrowing from another color channel. You will work with this group later in this lesson.

Figure 6.4
The puzzling combination of buttons and formulas that make up the Channels group.

Secondary Group

Secondary color correction enables you to make real-time adjustments to parts of an image defined by hue and saturation values. The Secondary group is the group that enables the classic demo of turning a blue object green, as shown in Figure 6.5, from the Symphony Help file.

Figure 6.5
Color replacement performed with the Secondary group.

Marketing for most NLEs and compositing applications would have you think this is far more common than it is. In reality, it's just an easy demo. More commonly, these tools are used to alter skin tones, to enrich the color of the sky or grass, and to de-emphasize background objects that may distract the viewer from the important things in the frame, such as the actor. The Secondary group is shown in Figure 6.6.

These controls are designed to enable you to make an input color selection, called a *vector*, and then an alternative output color selection. The process is similar in concept to pulling a chroma key, except that instead of turning a green background transparent, you're changing it to, say, blue. This group is covered in depth in the next lesson.

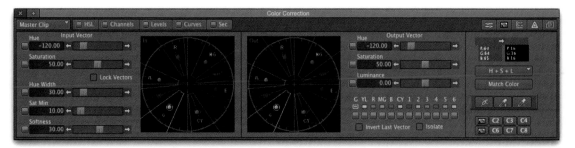

Figure 6.6
The Secondary group, with default values.

Buy One Correction Tool at a Time

In Symphony, the corrections made to an image are cumulative, giving you the flexibility to use whichever tool you wish, in whichever order suits you best. Over time, you will no doubt develop your preferences for which tool you use for which task. But remember, stay flexible in your thinking! Doing so will make you a better problem-solver in the grading suite.

So, how do you cultivate this flexible mindset? When I was learning still photography, I read a great bit of advice from a photographer I admired. He said, "Do yourself a favor. Even if you have the money to buy a whole kit of lenses, buy only one lens every six or eight months. Then *live* with it. Shoot everything you can with that one lens. This will force you to really learn everything that lens can do. If you get them all at once, you'll never know!"

Working with the grading tools in Symphony is like having a whole kit of lenses right off the bat. It's easy to always reach for the tool that makes a given task seem easiest. (Color-balance problem in the blue channel? That's fixed in Curves.) The danger in this is that inevitably, you'll come to a shot that is too complicated—a shot in which you can't use HSL and Curves to set the tonal range, balance the shadows and highlights, tone down an object in the background, and create the final look. If you haven't learned the full extent of what each of the tools can really do, you'll be stuck and forced to compromise the image quality on that shot.

As you are learning in this course, each problem can be solved with a number of different tools and different techniques. Start by thinking about the overlap in the tasks that can be accomplished by each tool. For example, setting the luma range can be done in HSL, Curves, or Levels. Correcting an overall color cast could likewise be performed in all three. Then, despite your preferences, force yourself to work with an alternative tool—say, setting the luma range and overall balance exclusively with Levels—until you've developed a comfort level with it. (If need be, hide the other controls to prevent temptation.) It may never be your favorite, but when you're in a tight spot, you'll be glad you have the skills to approach the grade in a unique way.

Customizing the Color Correction Tool

Like many elements in the application, you can customize look and functionality of the Color Correction tool in Symphony. Although the variation of controls means that some groups are especially well-suited to solving particular color problems, each group can be used successfully to make a wide range of adjustments. Which group(s) you use is mostly a matter of personal preference. As such, if there are some tabs that you find yourself using very little and want to simply remove from the interface, you can do that.

To change the display of correction group tabs:

1. Click the **CORRECTION MODE SETTINGS** button, which is the middle button in the row found at the top-right corner of the Color Correction tool. The Correction Mode Settings dialog box appears as shown in Figure 6.7.

2. Deselect the unwanted tabs—for example, **CHANNELS** or **LEVELS**.

3. Click **OK** to close the Correction Mode Settings dialog box.

Figure 6.7
The Correction Mode Settings dialog box enables you to hide unwanted groups.

Let's look at one more setting while you're here. Avid invented the ChromaWheel and ChromaCurve displays—complete with trademark and patent to prove it. The idea of overlaying the color wheel and color gradient over the interface controls was novel and remains quite helpful for users new to the grading process. Some experienced colorists, however, may find the colorful displays distracting. Not to worry; you can remove those too. (See Figure 6.8.)

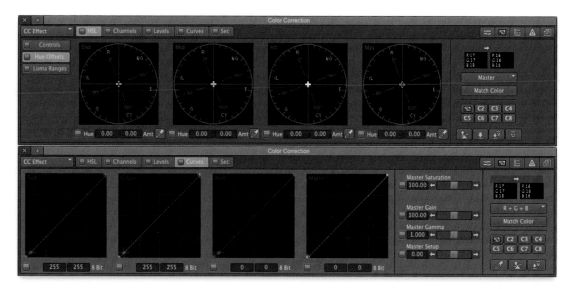

Figure 6.8
The HSL Hue Offsets and Curves groups, without the ChromaWheels and ChromaCurves displayed.

To hide the ChromaWheel and ChromaCurve displays on the Hue Offsets and Curves displays:

1. Click the **CORRECTION MODE SETTINGS** button. The Correction Mode Settings dialog box appears.

2. Click the **FEATURES** tab.

3. Deselect the **SHOW CHROMAWHEEL AND CHROMACURVE GRAPHS** option.

4. Click **OK** to close the Correction Mode Settings dialog box.

Note: There are additional settings worth exploring, including the Units tab, where experienced colorists may choose to change the values on the internal scopes to mV instead of bits. For more information on all settings options, look up "Correction Settings" in the Symphony Help files.

Keyboard Shortcuts for Efficient Grading

Avid Symphony 6.0 marks the first version that is integrated with a hardware grading panel. Grading on an Artist Color is most efficient, due to the dedicated controls and advanced capabilities, such as the corrected/uncorrected toggle and others already discussed. But, you are not out of luck if grading with a mouse alone.

Following are some keyboard shortcuts built into Symphony to speed the grading process. This is not a comprehensive list because a number of shortcuts specific to certain groups have already been covered in context.

- **Tab selection.** Press the Page Up and Page Down keys on the keyboard to scroll through correction group tabs.

- **Tab shortcuts.** The CC tab in the Command Palette contains 12 numbered Tab buttons: Tab 1, Tab 2, etc. These can be mapped to any key on the keyboard and programmed to correspond to any tab in the Color Correction tool, including subtabs. Most colorists tend to use the same tools repeatedly during grading, and these provide you direct access to the tools you use most. These buttons have no default associations and must be programmed to select the tab of your choice.

  The process of programming a tab is identical to that of saving a correction to a bucket; use the Alt (Windows)/Option (Mac) modifier to program the key. For example, if the Tab 1 button has been mapped to the F5 key on your keyboard, and you want Tab 1 to select HSL Master controls, you would activate the HSL Master controls, then press Alt+F5 (Windows) or Option+F5 (Mac) to program the key. F5 could then be used to jump directly to the HSL Master tab.

- **Text boxes.** When a control tab with text boxes is active, the Tab key will cycle through the text boxes and option buttons. Press Shift+Tab to cycle in the opposite direction. When a text box is active, you can type numbers to enter a specific value. Or, the Up Arrow and Down Arrow keys will increment the numbers by one. When a option button is highlighted, press the space bar to activate the button.

If you are grading without an Artist Color, use these shortcuts to do more with the keyboard and less with the mouse. You will definitely be faster for it!

Understanding the Symphony Grading Workflow

It's not enough to identify the various tools, nor even to know how each works. You need to know how these tools work *together*. This is where the real power of Symphony lies. In a word, it's about *relationships*.

The Interaction of Color Correction Groups

The full Avid Symphony color-grading toolset is organized in the Color Correction tool, with the exception of several effects that can be used for grading purposes. (These are discussed in Lesson 8, "Intraframe Effects: Avid's Hidden Secondaries.")

You can make adjustments to each of the correction groups, in any order, and the system will simply process and display the cumulative result of the corrections. This gives you the flexibility to work however you are most comfortable.

Note: In the beginning, I recommend following the grading process you're learning in this course, but over time you'll adapt this into your own personal method.

The industry-standard approach that has been refined over time is as follows:

1. Set the base grade using primary adjustments to establish the tonal range and balance the overall image.

2. Perform secondary corrections to address specific problems and/or stylize the image.

3. Finalize the grade with additional secondaries to direct the viewer's eye to the important elements in the shot.

The primary grading tools in Symphony allow for such precise control that they can be used for tasks that would be considered secondary corrections—think HSL or Curves. The key to doing this successfully is in being able to make multiple passes at an image using the same toolset. Relationships enable you to do just that.

A *correction relationship* in Symphony defines how a correction relates to the media. Unlike Media Composer, which can only apply color correction as effects, Symphony corrections can be linked to the source media itself, to the sequence media, or applied as a correction.

The Relationship Menu

The controls in the Color Correction window, as you know, are organized hierarchically. The highest level of the hierarchy is the correction relationship, defined in the Correction Type menu, shown in Figure 6.9.

Figure 6.9
The Correction Type menu.

The first section of the menu contains source relationships. The second section of the menu contains program relationships. The third section is the CC Effect, or color correction effect, section. Source relationships apply the correction to the selected source material. Program relationships can be applied to sequence segments or entire tracks in the Timeline. Finally, CC Effects are applied only to sequence segments. The CC Effect is the only type of correction that can be applied by Media Composer.

Tip: As a rule of thumb, select a source relationship if you are restoring the original look of the scene. Select a program relationship if you are modifying the look of a scene.

Once you define the relationship by making a selection from the menu, Symphony will maintain that selection as you grade the sequence. There is no need to stop and redefine the relationship as you go along.

When you make a selection in the Correction Type menu, the full complement of correction groups is available for that particular relationship. Any adjustments you make stay with that relationship. When the selection is changed to a new relationship, the Color Correction tool resets, enabling you to start with a clean slate for the new correction. Considering that you can have up to three active relationships at a time, and five correction groups to work from, the flexibility of the tool is profound.

Note: Other grading applications, such as Apple Color and DaVinci Resolve, have similar concepts expressed through different models. In Apple Color, the closest equivalent would be the grading rooms. In DaVinci, the comparison would be to sequential nodes.

Notes from the Colorist: Relationships and Genre

When you start a project, take a moment to think about the source-side relationship you want to use. To help frame your thinking, the genre of the shooting style may help considerably. A documentary or reality shooting style tends to have lots of disjointed shots from a single camera—indoors, outdoors, lot of movement. All this variation suggests that a single grade won't hold up across multiple shots. Master Clip or SubClip is probably a better choice than Src Tape. If you're shooting a concert with locked off cameras shooting continuously, however, choosing Src Tape could save you hours of work.

—pi

Any relationships that have been modified are underlined in the menu. In the previous figure, Figure 6.9, Src (Source) Tape and Prog(ram) Segment have corrections. This is a typical example. A base grade has been applied to a segment using a source tape relationship, which also automatically applies the same correction to all other clips from the same source tape. Then, a program segment correction was applied to the segment to finalize the look. Using relationships, you can layer up corrections to achieve a final grade.

Identifying Relationships in the Timeline

In Lesson 1, "Color Grading Fundamentals," you learned that Symphony corrections appear in the Timeline by default as a dotted green line running along the bottom of the clip. This is the result of the default relationship being Src Segment.

The only control in the Timeline that is specific to color correction is the Color Correction option in the Timeline Fast menu. When you choose Color Correction, a segment in the Timeline that has source color correction exhibits a green line at the bottom of the segment. A segment that has program color correction exhibits a blue line at the top of the segment. A green dot also appears in the middle of the segment, indicating the presence of an effect.

Note: The green dot indicating a Symphony correction is identical to the green dot that indicates the presence of a motion adapter, applied automatically to media of a different frame rate from the project. If you're confused, use the Color Correction option in the Timeline settings to verify whether a correction is present on the segment.

A dotted line indicates a correction that applies only to that segment (source segment or program segment relationship). A solid line indicates a correction that applies beyond the individual segment (source tape, source clip name, master clip, subclip, or program track). Figure 6.10 illustrates several relationships displayed in the Timeline.

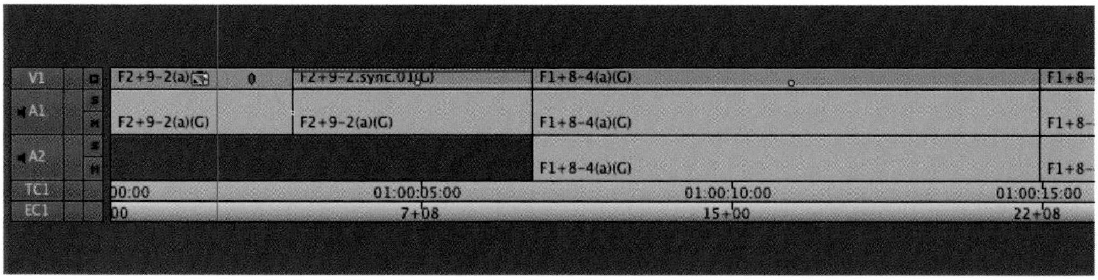

Figure 6.10
Symphony color relationships displayed in the Timeline.

When you color correct a clip in the Timeline, a Color Correction Effect icon is automatically added to the segment. You will use correction relationships throughout the remainder of this book to give you an opportunity to explore and understand them more fully.

Understanding the Levels Group

The main purpose of the Levels group is to adjust the tonal range of an image. It can also be used to successfully neutralize color casts. In many respects, the Levels group is a more refined and specialized version of the Gain, Gamma, and Setup controls in the HSL tab, coupled with the Curves capacity to adjust individual color channels (red, green, and blue).

Levels and Color Space Processing

The Levels group is unique in that it supports processing in both the YC_BC_R and RGB color spaces:

- The Composite and Luma tabs process in YC_BC_R color space.
- The Red, Green, Blue, and Master tabs process in RGB color space.

The results will be different depending on the color space used. For adjustments processed in RGB color space, both the luma and the chroma components of the signal are affected. Visually, the colors appear more saturated from RGB adjustments than they do with luma adjustments. However, you also run the risk of creating a final signal with unacceptably high composite voltages.

Note: Because YC_BC_R adjustments are done before RGB adjustments, any limiting done to the composite signal can be overridden by an adjustment in the Red, Green, Blue, or Master tab, or by an adjustment in the Curves group.

In this section, you will start working with the Levels group to build familiarity with this useful tool.

Performing Primary Corrections with Levels

In this section, you will make adjustments to the input or output histogram by dragging the Black Point, White Point, and Gray Point triangular sliders. You will also make adjustments to the curve graph on each channel. You may choose to use either control exclusively, if you wish. Depending on previous experience, you may find one more intuitive than another. The adjustments described here can be accomplished either way.

As you work, here are some key points to keep in mind:

■ You should generally set Input values before setting Output values.

■ If you change the Input setting, the system *clips* excessive luminance values.

■ If you change the Output setting, the system *remaps* luminance values.

■ To increase the image's tonal range, use the Input setting; to reduce the image's tonal range, use the Output setting.

■ You generally set the value for the Input setting to approximate the camera's view when the footage was shot. (When you color correct an image, you typically want to maximize the tonal range.) Often, the Output values are changed to add a stylistic look to the image.

Note: Where appropriate, Input and Output values will be noted in the directions if you wish to perform precisely the same correction as I do. The Black Point, Gray Point, and White Point values will be labeled as BP, GP, and WP. For example, after making an adjustment to the Black Point on the Master histogram, the slider may have an associated Input value of 138 and an Output value of 159; this would be noted as (BP: 138, 159). The same nomenclature will be used regardless of the color channel on which the adjustment is made.

To begin working with the Levels group:

1. Open the project AVID COLOR GRADING (239) and the bin 6_SYMPHONY TOOLS.

2. Load the sequence 6_SYMPHONY LEVELS_ROOFTOP. This is a familiar sequence. You graded it in Lesson 3, using HSL controls.

3. Enter COLOR CORRECTION mode.

4. Set up the Composer monitors to display the Y WAVEFORM on the left, RGB PARADE in center, and CURRENT on the right.

5. Verify that the Timeline is set to FULL QUALITY.

6. Click the LEVELS tab.

Note: The Artist Color controller does not have dedicated controls for use with the Levels group, nor with the Channels group. To use it in this section, press the Nav button then press the Levels soft knob. Then press F6 to activate Mouse mode. The center trackball will now control the mouse pointer; R3 and R4 function as left- and right-click buttons. Press F6 again to exit Mouse mode.

To set the tonal range using Levels:

1. Click the RELATIONSHIP menu and select SRC TAPE. Many of the shots in this sequence have the same image problems and come from the same tapes. Use that to your advantage!

2. Advance the position indicator to the fourth shot, **C3-1**. This shot is an extreme close-up of Agent Sierra in the control room, talking on her headset to Zero as she watches the monitors. (See Figure 6.11.) This is a good image to start with.

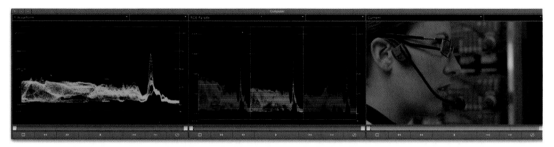

Figure 6.11
Improve the image of Agent Sierra by setting the tonal range.

3. Play the shot and analyze it in the scopes. You will notice that the image is flat. There's a slight yellow cast in the shadows, possibly extending into the midtones and beyond (you won't know really until you expand the tonal range) as well as a bright blue reflection in the background, distracting you from the subject's face. The histogram displays confirm that the image is dark and flat. All the values are piled up below the midpoint.

4. In the Levels group, click the MASTER sub-tab. You will use histograms and the master curve to set the luma range.

   Looking at the Y Waveform, you see that the black point sits several percentage points above 0%. To avoid clipping any detail in the shadows, use the Output Black Point slider.

5. Click the OUTPUT BLACK POINT text box; then repeatedly press the DOWN ARROW key. Watch the Y Waveform; stop when the traces reach **0%** (**BP: 16, 8**).

6. Drag the INPUT WHITE POINT slider to the left until the peak on the Y Waveform approaches **100%** (**WP: 160, 235**). Technically, you have set the brightest white in the source image to 160 bits and clipped all values above it. This *should* substantially brighten the image. Figure 6.12 shows the adjustment.

Tip: Use the Input controls to clip off empty portions of the source signal that contain no data. This enables the system to spread the portion with data across the full luma range. Be careful not to clip portions of the signal that contain the image, or you'll lose detail in those regions.

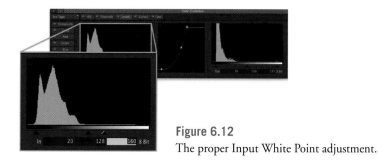

Figure 6.12
The proper Input White Point adjustment.

The problem is, the image isn't brighter at all! Quite the contrary, the image looks darker and a good deal worse. To understand what's going on, look at what's happened in the master curve, also visible in Figure 6.12. The gray point stayed in its original location, acting as a pivot point. This has caused a strong bend in the shadow portion of the curve, depressing the values of all tones below the midpoint. To make matters worse, the input histogram shows that nearly all values in the image are still below the Gray Point slider value, which is 128.

Note: The input histogram never changes; the output histogram updates as changes are made.

7. To fix the tonal values, drag the gray point to the left. As you do, the image will brighten dramatically. Moving the control point horizontally changes the Input value; moving it vertically changes the Output value. Play with the position of the control point to set a good tone to the subject's skin. To keep it a little moody, set the tones a bit on the darker side (**GP: 86, 107**).

8. The tonal range is shaping up, but the bright spot on the cabinet is starting to look electronic in the client monitor, meaning you have pushed them too far. (See Figure 6.13.) To fix this, click in the **INPUT WHITE POINT** text box; then press and hold the **UP ARROW** key, watching the bright spot on the cabinet. Release the key when a more natural gradient has been restored (**WP: 178, 235**).

Figure 6.13
A good luma range, but the highlights are overdriven.

Well done! Next, you need to correct the overall balance. A careful analysis of the RGB Parade indicates two problems, both on the blue channel. First, there's a yellow/red cast to the blacks and darker midtones. This can be seen in the lowest blacks on the right side of each channel, corresponding to the black wall in the frame, and in the group of traces between 15 and 30% that represent the equipment behind her. Second, the bright blue reflection on the background rack is also distracting and needs to be reduced. You can address both of these with the blue channel Level control.

To correct the balance of C3-1 using Levels:

1. Click the **BLUE** tab to activate it. The highlight spike is the more extreme problem and will require the larger adjustment, so start there. You can tweak the curve for midtones and shadows after.

2. Drag the **WHITE POINT** control straight down, watching the RGB Parade until the highlight spike is approximately even with the green channel (**WP: 235, 179**).

3. Slide the **GRAY POINT** control down the curve and to the right, straightening the curve, as shown in Figure 6.14. Watch the traces that represent the gray equipment in the background, as these should be balanced. Also, keep an eye on the subject's skin (**GP: 90, 84**).

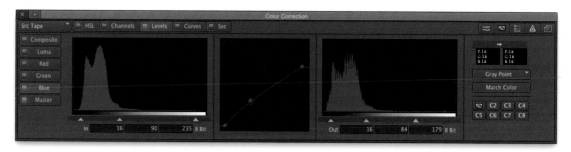

Figure 6.14
Adjustments to the blue channel correct the blown-out blue highlight.

4. Drag the **BLACK POINT** control in the curve graph slightly up and to the right, increasing the contrast of the blacks and clipping them to **0%** (**BP: 29, 22**).

5. Toggle the **BLUE** enable button off and on to see the result of the blue channel adjustment. There's not a big difference, but the blue highlight is definitely improved.

6. Toggle the **LEVELS** enable button off and on to see the result of the full correction. A nice improvement! At this point, the image is looking quite good; it's probably time for you to move to another tool to really improve it. Figure 6.15 shows the image before and after the Levels adjustments.

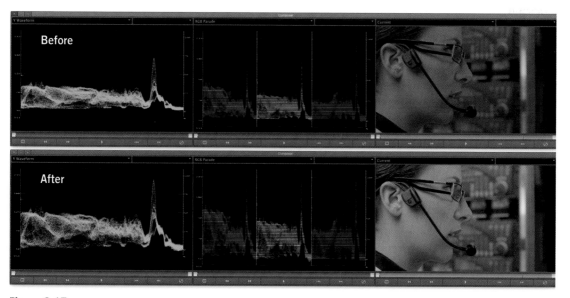

Figure 6.15
Shot C3-1, before and after the Levels adjustments.

7. Change the left Composer monitor to the **Vectorscope** to check the subject's skin tones. Sure enough, the Vectorscope shows a yellow hue shift to the image, most notable in the skin tones.

8. Select the **HSL > Controls > Master** tab.

9. Shift-drag the **Hue** slider to the right, watching the subject's skin tone on the monitor. Settle on a value where her skin looks right to you. See Figure 6.16 (**Hue: 5.00**).

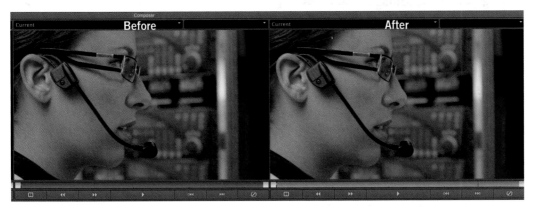

Figure 6.16
Sierra's skin tone is improved by the hue adjustment.

10. Nice work! This shot is looking significantly improved. Now verify the grade for the other six segments you corrected in the process, thanks to the Src Tape relationship!

Leveraging Source Relationships

Let's look at another example to continue practicing with Levels and further explore the power of source relationships.

To grade the next shot:

1. Continue working with the same sequence, **6_Symphony Levels_Rooftop**.

2. The sequence includes a number of shots of Agent Zero from behind, and/or in profile. Grade one of the close-ups as the reference shot. To begin, verify that the **relationship** menu is still set to **Src Tape**.

3. Move the position indicator ahead several segments to shot **B3-3**. The image has minor luma-range and balance issues. You will correct them with Levels.

4. Select the **Levels > Master** tab.

5. Using the Master controls, set the tonal range. Consider darkening the midtones a bit to keep things contrasty and tense (**BP: 16, 16**; **GP: 86, 84**; **WP: 161, 235**). The adjustment is shown in Figure 6.17.

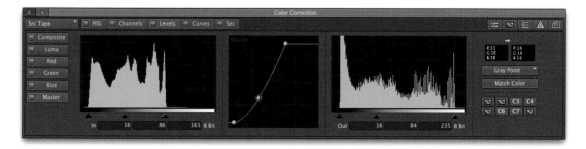

Figure 6.17
The Master Levels adjustment to set the tonal range for shot B3-3.

6. The tonal range looks good, but there's a slight red cast, visible on both his face and the buildings in the background.

7. To fix this, first select the **RED** channel, then adjust the **GRAY POINT** setting to correct the red cast (**GP: 98, 95**).

8. Toggle the correction on and off to see the before and after. Play the image to see it in action. It's looking good! (See Figure 6.18.)

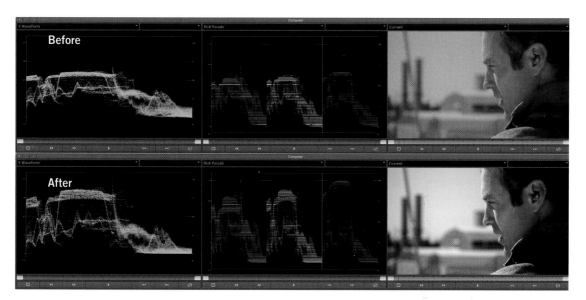

Figure 6.18
A much improved shot B3-3 after Levels primary correction.

9. Take a moment to review the sequence again. "Houston, we have a problem." Far too many segments received these adjustments, including the first two shots, which are of Gemini walking in the hall. Obviously there were more clips in the sequence from this tape than you thought. Okay, lesson learned: Verify the sources *before* setting a source relationship.

Tip: Always verify the sources of your clips before applying broad-based source corrections such as Src Tape.

10. Save the template to correction bucket **C1**. (No sense throwing the baby out with the bathwater!) Then, use the **EDIT > UNDO/REDO** list to undo those corrections.

Note: Deleting the effect applied by a source correction will remove the effect only from the current segment, leaving it in place on all other segments. Generally that's preferable. In this case, however, it won't solve the problem.

11. From the **TIMELINE FAST** menu, choose **CLIP TEXT > SOURCE NAMES**. Enlarge the **V1** track until the source names are visible. Scrubbing through the Timeline, you'll see that many of the clips are from the tape VT103 but contain a variety of images.

12. Open the **RELATIONSHIP** menu and choose **SRC MASTERCLIP**, a safer choice for this segment.

13. Apply the correction template from the bucket. Only one other shot has received this correction, which is appropriate.

Well done. The images are looking great!

Understanding the Channels Group

Channels is a specialized tool for repairing damaged video signals. In it, you have the ability to modify signals by adjusting how the RGB primaries are generated. Channels may be the least understood of Symphony's advanced tools, perhaps because the Channels group is not the kind of thing you can just start noodling with and have a good chance of figuring it out. Once you see how it works, however, you'll recognize that it's not as complicated as it might appear.

Poorly exposed images often have one channel that is damaged more than the others. If an image is underexposed, typically the blue channel suffers. If the image is overexposed, frequently the green channel will be clipped and lose detail in the highlights.

The information lost in one channel, however, is frequently still present in another; the damaged channel can be re-created by blending in information from the stronger channels. In some cases, especially if there was in-camera clipping on one of the color primaries, these controls may mean the difference between a usable shot and an unusable one.

You might say Channels adjustments are a bit like plastic surgery. You are performing a cosmetic operation that, when done correctly, can produce breathtaking results. When done poorly, however, the results can leave you wishing you had left well enough alone! But, take it a step at a time, following the directions here, and you'll get to a pleasing result.

Identifying the Channels Controls

Figure 6.19 shows the Channels group. Two vertical bars divide the group. The left section contains Preview control buttons, used to select a view of the input or output signals for individual component channels, as well as Master Input and Output. The center section holds the channel blenders.

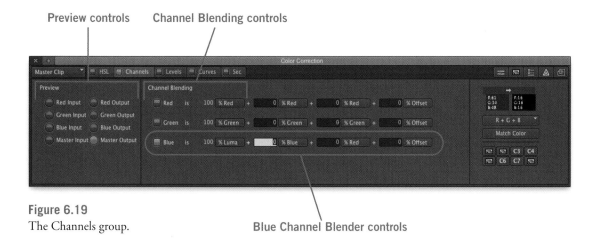

Figure 6.19
The Channels group.

Use the Preview controls to diagnose which channel needs repair, and which will be the donor channel(s). When a Preview button is selected, the Current monitor displays the channel signal as a monochrome image. From this, you can determine the strength of the signal, check for noise and clipping, and compare it to other channels. After a diagnosis is made, you perform the operation using the channel blenders.

The red, green, and blue channels can be reconstructed out of positive or negative percentages of the following signals, available in drop-down source menus on each channel blender:

- Red
- Green
- Blue
- Luma
- Cr
- Cb
- Offset

Up to four signals can be blended to create the new color channel. For each, values between –200% and +200% are supported. In addition, a positive or negative offset can be applied to the end result. You can also choose to invert any of the signals. This is identical, however, to entering a negative number for a blending percentage.

Key concept: Identify strong components of the video signal; then use those to fortify the weaker signals.

Repairing Damaged Signals with Channels

Let's walk through the process of channel repair to better grasp the process and potential results.

To repair a shot with Channels:

1. Open the project AVID COLOR GRADING (239) and the bin 6_SYMPHONY TOOLS.

2. Load the sequence 6_SYMPHONY CHANNELS.

3. Enter COLOR CORRECTION mode.

4. Set up the Composer monitors to display the VECTORSCOPE on the left, RGB PARADE in the center, and CURRENT on the right.

5. Verify that the Timeline is set to FULL QUALITY.

6. Click the CHANNELS tab.

7. Select SRC SEGMENT in the RELATIONSHIP menu.

8. The sequence contains one shot, DELIVERY60-TAKE20440-. Play the shot; then take a moment to analyze the image visually using the scopes. See Figure 6.20.

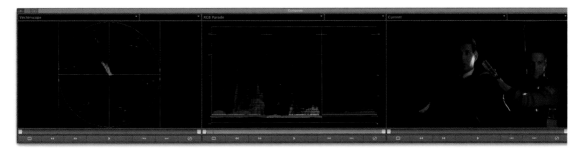

Figure 6.20
The original shot has obvious luma and chroma problems.

The image is underexposed, with an excessive red cast. In context, the actors are being lit by the stage lighting of the burlesque dancers, so some cast is acceptable, but not this much. Looking at the RGB Parade, it's clear that the blue channel is the weakest.

9. Select the **RED INPUT** preview button. The red channel monochrome is displayed in the Current monitor.

10. Play the shot, viewing only the red channel. Examine the image for exposure and noise as it plays.

11. Repeat the process for the green and blue channels. As expected from the initial analysis of the RGB Parade, the blue channel exhibits extreme problems. There is heavy noise throughout the image. The red channel has the strongest voltages, but also exhibits noise in the shadow areas. Surprisingly, the green channel is the cleanest.

12. To rebuild the image, you need to repair the blue channel and reinforce the green channel. Doing so should clarify the image and offset some of the red cast. To begin, select the **BLUE OUTPUT** preview button to see the results as you blend the other signals to repair the blue channel.

13. On the **BLUE** blender, set the first source menu to **%LUMA**. This remaps the entire luma signal back into the blue channel. The result is two-fold. First, the blue channel on the RGB Parade is much stronger, showing similar trace patterns to the other channels. Second, the Vectorscope trace has become a narrow line toward red-magenta, as shown in Figure 6.21.

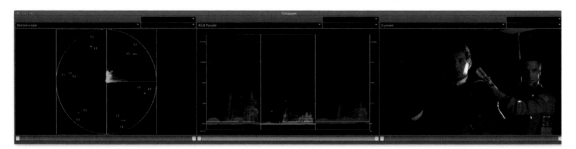

Figure 6.21
The initial blue channel adjustment.

14. To improve the signal balance, add more blue. To do so, set the second source menu to **%BLUE** and type **70** in the text field. This adjustment increases the trace spread on the Vectorscope but also creates a strong magenta cast. Correct this on the green channel.

15. Switch the Preview back to Master Output, then enable the **GREEN** channel blender.

16. Leave the first source menu on **100% GREEN**. In the second menu, choose **LUMA** and type **60** in the text field.

17. Finish the correction on the **RED** channel blender. In the third menu, choose **OFFSET**, and type **−2** in the text field, as shown in Figure 6.22.

Figure 6.22
The final Channels adjustment and image results.

Tip: You don't need to know the final formula of a Channels correction when you start! The process of repairing signals involves incrementally building the signal by adding component signals. The selection and amount of these additions is directed by how the scopes respond to each change.

Nice work! The image after Channels adjustments has a more reasonable balance. The goal isn't to achieve a final grade. Rather, the image is improved, and most importantly, it has stronger signals on all three channels that will hold up to further grading using other correction groups.

Notes from the Colorist: Why Symphony Changes How You Grade

Avid Symphony doesn't just give you more tools to use. Symphony changes the way you grade. Think about it: Using Media Composer's core color-correction tools, it can be very tedious and time-consuming to do anything but make overall changes to the image. Yes, you can make changes to broad tonal ranges (shadows, midtones, highlights) or even within very narrow tonal ranges of a specific color channel using Curves. But to isolate the sky at magic hour and alter it? And instantly propagate that change every time that shot appears on the Timeline? Nope. Not easy at all.

Symphony Changes How You Think About Grading

Unlike with Media Composer, you don't have to dial in the overall shot and sacrifice one part of the image (the color of the grass) to save another part of the image (skin tone). Using Symphony's Secondary controls, you can perform a primary grade to enhance the look of the grass (if you're grading a commercial for lawn products) even if it throws off the look of skin tones. This is because Symphony enables you to step into Secondaries to isolate those skin tones and control them independently.

Think About Grading in Passes

Of course, with great power comes great responsibility. It's tempting to impose the full power of Symphony on every single shot. Resist the urge. Don't feel compelled to fix every single element of every shot at that very moment in time. Rather, you can do an overall balance and a tweak on the primary focus of the shot. And then? Move on. When you finish a scene or an act, check the clock to decide how much time you have left to go back and make further refinements on key scenes that really need it.

Additional Thoughts on Secondaries

As mentioned, secondaries aren't just for turning a red shirt blue. If that's your initial inclination, I'm suggesting you broaden your use of this tool. Some key elements you'll find yourself controlling include skin tones, grass, sky, water, and brand colors (for product shots). Some not-so-key elements you'll find yourself de-emphasizing include walls, practical lights, and general visual distraction.

—pi

Review/Discussion Questions

1. What is the difference between the HSL Controls in Media Composer and Symphony?

2. How many luma ranges can be adjusted using the Gain, Gamma, and Setup controls in Symphony?

   a. 3

   b. 6

   c. 9

   d. 12

   e. None of the above

3. What is the purpose of the Luma Ranges controls?

4. Which of the following could be used to set the tonal range and balance a shot?

   a. HSL

   b. Levels

   c. Channels

   d. Curves

   e. Secondary

5. What are the differences between working in the curves graphs in Levels and those in the Curves group?

6. How can correction relationships speed the correction process?

7. How do source and program relationships interact on a segment?

8. A segment in the Timeline shows a solid green line on the bottom and a dotted blue line on the top. What type of correction effect(s) has been applied to the clip?

9. What is the Channels group used for?

10. Name three advantages to grading on Symphony over Media Composer.

Lesson 6 Keyboard Shortcuts

Command/Action	Result
Page Up/Page Down	Changes the active correction group tab within the Color Correction tool
Tab	Activates the next text box in the current correction group tab, moving left to right, top to bottom
Shift+Tab	Activates the previous text box in the current correction group tab, moving left to right, top to bottom.
Up Arrow/Down Arrow	When a text box is active, increments the value by one point
Tab 1, Tab 2, etc.*	Switches directly to the user-defined tab within any correction group in the Color Correction tool
Option+click (Mac)/Alt+click (Windows) on the Tab 1, Tab 2, etc., keys in the Command Palette*	Maps the currently active tab in the Color Correction tool to the key being clicked

* These functions can be mapped to the key of your choice. For information on how to map your keyboard, see the article "Mapping User-Selectable Buttons" in the Media Composer or Symphony Help.

Advanced Grading with Symphony Tools

In this exercise, you will practice the techniques for repairing channels and explore the use of relationships to speed the grading process.

Media Used:

Avid Color Grading (MC239) project > 2_Exercise Bins folder > Ex6_Symphony Tools Exercise bin > Ex6_Channels Corrections sequence, Ex6_Symphony Grade_Hallway sequence

Duration:

60 minutes

GOALS

- Use Channels to repair shots in the context of a sequence
- Leverage color-correction relationships to speed up the grading process
- Set the tonal range using Levels
- Repair images using Channels

Practicing Channel Repair

In this section, you will grade a short sequence of images. At least two of the shots will require Channels corrections. In addition, these shots exist on two tracks, and have been composited using Picture-in-Picture effects (PIPs). Grade the sequence to establish a more consistent tonal range and cast to the image.

Here are some key points to keep in mind:

- Some variation in luma and chroma between shots is permissible, even desirable.

- Remember, corrections are always applied to the highest active track. Because this is a multilayered sequence, you will need to change the active tracks as you go.

- Perform the initial primary corrections on the shots using the Step In command. This will bypass the PIP, enabling you to see the full-frame image and to use the scopes to analyze each shot individually.

- Step out of the PIPs to see how the corrected images compare with each other. Because source corrections are applied under other effects, you can make final adjustments to the color in this view.

To begin the exercise:

1. Open the project AVID COLOR GRADING (239) and the bin EX6_SYMPHONY TOOLS EXERCISES.

2. Load the sequence EX6_CHANNELS CORRECTIONS.

3. Grade the sequence using the full complement of skills you have learned to this point.

Relationship Grading

In this section, you will grade a familiar sequence. It is the hallway scene in which Zero accosts bad guy, Gemini, and steals the nuclear launch key. You graded this sequence in the previous lesson, so you should be familiar with the footage and its image problems.

This time, grade the scene using source relationships rather than templates to speed the process. Use the correction tools of your choice—you have quite a few options now. Remember the advice about buying one lens, though. You just bought Levels; try using it as much as you can!

Here are some key points to consider as you grade:

- You are still performing primary grades. Your goal is to establish a good tonal range and balance the image. Grade *toward* a desired look, but don't try to finish it.

- Work quickly. Rely on your scopes to help extend your "60 seconds."

- Shot matching is still key. These shots need to match.

To begin the exercise:

1. Open the project AVID COLOR GRADING (239) and the bin EX6_SYMPHONY TOOLS EXERCISES.

2. Load the sequence EX6_SYMPHONY GRADE_HALLWAY.

3. Grade the sequence using the full complement of skills you have learned to this point.

Performing Secondary Corrections in Symphony

Secondary grading tools are powerful additions to your grading toolset. They enable you to make precise adjustments to correct, enhance, or de-emphasize certain regions or image elements. In this lesson you will learn ways to define the region of interest for manipulation, and two of the secondary correction tools available in Symphony.

Media Used: Avid Color Correction (MC239) project > 1_Lesson Bins folder >
7_Secondaries bin > 7_Secondary Corrections sequence

Duration: 60 minutes

GOALS

- Define secondary corrections
- Identify the Media Composer and Symphony tools for secondary corrections
- Explain color-correction relationships
- Use the Secondary group to make chroma-qualified secondary corrections
- Use the Luma Range controls to make luma-qualified corrections with HSL

Understanding Secondary Corrections

Secondary corrections, a.k.a. secondaries, are those corrections made to the image after the primary corrections set the tonal range and balance the image. Unlike a primary correction, which affects the entire image, secondaries affect only a portion of the image. Secondary corrections include a wide range of tasks from performing shape-based spot corrections, to adding gradients and vignettes, to color replacement, to stylizing the look of the shot. Both Media Composer and Symphony include a number of tools that are, by definition, secondary grading tools, only one of which carries the name Secondary.

Identifying Avid's Secondary Correction Tools

This section provides an overview of the tools included in Media Composer and Symphony. This lesson will teach you two tools used for secondary color correction that are available only in Avid Symphony. Those not covered in this lesson are covered later.

Secondary Group

Avid Symphony provides a 12-vector secondary color corrector, shown in Figure 7.1. As discussed, this group enables a specific type of secondary correction: adjustments to parts of an image defined by hue and saturation values. This tool will be covered in depth in this lesson. In technical terms, the Secondary group enables chroma *qualified* manipulation and substitutions. You'll explore the concept of qualification in a moment.

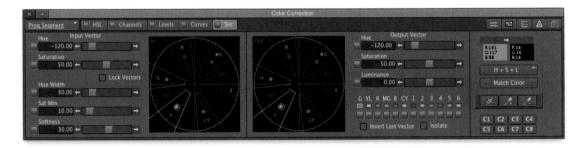

Figure 7.1
The Secondary group.

HSL Luma Ranges

Identified in the previous lesson, the HSL Luma Ranges controls are another Symphony-only feature. They enable you to redefine the values assigned to the regions of highlight, midtone, and shadow within an image. Doing so customizes the impact of HSL adjustments on the current image. In this lesson, you will use HSL Luma Ranges controls to perform secondary corrections.

Paint Effect

The Paint Effect is Avid's multipurpose image-painting tool, available in both Media Composer and Symphony. Found in the Image category, the Paint Effect (see Figure 7.2) can be used to create a wide array of effects, from rotoscoping and scratch removal, to blurs and mosaics, to gradients, to vignettes, to spot corrections. The uses of the Paint Effect for color grading are covered in the next lesson.

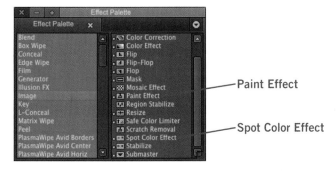

Figure 7.2
The powerful and versatile Paint Effect, along with the Spot Color Effect.

Note: To learn more about the full range of effects created with the Paint Effect, check out the companion book in this series, *Media Composer 6: Advanced Effects and Compositing*.

Spot Color Effect

Any guesses what the Spot Color Effect is used for? As its name implies, this effect is used to perform corrections to specific regions of the image—typically small ones. The Spot Color Effect is also grouped in the Image category of the Effect Palette (refer to Figure 7.2), and is covered in the next lesson. At one time, the Spot Color Effect was available only in Symphony, but recent versions of Media Composer now include it as well.

AniMatte

Though AniMatte is not a color-manipulation effect, it is commonly used to create secondary corrections. AniMatte is Avid's built-in effect for cutting custom mattes in an image. It is found in the Key category of the Effect Palette. You can use AniMatte to create spot corrections by stacking two layers of the same clip on top of each other and cutting a matte to reveal a portion of the lower clip, which would be graded differently. AniMatte is available in both Media Composer and Symphony, and is covered in depth in the next lesson.

Understanding Qualification

You can't have a discussion about secondary corrections without understanding qualification. Simply, *qualification* is the manner in which you define a region of interest within the image to isolate it. If you can isolate it, then you can manipulate it independently of the rest of the image. The success of any secondary corrections depends on how well you qualify the portion of the image you want to adjust.

There are three ways to qualify a region or object for secondary corrections:

- Luma qualification
- Chroma qualification
- Shape-based qualification

Luma and chroma qualification are procedural operations. The advantage of a procedural operation is that it automatically selects all pixels within the image that fall within the defined limits of the qualification. Remember: You're working with moving images. As the image changes from one frame to another—which is to say, the pixel values change—so do the pixels that meet qualification. In practical terms, if the secondary correction is improving the actor's skin tone, the effect doesn't need to be adjusted on every frame as the actor moves and speaks. The adjustments are automatically applied to the pixels that meet the skin tone qualification of luma and/or chroma values.

The disadvantage of luma and chroma qualification is that the area you want to correct must be distinct from the rest of the image. If the actor in question is sitting next to a wall of similar luma values or hue, the secondary correction to improve his skin color could easily change the wall as well.

You perform shape-based qualifications by literally drawing a shape to define the region of interest. The advantage (and disadvantage) of shape-based qualification is that it is defined by a shape that must be manually drawn and adjusted, and is not dependent on the pixel values contained within it. Keyframes can be used to change a shape's form and position in the frame, or you can adjust it semi-automatically by linking it to tracking data.

In Symphony, you perform luma qualifications using the HSL Luma Ranges controls. Chroma qualifications are performed using the Secondary group to isolate elements based on hue and saturation. You perform shape-based qualifications using Avid's Intraframe effects—Paint, Spot Correction, and AniMatte.

All three types of qualification are useful. It really depends on the image you are grading as to which will serve you best at that moment. Frequently, you will need a combination of these to accurately qualify the region of interest.

Understanding Luma Ranges

The HSL Luma Ranges controls are not exclusively for secondary color correction. They can, and are, used to make broad changes to the image. However, the specificity of the controls coupled with the time required to adjust them on a shot-by-shot basis means they are more naturally used as secondary tools—hence their inclusion in this lesson. Like any tools or workflow techniques taught in this course, you will naturally adapt them to fit what works best for you.

Let's start by identifying the controls. The Luma Ranges tab is the third tab in the HSL group. As stated, three tabs subdivide the Luma Ranges tab, one for each of the luminance ranges: Highlights, Midtones, and Shadows. A graph illustrates the selection curve that defines each of the luminance ranges, with all three curves always visible. The curve for the currently selected range—say, Midtones—is displayed with a white line. The lines representing the other luma ranges are displayed in gray, as shown in Figure 7.3.

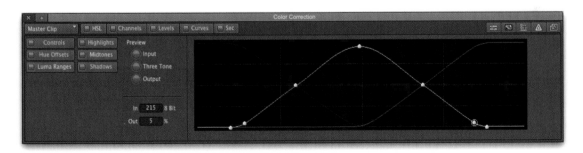

Figure 7.3
The Luma Ranges controls, with the Midtones curve active.

The graph plots brightness values from 0 to 255 on the horizontal axis and the relative percentage of shadows, midtones, and highlights on the vertical axis. The system defines a luminance range as the area in the graph where the curve for that range is highest in the graph. (The default curves are visible in Figure 7.3.)

Changing the luma range has no impact on the image *per se*; rather, it controls what parts of the image will respond to other HSL adjustments. By changing the width of the curve horizontally, you expand or contract the range of values included in that luma range, as shown in Figure 7.4. By moving the control points up and down, you control the amount of influence, or amount of correction applied, to that region. A point at the top means 100% of the correction is applied; a midpoint means 50% is applied; and so on. This enables you to roll off a correction across a range of luminance values. The brightness values that correspond to the active point in Figure 7.4 will receive 50% of a midtone adjustment and 50% of a highlight adjustment.

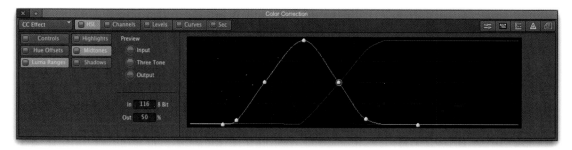

Figure 7.4
Changes to the Luma Range curve have expanded the highlights and a compressed midtone range.

Key Concept: Adjusting the HSL Luma Ranges doesn't have any impact on the image. Instead, it changes which parts of the image respond to highlight, midtone, or shadow adjustments performed with HSL tools.

This would all be very esoteric without a way to see how the changes to the curve translate to the image you're grading. For that, refer to the Preview option buttons —in particular, the Three Tone button. When this button is enabled, the video image in the Current monitor changes to a three-tone display, which shows the shadow regions in black, the midtone regions in gray, and the highlights in white.

Figure 7.5 shows a video frame and its three-tone display with standard luma range curves. Notice how the sky is divided between highlight and midtone, while the cityscape is a complicated mess of midtone and shadow.

Tip: The Three Tone preview is a great reference to see where HSL changes will affect your image. If you're ever unsure of where the HSL adjustments are hitting a complex image, take a quick peek at the Three Tone preview.

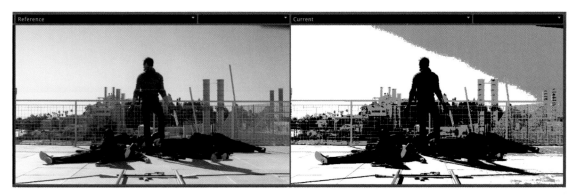

Figure 7.5
The shot of Zero on the rooftop with default luma ranges, shown in Three Tone preview.

In Figure 7.6, the luma ranges have been altered to expand the highlights and compress the midtones. This result in the Three Tone preview is dramatic. The sky is almost uniformly highlight (except for the upper-right corner, where the matte box intrudes into the frame), as is the rooftop and Zero's gun. Zero himself and the dead goons are almost entirely in shadow. Their shadows, the buildings in the background, and the fence are now defined as midtones. With the ranges redefined, you can easily see where the HSL shadow, midtone, and highlight adjustments will have the greatest impact.

Figure 7.6
The shot of Zero on the rooftop with an expanded highlight range and a compressed midtone range.

If you find yourself thinking this is *very detailed*, you're right! This type of adjustment is not something you do for every shot—and perhaps not very often at all. You may choose to make your initial HSL adjustments with the default luma ranges in place, and only adjust luma ranges if there are problematic areas in the shot that aren't responding well. These problem areas typically lie in the transition values between default luma ranges. Adjusting the ranges can quickly clarify the tonal values within a luma range, making the HSL more effective in correcting the shot.

Note: Adjustments to the luma ranges can also be made before other HSL adjustments. This is helpful if you're working on a complex image and want to simplify it from the start.

For more information on fine-tuning luma ranges, particularly at the transitions between regions, see the Symphony Help article, "Understanding the Luma Ranges Graph."

Using Luma Ranges

In this section, you will make corrections and image adjustments using the HSL controls. These adjustments will be controlled by changes you make to the luma ranges.

Tip: The Luma Ranges controls are not accessible through the Avid Artist Color controller. However, you can keep your hands on the controller! Press F4 to toggle to Mouse mode and make your adjustments to the Luma Ranges curves using the center track ball.

Like all correction groups in Symphony, changes to the luma ranges are applied based on the relationship. If you happen to be working with an image that is very characteristic of the tape or scene, you could set the luma range for all the shots in the scene. Corrections governed by luma ranges will be applied, at most, to the source master clip or subclip; typically, they are applied to the source or program segment.

Note: In many video workflows, a subclip represents an individual shot or even a small excerpt such as a sound bite. In a traditional telecine-based film workflow, however, a subclip frequently represents a reel and, by extension, a scene—hence its inclusion in the list of relationships.

Making Adjustments Using Luma Ranges

In this section, you will continue working with the same images as in the previous section, further refining them.

To set up for this exercise:

1. Open the project **Avid Color Grading (239)** and the bin **7_Secondaries**.

2. Load the sequence **7_Secondary Corrections**.

3. Enter **Color Correction** mode.

4. Set up the Composer monitors to display the **Vectorscope** on the left, **RGB Parade** in the center, and **Current** on the right.

5. Set the **Video Quality** menu to **Full Quality**.

To begin working with luma ranges:

1. Review the sequence. This is a familiar sequence of shots. You graded them in Lesson 3, "Establishing the Base Grade," using HSL controls. Markers on the sequence indicate the exact frames used for screenshots in the lesson.

2. Move the position indicator to the first shot in the sequence. It is the wide dolly shot of Agent Zero on the rooftop, having just assaulted the bad guy stronghold. (See Figure 7.7.)

Figure 7.7
The now-familiar shot of Agent Zero on the roof.

3. Set the black point using the **MASTER SETUP** control. Then balance the blacks using the **SHD HUE OFFSET** wheel.

   To finalize the look for this shot, the director wants a piercing blue sky to be the dominant color. It should stand out against the rest of the image. To create this effect, adjust luma ranges to qualify the sky, as demonstrated in the previous section.

4. Click the **HSL** tab and select the **LUMA RANGES** tab.

5. Set the relationship to **MASTER CLIP**.

6. Change the **PREVIEW** setting to **THREE TONE**. The contents of the Current monitor change to a three-tone representation of the image, illustrating the shadows in black, midtones in gray, and the highlights in white.

7. Click the **HIGHLIGHTS** tab.

8. Drag the control points in the graph to reshape the highlight curve, expanding it to the left as shown in Figure 7.8. As you do, watch the changes to the sky.

Tip: **You may find it quicker to make changes to the Luma Ranges graph if you delete some control points. To delete a point, simply click on it and press the Delete key. The tradeoff is the curves are less refined with fewer points.**

Figure 7.8
Expand the highlight range to include more of the sky.

9. Click the **MIDTONES** tab.

10. Drag the control points to compress the midtone range toward the shadows.

11. Repeat the process in the **SHADOWS** tab. The finished curves and Three Tone preview should appear similar to Figure 7.9.

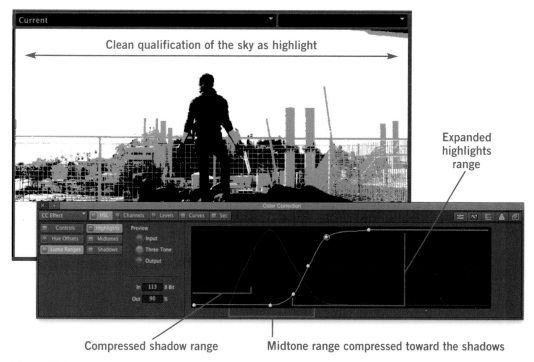

Figure 7.9
Expand the highlight range to include more of the sky.

Good! You've qualified the sky as highlights. Now you're ready to make your adjustments.

Tip: Having spent the time reshaping the luma curves, save a template. As noted in Lesson 5, "Matching Shots," that template can be applied exclusively to the Luma Ranges tab of another correction, without overwriting any other values. A huge timesaver!

12. On the **Luma Ranges** tab, change the **Preview** setting back to **Output**.

13. Click the **HSL > Controls > Highlights** tab.

14. Boost the **Saturation** setting to approximately **165**.

15. Click the **HSL > Controls > Shadows** tab.

16. Reduce **Saturation** setting to approximately **75**.

17. Click the **HSL > Luma Ranges** tab again.

18. Toggle the **Preview** button between **Input** and **Output** to see the impact of the HSL adjustments.

Note: As you know, there are other ways to toggle the adjustment. The advantage of using the Input and Output buttons in this context would be to further refine the curves if need be.

Because you used a master clip correction, the third shot in the sequence received the same correction. Before moving on, you'll need to verify that the adjustments have not caused any unexpected problems in this image.

19.   Move the position indicator to the third shot in the sequence, **B1-3**.

20.   Examine the image for unforeseen problems caused by the correction. Toggle the correction to see the corrected and uncorrected image.

Nice work. You will continue to explore the advantages and limitations of qualifying a selection with the luma ranges throughout this lesson. For now, let's examine chroma qualifications with the Secondary group.

Key Concept: Luma ranges can be used to perform luma qualification, allowing for secondary corrections to specific regions. However, this requires sufficient luma separation of the target area from other regions of the image.

Exploring the Secondary Group

The Secondary group is a 12-vector secondary color corrector. Adjustments are made using six standard color vectors and six custom color vectors. Start by familiarizing yourself with the controls of the Secondary group, shown in Figure 7.10. As you can see, the Secondary controls are divided in the middle. The left panel defines the input vector, or color selection; the right panel defines the output vector.

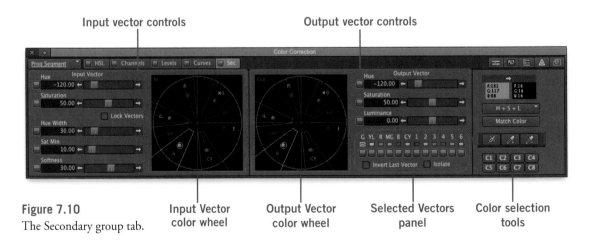

Figure 7.10
The Secondary group tab.

Input vector controls

Output vector controls

Input Vector color wheel

Output Vector color wheel

Selected Vectors panel

Color selection tools

Input Vector Controls

The input vector controls include the following control sliders for fine-tuning the vector selection:

- **Hue.** This control adjusts the vector's hue midpoint. The parameter supports values between −180º and +180º with 0º equivalent to pure red.

- **Saturation.** This control adjusts the vector's saturation midpoint. The parameter supports values between 0 and 100 with 0 representing no saturation and 100 representing full saturation.

- **Hue Width (custom vector).** This control specifies the number of degrees of arc—that is, the range of hues—for a standard vector's hue. Values range between 0º and 180º.

- **Sat(uration) Min(imum) (standard vector).** This control sets the minimum saturation value for the vector. Use this vector to remove colors with a low degree of saturation, such as reflections and noise, from the vector.

- **Sat(uration) Width (custom vector).** This control specifies the length of the vector's saturation axis. The vector supports values between 0 and 100.

- **Softness.** This control adjusts the vector's softness. The parameter supports values between −255 and +255. Positive softness increases the hue and saturation values selected to include those beyond the vector boundaries. Negative softness decreases the blend of hue and saturation values to remove those within vector boundaries. A value of 0 creates a hard edge at the vector boundary.

Tip: The Hue and Saturation settings define the base values of the vector; the other settings determine the degree of tolerance used to qualify other tones for the vector.

Output Vector Controls

The output vector controls determine how the input vector is altered for output. They are as follows:

- **Hue.** This control sets the new hue for the selected vector.

- **Saturation (standard vector).** This control sets the saturation offset for the selected vector. The change in saturation for standard vectors is the difference between the input and output Saturation parameters. If you are unable to increase the saturation as much as desired, lower the input Saturation parameter.

- **Saturation (custom vector).** This control sets the new saturation for the selected vector. There is no offset interaction between the input and output Saturation parameters for custom vectors.

- **Luminance.** This control raises or lowers the luminance for the selected vector. The parameter supports values of −10 to +10. Each unit of value is equivalent to a potential shift of 1mV. Depending on the selected color, the actual shift may be less than 1mV.

Vector Color Wheels

A color wheel on either side of the center divider shows a graphical representation of the input and output vectors. There is a standard set of vectors displayed by default. Preconfigured custom vectors, as well as a user-defined vector, can be displayed on the graph. Figure 7.11 shows the various display options of the vector color wheels.

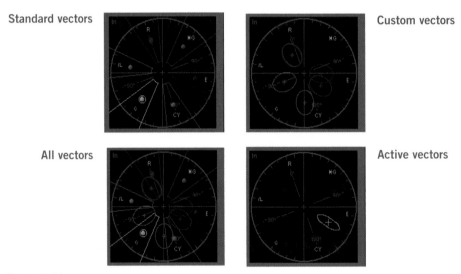

Figure 7.11
The color wheels can be set up to display some or all of the input and output vectors.

Note: To change the vectors visible on the color wheels, open the Correction settings, select the Features tab, and select the pop-up menu Secondary Vectors.

The shape of a vector is important because it defines the range of hue and saturation values the vector contains. Standard vectors always appear as wedges on the color wheels. The hue range of the vector is defined by the width of the wedge. If you increase the Hue Width value, you include a broader range of colors in the vector, and the wedge will cover a wider arc on the color wheel. Standard vectors have no upper limit to saturation.

Custom vectors appear as ellipses. The preconfigured custom vectors are set up for common colors, such as flesh tones, grass green, and sky blue. Their shape and position is fully adjustable; the two axes of the ellipse are defined by the range of hues and the range of saturation covered by the ellipse. When you define a vector by sampling the colors in the image, the custom vector in that hue range is automatically selected and adapted to your sample values.

In addition to the boundary line, each vector includes a center point that marks the base hue and saturation values for the vector. This can be manipulated directly on the color wheel or through the Hue and Saturation sliders.

Note: The center point of standard vectors appears as a solid circle, similar to the control points seen on curves. The center point of custom vectors appears as a crosshair. Both can be manipulated by dragging.

Selected Vector Panel

The Selected Vectors panel at the bottom of the output side indicates which vectors are active. It is most common to activate a vector by clicking the vector control point on the color wheel or by sampling a color from the image (which activates a custom vector). The white outline around the color swatch indicates which vector is selected for manipulation. The enable buttons indicate which vectors are active, acting on the image.

Tip: Like all enable buttons in Avid, the enable buttons on the vectors can be used to toggle the vector's active state—useful for seeing its impact on the image. They can also be reset using the standard shortcut Option-click (Mac) or Alt-click (Windows).

Order of Vector Processing

The Secondary group provides controls for making hue, saturation, and luminance adjustments to as many as 12 distinct color ranges in a shot, meaning all 12 vectors can be active at the same time. (Needless to say, it would be a very complicated correction!) Most users work with no more than two or three at a time. Even still, any time you are working with more than one active vector, it is important to understand the order of processing.

Vectors are processed one at a time, from left to right. The output of one process is fed into the next. This order of processing is important because if the output hue of one vector shifts the colors into the input range of a downstream vector, the final result could be different than intended.

For example, if the R vector is used to change a red car to blue, and the B vector is used to change the hue of the sky, the B vector would also alter the color of the car. Granted, this is an unlikely example in the real world (the production company probably wouldn't have shot the wrong-colored car for the commercial), but it makes the point.

The standard vectors are labeled and configured to correspond to the six primary and secondary colors of the color wheel: (G) green, (YL) yellow, (R) red, (MG) magenta, etc. However, you can redefine the target hue of any standard vector, regardless of its label. If it's important that a given correction happen last in the processing chain—for instance, altering the color of the green grass—you may wish to use a vector farther to the right, such as CY. In this regard, it may be helpful to think of the letters simply as labels rather than colors.

Note: The color swatch under the vector label will update dynamically to show the current color defined by the vector.

You must also take into consideration the order of processing when using the Invert Last Vector setting. This setting applies to the last active vector—whichever is active farthest to the right. I will discuss this setting in greater detail later.

Performing Vector-Based Corrections

Like anything, real understanding of these tools comes from using them. In this section, you will perform three corrections: one using standard vectors, another with custom vectors, and one using an inverted vector.

Using Standard Vectors

To explore the operation of performing secondary corrections with standard vectors, let's continue with the grading process. You will continue to work with the same sequence.

To set up for this exercise:

1. If it's not open already, open the project AVID COLOR GRADING (239) and the bin 7_SECONDARIES.

2. Load the sequence 7_SECONDARY CORRECTIONS.

3. Enter COLOR CORRECTION mode.

4. Set up the Composer monitors to display the RGB PARADE on the left, CURRENT in the center, and REFERENCE on the right.

5. Set the VIDEO QUALITY menu to FULL QUALITY.

6. Set the reference frame to the wide shot you graded in the previous section, **B1-3**.

7. Move the position indicator to the fourth shot in the sequence, **B3-3**. This is a familiar shot: the close-up over-the-shoulder of Zero talking through his earpiece to Agent Sierra, back in master control. (See Figure 7.12.) You'll use an alternative approach here to create the same effect of saturating the sky that you did in the previous section using luma ranges.

Figure 7.12
Perform a secondary correction to match the sky to previous shots.

8. Use the correction group of your choice to perform a quick primary grade: Set the tonal range, placing the white point at approximately **75%**, and balance the image.

On this image, a secondary is a better approach because you cannot easily isolate the sky and foreground with luma range. As shown in Figure 7.13, there's too much overlap between the luma values of the sky and Zero's face.

Figure 7.13
Overlapping luma values exclude this image from luma qualification.

Notice how the highlights extend onto his forehead, nose, and cheek. Any adjustment to the highlights, such as boosting saturation or using a hue offset to enrich the blue, would adversely affect Zero's face—the most important element in the shot. In contrast, there are no blue values in the rest of the image, making it an ideal candidate for chroma qualification.

To perform a secondary correction with standard vectors:

1. In the Color Correction tool, click the **Sec** tab, if it is not already active.

2. In the Selected Vectors panel, click the blue color chip, and the enable button below it. The white highlight moves to the blue chip, indicating that it is active for manipulation. Normally, you could skip manually enabling the vector, because it would enable automatically with your first adjustment, but we want to see the default values first.

3. Click the **Isolate** check box. The image immediately changes. Only the hues contained within the vector remain in the image. The remainder of the image appears as desaturated grayscale, as shown in Figure 7.14. Using the Isolate control, you can easily see where the adjustments will affect the image.

Figure 7.14
The default hues of the blue vector encompass most of the sky. Hues not included appear desaturated.

Only a small portion of the sky is included by default; the lighter portions of the sky are not. You will need to alter the input vector settings to include those.

4. In the Input Vector panel, click the **Lock Vectors** check box. Locking the vectors makes hue selection easier by keeping the values the same between input and output. If they were not locked, changing the input vector only would create a delta between the two values and the Composer window would show the resulting effect. When you're more familiar with the controls, you may choose to work this way for expediency.

Tip: Using Lock Vectors is especially helpful in client sessions. Otherwise, clients may misinterpret what they're seeing in the Composer window and think you are selecting the wrong color or making an unwanted change. It's usually better to avoid the issue altogether and work with Lock Vectors active.

5. The sky in your image has more green than the default vector. Shift-drag the input **Hue** slider to the right, to approximately **127**. This shifts the base tone of the vector toward cyan. In the Composer monitor, the sky is now more evenly selected.

6. Shift-drag the input **Saturation** slider to the left, reducing the value to approximately **40**.

7. Drag the **Hue Width** slider to the right, stopping at approximately **70**. This increases the range of blue/cyan tones included in the vector.

8. Reduce the **Sat Min** setting to **0** and increase the **Softness** setting to approximately **150**.

   These adjustments are very aggressive, qualifying a wide range of blue/cyan tones in the image, including pixels with no saturation values.

Note: Softness is a hue/saturation value adjustment, not a spatial adjustment. Increasing Softness may enlarge the selection if adjacent values are similar, but it does not soften the matte generated by the vector.

9. Examine the image. The input vector has qualified portions of the image that are undesirable, as shown in Figure 7.15. The smoke stacks and the subject's shoulder show blue spill, where subtle blue tones in these areas have been qualified. This is not acceptable.

Tip: In qualifying a vector for secondary correction, it is just as important to note the regions that are *excluded* as those that are included.

Figure 7.15
The qualification is too broad, including pixels that should not be altered.

10. Adjust the controls to constrain the input vector. Use the following as guides. When you're finished, the qualified area should look similar to that shown in Figure 7.16.

- **Hue Width: 30.00**
- **Sat Min: 10.00**
- **Softness: 45**

Now you are ready to create the effect. Remember, the goal for the image is a piercing blue sky. However, because the view of the sky in this shot is closer to the horizon than in the reference shot, be realistic about the region of the sky you are comparing. Analyze the difference between the two. There is a hue offset between the two sky tones, and the sky in B3-3 is darker than the horizon transition area of the reference image.

Tip: If you're unsure about what you're seeing, you may want to use the Color Match eyedroppers.

Figure 7.16
The properly qualified sky, ready for adjustment.

As you make the following adjustments, eye-match the two images. If you have one, watch the broadcast monitor. Remember, you can press the Esc key to quickly toggle the image visible on the broadcast monitor.

To perform the secondary correction:

1. Deselect the **LOCK VECTORS** check box.

2. Disable the **ISOLATE** vector setting.

3. Shift-drag the output **HUE** slider to the right, shifting it toward cyan, until you reach approximately **130**.

4. Shift-drag the **LUMINANCE** slider to the right, increasing its value to approximately **4.30**.

5. Play the shot, watching for artifacts, or digital noise, in the areas of the adjustment. If artifacts are present, reduce your adjustments. If not, move on!

Tip: Be especially aware of creating noise in the image when performing secondary corrections. While it's always a concern when grading, secondary corrections can easily stretch an image to its limits. If the compression used has little latitude, you'll quickly start to see noise in the image.

6. Toggle the correction to see the difference. It's subtle, but clearly improves the shot. Figure 7.17 shows the image before and after the secondary correction.

Figure 7.17
The image, subtly improved by secondary correction, now matches the sequence.

Notes from the Colorist: Secondaries Have Their Limits

If there is one caution I have to offer when performing hue and saturation isolations for manipulation, it's this: Be careful when making big luma adjustments. If you isolate sections of the image based on their hue and saturation and make a drastic shadow, gamma, or high-light adjustment, watch the edges of the isolations. Subtle tweaks usually look great. Really big luminance adjustments, however, tend to introduce fringing or posterization. The best way to identify these artifacts is to watch the shot play down.

As with other bits of advice I've offered, I'm not saying you shouldn't try making big moves. I'm saying to try it but to verify with your own eyes that you're not introducing new problems.

—pi

Using Custom Vectors

In addition to the standard vectors, the Secondary group allows you to create as many as six custom vectors. In the Secondary group, special color-selection buttons are available in the Match Color panel to make an initial vector selection or to modify an existing vector, as shown in Figure 7.18.

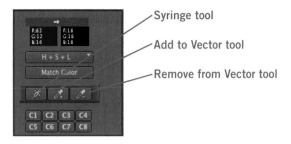

Syringe tool

Add to Vector tool

Remove from Vector tool

Figure 7.18
The color-selection buttons, used for creating a custom vector.

These buttons are as follows:

- **Syringe.** This reads a range of adjacent colors and creates a vector to represent them.

- **Add to Vector.** This adds the clicked-on color to the range of colors represented by the vector. If the clicked-on color is too far outside the vector, this tool may not alter the vector.

- **Remove from Vector.** This attempts to remove the clicked-on color from the range of colors represented by the vector. If the clicked-on color is not on the edge of the vector, this tool may have no effect on the vector.

Note: It's possible that the syringe will determine that an enabled vector you are already using is the most appropriate for the range of colors you sampled. In that case, it will replace that vector with a new vector. If this happens, undo, and then try to select a different range of colors or manually create the vector instead.

When using these tools, there are two basic approaches to creating the vector:

- Sample a broad range of values to create the vector, then remove unwanted colors from the vector.

- Sample a narrow range of values, then add additional values to complete the vector selection.

Both approaches are equally valid; the most efficient one will often be determined by the nature of the selection. If selecting the sky, for instance, as you did in the previous section, the first approach of selecting a broad range may be best. If you instead want to adjust the blue paint on a building without affecting the sky, it would be better to select a very narrow range. Either way, you can always use the manual controls to further refine the results of the vector.

In this section, you will use these tools to make and modify a vector selection. Continue working on the same sequence.

To set up for this example:

1. If it's not already, open the project **AVID COLOR GRADING (239)** and the bin **7_SECONDARIES**.

2. Load the sequence **7_SECONDARY CORRECTIONS**.

3. Enter **COLOR CORRECTION** mode.

4. Set up the Composer monitors to display the **VECTORSCOPE** on the left, **CURRENT** in the center, and **RGB PARADE** on the right.

5. Set the **VIDEO QUALITY** menu to **FULL QUALITY**.

6. Select **PROG SEGMENT** from the RELATIONSHIP menu.

7. Move the position indicator to the last shot in the sequence, **MVI_6166**, shown in Figure 7.19.

Figure 7.19
A surrealistic shot of the dreaded Mysterion.

This is a new shot—an ultra-wide close-up of Mysterion, shot with a fish-eye lens. He is sitting in a chair in the desert, laughing maniacally, and looking directly into the camera. The shot is surrealistic and is part of the sequence in the film where Agent Zero experiences a hallucinogenic dream.

Performing a quick analysis, the shot looks good overall. It has strong contrast, filling the luma range, and appears balanced. To support the intended surrealism, the only adjustment that's needed is to boost saturation.

To grade the shot using custom vectors:

1. Click the **HSL > Controls > Master** tab.

2. Boost the **Saturation** setting to approximately **155**.

   That definitely boosts the crazy factor. The sky has that piercing blue the director wants, and Mysterion's gloves pop off the screen as a brilliant, ruby red. The only problem is that the increased saturation is making Mysterion look more like a happy, red-faced drunkard than a diabolical madman. Let's tone down the color in his face.

3. Click the **Secondary** tab.

4. Click the **Syringe** tool to select it.

5. Move the mouse pointer to the Current monitor. The pointer changes to a syringe.

6. Drag the tip of the syringe over Mysterion's face—the area of color you want to sample. Try to sample the various tones in his face as completely as possible. Release the mouse button when you have finished sampling.

7. Deselect the **Syringe** tool when finished. This prevents accidental sampling that could change an existing vector.

Note: The syringe samples every color value its tip passes over. The input color swatch in the Color Match control updates as you drag the syringe to show the most recently sampled color.

When you finish sampling the image, the system does three things, as shown in Figure 7.20:

■ It selects and enables the vector it considers most appropriate for the range of colors you have sampled. Typically, this is a custom vector, but it may activate a standard vector instead.

■ It adjusts the input and output vector parameters to include the full range of colors you sampled.

■ It enables the Isolate button so that only the colors represented by the vector you defined are visible in the monitor.

Obviously, you need to tweak the vector. More than just Mysterion's face, all the desert sand and even portions of his gloves have been included in the selection.

Figure 7.20
The vector selection from a full sample of Mysterion's face.

To modify the vector:

1. Select the **SUBTRACT COLOR** tool.

2. In the Current monitor, click the desert sand. The system will remove the specific tone from the color vector. In the monitor, a portion of the desert sand will become desaturated.

3. Repeat step 2 until all the sand is removed from the vector, then deselect the **SUBTRACT COLOR** tool.

   It's quite possible that Mysterion's face now has blotches of desaturation where tones matching the sand have been removed from the vector. Portions of the gloves are likely still selected in the vector. You will need to further refine the vector manually.

4. Select the **LOCK VECTORS** check box.

5. If necessary, drag the center point (crosshair) of the input vector to center it on the skin tone range on the color wheel. (Think about the position of the I-line on the Vectorscope.) As you drag the center point, the image will update in real time to show the results. You can also Shift-drag the **HUE** slider to make fine adjustments (**HUE: −9.50**; **SATURATION: 32.00**).

Tip: Centering the vector within the desired range of hues results in more predictable behavior and helps ensure that there aren't any pinholes (that is, tiny areas of unselected pixels) in the desired color range.

6. Adjust the **HUE WIDTH** setting to approximately **12.00**.

7. Adjust the **SAT WIDTH** setting to approximately **52.00**.

These two manual adjustments constrain the vector to a very narrow range of hues but permit a broad range of saturation values within those hues.

As shown in Figure 7.21, in the final vector selection, the sand and most of the gloves are now removed from the vector. Note that a small portion of the shadowed side of the gloves remains selected in the vector, while the darkest shadows of his face have been excluded. Neither of these will be of consequence.

Figure 7.21
The proper vector selection for Mysterion's face.

8. Deselect the **LOCK VECTORS** check box.

9. Watching the Vectorscope and the client monitor, drag the **HUE** slider to the left, decreasing red until the skin tone is proper (**HUE: −12.00**).

10. Finish the correction by reducing the output **SATURATION** setting to approximately **25.00**.

11. Deselect the **ISOLATE** vector setting to see the face in context.

12. Toggle the **Sec** enable button to see the before and after, as shown in Figure 7.22.

Figure 7.22
Mysterion's face appears more natural after the correction.

13. Play the footage, checking for noise or artifacts. Looking good! There is, however, one final problem: the gloves are *too* saturated. You want them to pop, but the Vectorscope indicates that the saturation level is exceeding 100%. Depending on the final display device used to view the film, this could cause blooming.

14. Enable the **R** vector by clicking its center point on the input vector wheel. (If you are not displaying standard vectors, click its color swatch and enable button in the Select Vector panel to activate it.)

15. Select the **Isolate** setting. The Composer monitor shows both the skin tones selected by your custom vector and the red hues selected by the R vector. This is normal.

16. Reduce output **Saturation** setting until the traces on the Vectorscope reach the 100% vector box—approximately **43.00**.

17. Deselect the **Isolate** setting.

18. Toggle the **Sec** enable button to see the before and after. Play the clip and watch it in your client monitor.

Creating the Pleasantville Effect

The 1998 film, *Pleasantville*, starring Tobey McGuire, Jeff Daniels, and Joan Allen, was a visually innovative film that began in black and white and, over the course of the film, added color. The addition of color, however, was linked to modern social views held by the characters. Only those who embraced the new paradigm were displayed in color. As attitudes changed, more characters appeared in color. For portions of the film, only the protagonists are in color, while the background sets and other characters still appear in black and white. The look, traditionally known as *limited palette*, has become known as the *Pleasantville* effect. Figure 7.23 shows a limited palette of red and yellow on the shot of the landing helicopter. (To see images from the film *Pleasantville*, visit IMDB.com.)

Figure 7.23
The *Pleasantville* effect on the helicopter landing shot.

The limited palette effect continues to make appearances in productions. At the time of this writing, Chase Sapphire commercials are being produced using it. As you've seen, Symphony creates this look automatically using the Isolate vector setting. While intended as a selection tool, it can be used to create this special effect. To create the effect, simply leave Isolate vector enabled on the shot(s) after defining the vectors. For playout, export, render, and Digital Cut, the shot will display the effect.

Inverting the Last Vector

As mentioned, the Vector Selection panel contains an Invert Last Vector button that changes the behavior of the right-most enabled vector in the panel. When this button is selected, the vector inverts; all the colors outside the vector are affected, while the colors defined by the vector are left unaffected. The most common use of this function is to utilize the vector as a hold-out mask, making an adjustment to everything in the image *except* those hues defined by the vector. In this section, you will make just such an adjustment.

Tip: You could compare this to alpha channels. Inverting a vector is like inverting the vector's alpha channel.

To perform a secondary correction with an inverted vector:

1. If it's not open already, open the project **Avid Color Grading (239)** and the bin **7_Secondaries**.

2. Load the sequence **7_Secondary Corrections**.

3. Enter **Color Correction** mode.

4. Set up the Composer monitors to display the **Vectorscope** on the left, **Current** in the center, and **RGB Parade** on the right.

5. Set the **Video Quality** menu to **Full Quality**.

6. Select **Prog Segment** from the **relationship** menu.

7. Move the position indicator to the second shot in the sequence, **C3-1**, shown in Figure 7.24.

Figure 7.24
Agent Sierra in the control room.

8. This is a now-familiar shot, so I won't take the time to analyze it again. Use the grading tools of your choice to perform a quick base grade, setting the luma range and balancing the shot. Or, pull a quick template from the same shot in a previous lesson sequence and apply it.

The goal for the shot is two-fold: To emphasize the subject's face by de-emphasizing the background and to shift the colors of the background image while maintaining her facial tones. As the story goes, budgets were slashed and the production can't afford VFX shots to replace the green and blue information displays on the background gear, so the director at least wants them to be different colors.

9. Click the **Sec** tab.

10. Click the **Syringe** tool and drag to sample Sierra's cheek and neck. The result is a clean chroma qualification of her face, with the exception of the monitor reflection. In this situation, that's acceptable. (See Figure 7.25.)

Figure 7.25
The vector isolation of Sierra's flesh tones.

11. Deselect the **Syringe** tool.

12. If necessary, select the **Lock Vectors** check box and use the manual controls to refine the vector selection. When you're finished, unlock the vectors and proceed.

13. In the Vector Selection panel, enable the **Invert Last Vector** setting. Both the vector and the color isolation in the Composer monitor invert. Now the selected area is the background rather than her face.

14. Darken the selection. To do so, lower the output **Luminance** setting to approximately **–2.00**.

Tip: If you reduce the luminance any further, you'll quickly see a harsh edge
between the affected and unaffected areas of her face due to the compression
of this media. If the line is too harsh, smooth it out by slightly increasing the
Softness setting.

15. Decrease the output **SATURATION** setting to approximately **12.50**.

16. Shift-drag the **HUE** slider to the right until the colors on the equipment
have a pleasing yellow and cyan tint (**HUE: 0.00**).

17. Play the clip to check for noise and artifacts. Toggle the **SEC** enable button
to see the before and after, as shown in Figure 7.26.

Great job! The director will be pleased.

Figure 7.26
The before and after shows a real difference here!

Notes from the Colorist:
The Dangers of Multitasking (and the Power of Focus)

Let's take a step back from colors and sliders, qualifications, and skin tones and talk about your overall color-correction session. Anyone who has ever done a significant amount of color grading inside an NLE will attest: Clients will throw you off track. You'll drop out of Color Correction mode to watch a few shots play down and then your client will start asking you to replace a sound effect, trim a shot, or look for B-roll that they suddenly recall.

Should You Stop Color Correcting to Address Editing Concerns?

As someone who's spent much of my career wearing both hats (editor and colorist), I've experienced this exact scenario. Generally, my answer is: No. Don't do it.

Don't underestimate the power of focus. You don't want to lose track of how you've been grading a particular sequence of shots or the concerns you've been addressing for the past hour. Your eyes are open and alert. You're using a different set of senses than when pulling sound effects or tweaking an edit. Contrary to popular belief, very few people are really good at multitasking; constantly switching between color grading, sound mixing, and editing is the post-production equivalent of just that. If you allow your client to push you into constantly switching tasks, you'll probably do all of them at a much lower level than you're capable.

The inverse of this is also true....

Should You Color Correct While You're Editing?

When you're editing, focus on story and timing. Put the pictures together in the order they need to be placed. If you need to take a moment to see if a shot can be saved, that's fine. But otherwise, forget about color correcting. Just edit. Clients have a tendency to try to throw you off your game, getting you to go down the rabbit hole of color correction while you're still figuring out the story. Don't be bullied into doing so. Focus on the task at hand and you'll get much better results. Besides, what's the point of color correcting a shot if it doesn't make the final edit? You'll have just wasted very valuable time.

Prepare Your Clients by Informing Them

When you start the color grade, give your client advance warning about this. Let them know where to look for the current timecode number and tell them to take notes. Educate your clients on your process. I think you'll find that even *having* a process will separate you from most of your peers.

Remember: Momentum while color correcting is huge. You always want to be moving forward. You never want to get bogged down. Yes, you have the full editing power of Avid at your fingertips; resist the urge to jump between tasks. Don't do this to your brain. Ask your client to take notes and save it for another day or the end of the color-grading process.

—pi

Review/Discussion Questions

1. Name three tools that can be used for secondary correction.

2. What is the purpose of qualification?

3. How can luma ranges be used to qualify a region for secondary correction?

4. What impact does changing the luma range have on the image?

5. What is the advantage of luma and chroma qualification? What is the disadvantage?

6. What type of qualification is performed with the Secondary group?

7. How many vectors can be simultaneously adjusted using the Secondary tool?

8. Which tool is used to define a custom vector?

9. Which parameter changes the size of the arc of a standard vector?
   a. Hue
   b. Saturation
   c. Hue Width
   d. Softness
   e. None of the above

10. Which parameter can be used to smooth the edge of the vector selection based on hue and saturation values?
    a. Hue
    b. Saturation
    c. Hue Width
    d. Softness
    e. None of the above

11. Which setting enables you to create the Pleasantville effect?

12. How can a hue within an image be changed to another?

Lesson 7   Keyboard Shortcuts

Command/Action	Result
Click the Correction tab enable button	Bypasses the correction in the tab, including any subtabs, permitting a view of the image without the correction. Parameter values are not reset.
Option-click (Mac) or Alt-click (Windows) the Correction tab enable button	Resets the values of all parameters in the tab, including any subtabs.

Performing Secondary Corrections

In this exercise, you will challenge yourself with more complex secondary corrections.

Media Used:

Avid Color Correction (MC239) project > 2_Exercise Bins folder > Ex7_Secondaries Exercise bin > Ex7_Secondaries_Poker Game sequence

Duration:

60 minutes

GOALS

- Perform secondary corrections
- Leverage color-correction relationships to speed up the grading process
- Set the tonal range using Levels
- Repair images using Channels

Overview

The poker scene is characterized by an overpowering red wall in the background of every shot. Your goal is to reduce the intensity of the red wall in the shots, maintaining the color and feel of the rest of the image elements, as shown in Figure 7.27.

Figure 7.27
A combination of secondary corrections reduces the intensity of the distracting red wall.

You graded this scene in the Curves exercise, in Lesson 4, "Grading with Curves." Either perform a quick base grade, or pull templates from the Ex4_Curves sequence to shortcut the grading process. Spend your time on the secondary grade, not the primary grading process.

As you work, here are some key points to keep in mind:

- The compression on these images limits their latitude. Be on the lookout for noise and artifacts. Go gentle with your adjustments!

- Don't try to fix the problem with one tool. Combine adjustments for greater success.

- Every image has shadows, midtones, and highlights. You may need to make dramatic changes to the luma range curves to isolate them.

- There are large overlaps between the skin tones and the wall. Take the time to define your vector well.

- Recognize where you can make compromises and where you can't. The audience won't always know what's missing—i.e., are her lips slightly less saturated in the final shot? Does it matter?

To begin the exercise:

1. Open the project AVID COLOR GRADING **(239)** and the bin EX7_SECONDARIES EXERCISE.

2. Load the sequence EX7_SECONDARIES_POKER GAME.

3. Perform secondary corrections to reduce the intensity of the wall.

Intraframe Effects: Avid's Hidden Secondaries

Intraframe effects enable the Avid colorist shape-based tools for vignetting, frame painting, spot corrections, custom matte cutting, and more—all linked to a flexible and accurate built-in Tracking tool. This lesson covers three of these effects, all available in both Media Composer and Symphony.

Media Used: Avid Color Grading (MC239) project > 1_Lesson Bins folder > 8_Intraframe Effects bin > 8_Intraframe Effects sequence

Duration: 60 minutes

GOALS

- Identify the common characteristics of Intraframe effects
- List Intraframe effects useful for shape-based secondary corrections
- Use various Intraframe effects to create secondary and spot corrections
- Keyframe Intraframe effects
- Use Avid's Tracking tool to animate Intraframe effects

Exploring Avid's Shape-Based Secondary Tools

In this lesson, you will explore the third and final type of secondary corrections: shape-based secondaries. Shape-based corrections, often referred to generically as *vignettes*, are a critical tool in finalizing a grade.

Built into both Media Composer and Symphony are a family of effects referred to as *Intraframe effects*. Each shares the same operating model and many of the same tools. Once you learn the first, the others are very easy to pick up.

Unlike luma or chroma qualification, these corrections are not procedural in nature. The region affected by the secondary correction will not automatically update as the image changes. Instead, these effects need to be keyframed, or linked to tracking data, to alter their size, shape, or position. In this lesson, you will learn to use three different Intraframe effects, each with unique capabilities and applications.

Understanding Intraframe Effects

The three Intraframe effects that have applications for color grading are as follows:

- **Spot Color Effect.** This contains the full range of luma and chroma controls available in the Color Effect. Used for spot-color treatments.

- **Paint Effect.** This is a multipurpose effects tool with 28 different image manipulation modes. For grading, the Paint Effect is used to create vignettes and gradients.

- **AniMatte.** Designed to cut custom mattes, AniMatte is used to create multi-layered correction effects.

All Intraframe effects function by altering the pixels within the shape, or region, you define using a palette of drawing tools. These effects are neutral effects. They're blank canvases. When you first apply the effect, there is no immediate change to the image. To create the effect, you first draw a shape, then manipulate the controls to change the effect on that region. The drawing tools include a standard array of shapes, as well as a collection of brushes, as shown in Figure 8.1.

You can create multiple shapes per effect—ideal for fixing multiple problems in the image with one effect. The shapes can also be grouped, can be ordered, and will interact with each other. To create a vignette, for example, one shape is created to darken the image, and another is created to define the brighter center. Intraframe effects produce very high quality results. All shapes are vector-based, and processed in 8, 10, or 16 bits, depending on project settings.

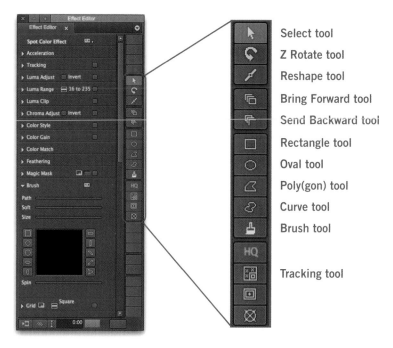

Select tool

Z Rotate tool

Reshape tool

Bring Forward tool

Send Backward tool

Rectangle tool

Oval tool

Poly(gon) tool

Curve tool

Brush tool

Tracking tool

Figure 8.1
The shape-creation tools of the Paint Effect, also available in other Intraframe effects.

Setting Up to Work with Intraframe Effects

Intraframe effects cannot be applied or manipulated in Color Correction mode. Instead, you work with these in the traditional Effect mode. This has several implications; as you would expect, there are some viable workarounds to mitigate the inconveniences:

■ Avid's internal scopes are not available outside Color Correction mode. This is a non-issue if you are working with external scopes. If not, the BCC Videoscope plug-in effect, found in the BCC Color & Tone category, can be added to a top filler track to provide real-time monitoring of scopes outside Color Correction mode. (Boris BCC plug-in effects are bundled with Avid Symphony purchases.)

■ Effect editing controls are not mapped to the Artist Color controller. If you are working exclusively with the Artist Color and no mouse, activate mouse mode on the Artist Color to work in the Effect Editor.

■ Outside Color Correction mode, you cannot toggle the grade, nor the individual effect, to see its impact on the image. Instead, using step in/step out can enable you to "look under" the effect to see the image without the effect in place.

To set up for working with these effects, it is helpful to have the Effects Mode button mapped to a key on the keyboard or, better yet, the Effects Editing workspace. If you are not working with your own custom user settings, take a moment to map those now.

To set up Media Composer for Effects editing:

1. Select **WINDOWS > WORKSPACES > EFFECTS EDITING**. The windows change to display the standard editing environment with the addition of the Effects Editor window.

2. Arrange the windows to fit your screen according to your preference. You may consider working with a single large monitor in the Composer window instead of with the standard two-up Source/Record monitors.

3. (Optional) To view a single monitor in the Composer window, drag the bottom-right corner of the Composer window, changing the dimensions of the monitor to a large square, as shown in Figure 8.2.

4. Select **WINDOWS > WORKSPACES > SAVE CURRENT**.

Figure 8.2
Effects mode, configured with a single, large monitor.

5. In the Project window, choose **SETTINGS > KEYBOARD**. Then double-click the **KEYBOARD** setting to open it.

6. Open the Command Palette by choosing **TOOLS > COMMAND PALETTE**.

7. If not already active, click the **BUTTON TO BUTTON REASSIGNMENT** option button.

8. Click the **OTHER** pane. Drag the **EFFECTS MODE** button to the **Y** key in the Keyboard window or another key of your choosing.

9. Click the **WORKSPACES** pane. Drag the **EE (EFFECTS EDITING)** button to the **F11** key in the Keyboard window or another key of your choosing.

10. From the Workspaces pane, drag the **CC (COLOR CORRECTION)** button to the **F12** key in the Keyboard window.

11. Close the Keyboard window and the Command Palette.

Now, when you press the Y key, it will open the Effects Editor; the F11 and F12 keys will toggle you between the Effects Editing and Color Correction workspaces, respectively. This is a real convenience if you need to move frequently between the two.

Note: If working on a Mac, you will need to disable the activation shortcuts for Mission Control and enable the use of F1, F2, etc., as standard function keys. Both are accomplished through the System Preferences > Keyboard setting.

Using the Spot Color Effect

As mentioned, the Spot Color Effect enables you to make precise color adjustments to a part of an image that you define using the Intraframe drawing tools. The Spot Color Effect contains the following parameters:

- **Acceleration.** This controls the degree of easing around keyframes. Values range from 0 to 100, with 100 being the maximum easing.

- **Tracking.** This enables you to link to up to four tracking points.

- **Luma Adjust.** These include Bright(ness), Cont(rast), and Invert.

- **Luma Range.** These include W(hite) Point, B(lack) Point, and Gamma. The embedded Fast menu selects between Computer RGB and 601/709 color values.

- **Luma Clip.** Settings include High (default of 235) and Low (default of 16).

- **Chroma Adjust.** Settings include Hue, Sat(uration), and Invert.

- **Color Style.** Settings include Post(erization) and Solar(ization).

- **Color Gain.** Settings include R(ed), G(reen), and B(lue), with individual control over the color gain for each channel. A default value of 100 denotes the value of the channel when the effect was applied; it can be reduced to 0 or increased to +200.

- **Color Match (Symphony Only).** Settings include Input and Output Color Match swatches, plus NaturalMatch selection.

- **Feathering.** Hor(izontal) and Vert(ical) settings control the amount of feathering, while the Bias setting balances the feathering inside or outside the shape. These are used to soften the edges of the shape for better blending.

- **Magic Mask.** Use the Magic Mask to create effects within the shape using the chroma and luma values as the criteria for edge detection. Controls include Hue, Sat(uration), Lum(inance), Gain, and Soft(ness).

- **Brush.** Select the brush shape, Soft(ness), Size, Spin (rotation), and Path. Brushes can be used instead of geometric shape-creation tools to create custom shapes.

- **Grid.** This setting displays format-specific framing guides.

Spot-color treatments are typically applied as a storytelling device, either to draw attention to a character or object or to de-emphasize competing objects in the frame. In this section, you will use the Spot Color Effect as an alternative approach to solving the problem of the bright red walls in the poker scene, which you worked on during the previous exercise.

To set up for this exercise:

1. Open the project AVID COLOR GRADING (239) and the bin 8_INTRAFRAME EFFECTS.

2. Load the sequence 8_INTRAFRAME EFFECTS.

3. If it's not set already, set the VIDEO QUALITY menu to FULL QUALITY.

4. Activate the Effects Editing workspace.

To create a spot correction with the Spot Color Effect:

1. Move the position indicator to the second shot in the sequence, **L1+2-2**. The CU shot of Zero talking with Kitty, shown in Figure 8.3, has the characteristic red background of this scene. You will darken the background to draw the viewer's eye to Zero's face.

2. Open the Effect Palette and select the IMAGE category.

Figure 8.3
Agent Zero gets lost in the background.

3. Drag the **Spot Color Effect** to the segment in the Timeline, **L1+2-2**.

4. Open the Effect Editor. The Effect Editor displays the Spot Correction parameters, as shown in Figure 8.4.

Figure 8.4
The parameters of the Spot Color Effect.

5. For this effect, you'll need to be able to draw outside the boundaries of the frame. Click the **REDUCE** button once. (The Reduce button has a magnifying glass with a minus symbol on it and appears in the bottom-right corner of the Composer window.) The image reduces to 75% size, revealing gray space around the image.

6. Select the **POLY(GON)** tool, shown in Figure 8.5.

7. You will need to draw a polygon around Zero's head and body that extends beyond the boundary of the video frame, as shown in Figure 8.5. First, decide where to begin the shape, such as the upper-left corner, and click to establish the first anchor point.

Figure 8.5
Use the Polygon tool to create a custom shape over the area to darken.

8. Move the mouse pointer. A straight line extends from the first point to the pointer location. Click to establish the second anchor point.

9. Continue around the image, outlining the background areas while excluding most of Zero. Don't worry if the shape isn't perfect.

10. Double-click the final point location to close the shape with a straight line connecting to the first control point. Alternatively, close the shape by hand by clicking the first control point.

11. In the Luma Range parameter group, reduce the **Gamma** setting until the background darkens sufficiently (approximately **–10**).

12. Next, adjust the **Feathering** to soften the edge (**Horz/Vert: 30, Bias = 70**).

13. Click the **Selection Tool** button. Then click in the gray space outside the image to deselect the shape to see the results of the adjustments.

Nice! Most often, a quick shape with lots of feathering is all you need. Sometimes, you'll need to tweak it further to perfect it. Let's look at how to do that now.

To refine a shape in the Spot Color Effect:

1. Click the **Reshape Tool** button. All control points become visible, with the active one solid, as shown in Figure 8.6.

Figure 8.6
Use the Reshape tool to refine the shape.

2. Adjust the control points to improve the shape. Here are some tips for doing so:

   ● Drag a control point to reposition it.

   ● Option-click (Mac) or Alt-click (Windows) a control point to convert it from an angle point to a Bézier point.

- Drag Bézier handles to change the angle and shape of the curves on either side of the point.
- Option-click (Mac) or Alt-click (Windows) the Bézier handles to toggle the locked versus independent relationship of the handles.

3. Click the **SELECTION TOOL** button. Then click in the gray space outside the image to deselect the shape.

4. Command-click (Mac) or Ctrl-click (Windows) the video image to zoom in. You need to examine the edges of the shape to see if it is unacceptably noticeable.

5. Press and hold **COMMAND+SHIFT** (Mac) or **CTRL+SHIFT** (Windows). The mouse icon changes to a hand. Drag the image to change the portion visible in the Composer window.

6. Click the **TIMECODE** track in the Timeline to exit Effects Mode.

7. With the position indicator still on **L1+2-2,** click **STEP IN** to see the underlying image *sans* effect. Alternate between the stepped in and stepped out views to see the impact of the adjustments.

The darkened background has definitely improved the image, as shown in Figure 8.7, but Zero's face still feels a bit dark. Brighten his face slightly with another shape.

Figure 8.7
The image is improving, but his face is still dark.

To brighten Zero's face:

1. Activate **EFFECTS MODE**.

2. If it's not already selected, click the **L1+2-2** segment to select it.

3. In the Effects Editor, select the **OVAL** tool.

4. Draw an oval over the lower two-thirds of Zero's face, excluding his forehead. His face will darken. By default, Symphony applies the last used settings to new shapes.

5. Select the **RESHAPE** tool.

6. Double-click the shape (a shortcut to activate the **RESHAPE** tool), then move the control points to reshape the oval to better match his face, as shown in Figure 8.8.

Figure 8.8
Define the region to "light" his face.

7. Feather the shape (**HORZ/VERT: 15, BIAS: 50**).

8. In the Luma Range group, increase the **GAMMA** setting to brighten Zero's face slightly. Be subtle. Remember, you don't want the effect to be consciously noticed by the viewer (**GAMMA = 2**).

9. Choose the **SELECTION** tool. Then click the **LUMA RANGE** enable button a couple times to toggle on/off the "light" on his face. Leave it enabled before moving on.

10. With the position indicator still on **L1+2-2,** click **STEP IN** to see the underlying image *sans* effect. Alternate between the stepped in and stepped out views to see the impact of the entire effect. (See Figure 8.9.)

Figure 8.9
The extra "light" on Zero's face finishes the grade nicely.

Notes from the Colorist: Keeping It Soft

There are two approaches to creating shapes to isolate areas of the picture:

- Draw very precise shapes around objects, with precision that almost reaches the level of rotoscoping, using many points to define the shapes.

- Draw very broad shapes around objects, sticking to circles or three-point ovals to create an irregular but not unnatural shape, and use very soft edges.

Both are valid approaches. Both are attempts to keep corrections inside (or outside) those shapes looking completely natural. The first type of approach works with hyper-detailed shapes. The second works in broad strokes.

Working between those two extremes can be very iffy; a small camera movement can betray the work you're doing. The right approach is often decided by the shot. When you're deciding what kind of shape to create, I have two bits of advice:

- The more precise the shape you use, the more you need to animate the shape frame by frame. Trying to keyframe shapes that need to precisely track the outlines of moving objects is a quick way to blow your deadline. If you begin down that path, be sure you have the time to finish what you start.

- If the shot's moving and you can't track it, go soft instead. Try using as few points as you can while keeping the edges of the shape very soft. It'll help blend your isolations into the rest of the image.

Of course, those are rules begging to be broken—and by all means, go for it. But if you find yourself spending too much time managing your shapes, simplify, simplify, simplify.

—pi

Using the Paint Effect

The Paint Effect is a versatile tool that can be used for a wide range of effects. In this section, you will learn to utilize it to create two common effects: a gradient and a vignette.

Creating Gradients and Vignettes

The principles you just learned about creating shapes with the Spot Color Effect apply to the Paint Effect as well. The shape-creation tools are the same. However, in the Paint Effect, you have a much broader range of modes that can be applied to the shape. The mode defines the type of effect being applied. A full list of Paint Effect modes is shown in Figure 8.10.

Figure 8.10
More than 25 modes are available in the Paint Effect.

Note: For more information on using the Paint Effect modes to create various effects, see the Help article "Paint Effect Modes."

To create a gradient:

1. Continue with the same sequence, **8_INTRAFRAME EFFECTS**. If it's not already set up, follow the directions in the previous section to get it set up.

2. Move the position indicator to **DELIVERY59-TAKE18513...**, the OTS shot of Zero looking at Mysterion in the distance. To better match this shot with the others, you'll create a gradient to recolor the sky and a vignette to draw the eyes to Mysterion.

3. Open the Effect Palette and select the **IMAGE** category. Drag the **PAINT EFFECT** to the **DELIVERY59-...** SEGMENT.

4. Sample the color of the sky before you add anything to it. To begin, click the **MAGIC MASK** color well; then drag the eyedropper to the top of the frame, where the sky has some color. Release the mouse button.

5. Draw a rectangle that covers the sky and mountains. The default mode is Solid and the color set to bright red, as shown in Figure 8.11. This is designed to be a visual aid to facilitate the drawing process.

Figure 8.11
The default bright red makes it easy to see the shape being drawn.

6. Click the **MODE** pop-up menu and select **OUTLINE** so you can sample the color of the sky.

7. Click the **MAGIC MASK** color well; then drag the eyedropper to the top of Zero's head, where the sky has the most color. Release the mouse button.

8. Change the **MODE** setting to **GRADIENT**; then open the **MODE** group by clicking its triangular opener. The gradient appears across the sky. Because the Magic Mask is already active, it excludes Zero's head.

9. Click the **ANGLE** slider; then type **90**. This sets the angle to 90 degrees, causing the gradient to appear darkest at the top and lighter at the bottom, as shown in Figure 8.12.

Figure 8.12
Magic Mask restricts the gradient to the sky only.

10. (Optional) Adjust the **MAGIC MASK** settings to refine the holdout region of Zero's head.

11. In the **COLOR** parameter, click the small button next to the color well to open the OS color picker. Use the controls to choose a bright, light blue for the sky to match the other shots.

12. Under **MODE**, reduce the **OPACITY** setting to better balance the gradient with the shot. The result is seen in Figure 8.13. Looks good so far!

13. Now let's build the vignette. The vignette is built by darkening the entire frame, then creating a holdout mask within it. To start, choose the **RECTANGLE** tool and draw another rectangle that covers the full frame.

14. Set the mode to **DARKEN**; adjust **OPAC(ITY)** to **100**, and **AMT** to **75**.

Figure 8.13
The shot before and after the gradient is applied.

15. Choose the **Oval** tool. Create a large oval across the key parts of the image. This will be used as a holdout mask to create the window within the vignette.

16. Set the mode to **Solid**. (You may wish to reset the color to bright red, rather than the sky blue you last used.)

17. Increase the feathering to **45**. The areas of greatest color concentration will be the clearest. (See Figure 8.14.)

Figure 8.14
Create the window within the vignette with an oval.

18. Change the mode to **ERASE**. This punches out the clear window, leaving the darkened edges in place.

19. The effect could be further improved by customizing the mask. Instead of a straight oval, reshape it to include the areas you want to emphasize—namely, Zero and Mysterion. Use the **RESHAPE** tool to adjust the shape to reduce the darkening on the back of Zero's shoulder and head, as shown in Figure 8.15. You may also want to tweak the **FEATHERING** settings.

Figure 8.15
Reshape the "window" within the gradient.

20. Close the Effect Editor.

21. With the position indicator still on **DELIVERY59-...**, click **STEP IN** to see the underlying image *sans* effect. Alternate between the stepped in and stepped out views to see the impact of the adjustments. (See Figure 8.16.)

Figure 8.16
The Paint Effect has made a big difference here.

Notes from the Colorist: The Art of Vignettes

Vignettes seem so simple, right? Create an oval, fill it with black, set your opacity, and you're done! Not necessarily. I have a few things for you to consider when you're creating vignettes:

- Apply the Spot Color Effect.

- Create a nice oval.

- Use one of these options to adjust the outside of the oval for the vignetting effect: Luminance, Darken, Color Adjust, or Color Gain.

Each of these tools will give you a different effect. And if you manipulate them correctly (darken the edges of the frame, and maybe desaturate them), they'll help draw the viewer's focus to the center of the vignette—but each in its own stylized way. It's a great way to add your own personal touch to what seems like a gimmicky effect.

Also, take a moment to consider Figure 8.15. It's a great example of creating interesting—but not too detailed—shapes. It helps hide the vignette.

Another technique I use all the time is to rotate the shape so the vignette is never quite parallel with the top and bottom of the screen. Again, this helps hide the vignette and makes it feel more natural and organic.

Finally, unless I'm trying to make the vignette very stylized—as part of a "look"—I know I'm creating good vignettes when I come back to a shot the next day and can't tell if there's a vignette on it. I'll then toggle back to the original shot and suddenly the vignette is completely obvious. When that happens, that's when I know I'm having a really good day.

—pi

Tracking Spot Corrections

The shots you've worked on to this point have been fairly static. Creating spot corrections for images with a moving subject in the frame isn't much more complicated, thanks to Avid's built-in tracking tools.

Many effects can be combined with tracking information to improve both the accuracy of the effect and the efficiency of creating it. Tracking data can be generated and tweaked in less time than it typically takes to keyframe similar movements. More importantly, the nuances of movement that are captured and translated to the effect through tracking can produce results that go completely unnoticed.

For this next effect, you will use the Tracking tool in conjunction with the Paint tool to create an effect on a moving image.

Note: Avid's Tracking tool is covered in depth in the companion book in this series, *Media Composer 6: Professional Effects and Compositing*. The corresponding class, MC205, available from an Avid Learning Partner, is highly recommended. The industry is changing, and more and more colorists are expected to do VFX and compositing work. The skills taught in that class are more valuable than ever!

To create a spot correction utilizing tracking:

1. Continue working on the same sequence, **8_INTRAFRAME EFFECTS**. If it's not already set up, follow the directions in the section "Using Spot Corrections."

2. Move the position indicator to the shot **MVI_8396.MOV**. The shot of the helicopter landing is part of the opening sequence. To draw the attention of the viewer, you will create more contrast on the helicopter itself.

3. Open the Effect Palette and select the **IMAGE** category. Drag the **PAINT EFFECT** to the shot **MVI_8396.MOV**.

4. Open the Effect Editor.

5. Press **HOME**; alternatively, drag the position indicator in the Composer window to the first frame of the clip.

6. Draw an oval that is roughly the size of the helicopter.

7. Select the **ROTATE** tool and rotate it to better cover the body and tail of the helicopter.

8. Soften the edges of the shape and focus the effect by increasing the **FEATHERING** setting to **18** and reducing the **BIAS** setting to **85**, as shown in Figure 8.17.

Figure 8.17
Define the effect region
with a solid shape.

Tip: When adjusting feathering to high amounts or on small shapes, use a solid
color. Doing so will let you see the effects of the feather and where the effect
will be most concentrated.

9. Next, you need to move the shape to match the helicopter's movement.
Click the keyframe at the end of the effect, visible in the effect position bar.

10. Move the shape to the new location of the helicopter.

11. Play the effect. Clearly, there are some problems. Not only does the effect
not match the movements perfectly, but the helicopter has also increased
in size and the shape hasn't. Rather than spend too much time keyframing,
fix both these issues simultaneously through tracking.

12. Click the triangular opener to open the **TRACKING** parameter group.

13. Click the enable button on the first tracking point. The Tracking Window
opens and a single tracker appears on the image, as shown in Figure 8.18.

14. Position the tracker on the nose window of the helicopter. The inner box
of the tracker defines the pixels to be tracked, and the outer box is the
tracking region.

Tip: The keys to accurate tracking is to give the tracker a high contrast group
of pixels to track and to set the search region to include any possible
movement of target pixels.

15. Because the helicopter gets bigger during the course of the shot, you'll need
a second tracking point to calculate the change in size, not just position.
Click the **CREATE NEW TRACKER** button.

16. Position the second tracker at the end of the helicopter's tail.

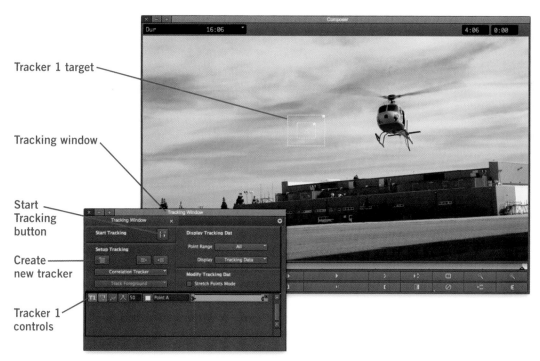

Tracker 1 target

Tracking window

Start Tracking button

Create new tracker

Tracker 1 controls

Figure 8.18
The Tracking Window and one tracker on the image.

17. Click the **START TRACKING** button. The system tracks the movement of the helicopter. When finished, the tracking data is displayed in the Composer window, as shown in Figure 8.19.

Figure 8.19
The trackers and data for the helicopter. (Note: The frame has been enlarged in these images for illustrative purposes.)

18. Close the Tracking Window and move the position indicator in the Composer window back to the first frame of the shot.

19. In the Effect Editor, enable the second tracking point in the Tracking parameter group.

20. Play the effect, watching the movement of the red shape. It should follow the helicopter's position and resize itself to match.

21. (Optional) If the tracking wasn't accurate, reopen the Tracking Window, delete the tracker that isn't accurate, and re-create it.

22. Change the mode to **Unsharp Mask**. The results of the image are seen in Figure 8.20.

Figure 8.20
The unsharp mask makes the helicopter pop.

Note: **The Unsharp Mask sharpens the image by increasing the contrast within the shape, especially at the perceived boundaries of objects within the shape.**

23. Play out the effect. If the unsharp mask is noticeable in the sky around the helicopter, increase feathering and/or reshape it for better blending.

Nice work!

Tip: **When adjusting feathering to high amounts or on small shapes, use a solid color. Doing so will let you see the effects of the feather and where the effect will be most concentrated.**

Using AniMatte to Create Spot Corrections

The AniMatte effect is found in the Key category. You can use the AniMatte effect to cut custom masks to composite images together. For color grading, this can be used to create multilayer spot corrections. Rather than compositing one image on top of another—to replace the background, for instance—you will use the AniMatte effect to composite one image onto itself. Each layer can be independently graded without concern how it might affect the other area. To create a custom matte with AniMatte, you will use the same shape-creation tools you used in the Spot Color Effect and the Paint Effect.

Although it is more work, this method of creating a spot correction can often create a better result. The full latitude of the shot is available for grading each region. Because you're not "stretching" the color information in different directions, you are less likely to introduce artifacts and noise into the image.

For this section, you will grade the familiar and problematic shot of Mysterion's girlfriend, Kitty, at the poker table. You've graded this shot with secondary corrections and already and know the challenges. Re-creating the grade with this method will enable you to recognize the differences in grading process and results.

To create a spot correction using AniMatte:

1. Continue working on the same sequence, **8_INTRAFRAME EFFECTS**. If it's not already set up, follow the directions in the section "Using Spot Corrections."

2. Move the position indicator to the first shot in the sequence, **K3+5-1**. It has been layered on top of itself, appearing on both V1 and V2. A simple primary correction exists on V1. The shot on V2, which will be used for the wall, has no correction applied.

3. Take a moment to examine the shot and consider how you might approach it: The goal is to diminish the intensity of the red wall while maintaining a proper grade on the faces of both Kitty and Mysterion. Mysterion is stationary through the shot; Kitty moves her head.

4. Move the position indicator to the first frame of the segment.

5. Open the Effect Palette and select the **KEY** category. Drag the **ANIMATTE** effect to the shot **K3+5-1** on V2.

6. Open the Effect Editor.

7. Your impulse may be to create a single large shape over all the important regions of the image, as shown in Figure 8.21. Instead, you should create separate shapes to correspond to the static and moving parts of the image, as shown in Figure 8.22. Use the **POLY** tool to draw and refine shapes around the characters.

Figure 8.21
A single large shape will be difficult to keyframe or track.

Figure 8.22
Independent shapes are easier to animate.

Tip: **Complex body movements are better handled with independent components. Track and correct the torso and limbs separately, like a marionette.**

8. Increase the feathering on each shape to soften the edges.

9. Shift-click all the shapes. Set the mode to **KEY OUT**. Immediately, the image changes, revealing the grade from V1 on their faces. You will need to examine and possibly refine the edges of the matte.

10. In the Timeline, Command-click (Mac) or Ctrl-click (Windows) the **VIDEO MONITOR** button on V2. The button turns green, indicating that you are soloing the V2 track, and the image changes to reveal V2 matte only, as shown in Figure 8.23.

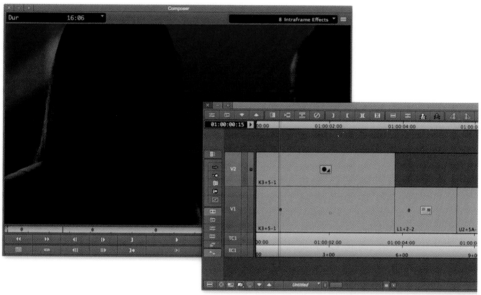

Figure 8.23
Solo the track with AniMatte to see the matte only.

11. (Optional) If needed, use the **RESHAPE** tool to refine the edges of the matte.

12. In the Timeline, again, Command-click (Mac) or Ctrl-click (Windows) the **VIDEO MONITOR** button on V2 to turn off solo.

13. Next, you'll need to track the movement of Kitty's face. Select this shape; then, in the Effect Editor, click the triangular opener to open the **TRACKING** parameter group.

14. Click the enable button on the first tracking point. The Tracking Window opens and a single tracker appears on the image.

15. Position the tracker on the edge of Kitty's right eye.

16. Because her head rotates on the Z axis, you'll need a second tracking point to calculate the change in size, not just position. Click the **CREATE NEW TRACKER** button.

17. Position the second tracker in the corner of Kitty's left eye.

18. Click the **START TRACKING** button. The system tracks the movement of Kitty's head. When finished, the tracking data is displayed in the Composer window, as shown in Figure 8.24.

Figure 8.24
The tracking data off Kitty's eyes will lock the shape to her head movement.

19. Close the Tracking Window and move the position indicator in the Composer window back to the first frame of the shot.

20. In the Effect Editor, enable the second tracking point in the Tracking parameter group.

21. Play the shot, watching the edges of the shapes for drift from their intended coverage area. Kitty's hair changes shape when she moves, but we only tracked her eye movement. The shape on her face doesn't maintain its coverage throughout the shot, as shown in Figure 8.25.

22. Move to the frame just before Kitty dips her head. Then click the **KEYFRAME** button to add a keyframe.

23. Move ahead approximately six or seven frames to the point where Kitty's movement stops. Add another keyframe.

Figure 8.25
The shape follows the movement of Kitty's head, but not the changes to her hair.

24. With this keyframe active, use the **Reshape** tool to adjust the shape over Kitty's face to better cover her face and hair. Solo the V2 track if necessary. (See Figure 8.26.)

Figure 8.26
Reshape the matte to cover Kitty's hair.

25. Click the active keyframe again; then press **COMMAND+C** (Mac) or **CTRL+C** (Windows) to copy its values.

26. Click the last keyframe in the track; then press **COMMAND+V** (Mac) or **CTRL+V** (Windows) to paste the values.

27. Scrub through the shot to verify the movement of the face shape.

28. Nice work! You can now use the matte to create the grade. Close the Effect Editor and enable **COLOR CORRECTION** mode.

29. Click on the shot **K3+5-1** on V2.

30. Using the HSL Master Controls, reduce the **SATURATION** to approximately **90** and the **GAIN** setting to **95**. The changes to the image are seen only on the background, and the resulting image is a very high quality grade. See the final image in Figure 8.27.

Figure 8.27
The finished grade.

Key concept: AniMatte can be used to produce very high quality spot corrections because the full latitude of the shot can be used for each region of the image.

Notes from the Colorist: Tracking, Shapes, and Chasing Rabbits

Do not underestimate the power of combining a good tracker with a shape for the purposes of color grading. I've worked in color-grading systems with terrible trackers and systems with terrific trackers; a terrific tracker changes the way you look at an image.

Keyframing can be both tedious and a time sink. A seemingly easy keyframing job can quickly devolve into a tedious frame-by-frame operation. But like a good chroma qualification, tracking can feel like a procedural operation that enables you to do interesting work such as isolating and grading a face, or even eyes on the face, as it moves through the frame. I encourage you to take the time to learn Symphony's tracker. It just might have a huge impact on the types of grades you attempt.

Tracking Shapes Can Raise the Level of Your Work

When you're happy with the overall correction of your image and your client asks if you can pull the faces up a bit more, you have a few choices:

■ You can go into Curves and try to lift the tonal range where the faces sit—but that brings up every part of the image in that tonal range, which may be harmful overall.

■ You can create an overall vignette that pulls up the faces, which often works on a static shot. But what if the faces are bouncing around the frame while the camera itself is moving? A big soft vignette will rarely solve that kind of problem.

■ You could draw a smaller oval, isolating the face a bit more precisely, and keyframe the oval. This works if you keep the shape nice and soft. Don't create an extreme grade if neither the face nor the camera is moving around too much.

■ You could draw a smaller oval, grade how you want—solving the specific problem the client is having—and track that oval to the face. It's a precise solution to a precise problem.

I like the last option the best. And it's almost always the first thing I attempt. Even on a simple shot, if the tracker nails the movement on the first pass, I'm done and I can move on. Fast. Efficient. What's not to like?

A good tracker (and Symphony has a pretty darn good tracker!) adds a level of precision to your secondary color grading, allowing for precisely targeted areas of isolation. But there's no reason to just stop with tracking faces, people, or objects.

Track the Camera to Re-light Your Footage

You can use your shapes to change the lighting of the scene and create pools of darkness where none existed before. It adds mood and interest while acting as a more subtle and natural version of a vignette. Colorists call this "re-lighting the scene."

It's as if we've placed our own flags in the scene—blocking some lights while letting others shine through. But there's a potential problem: The slightest tilt or the motion from a hand-held camera can completely reveal our artificial re-light. Tracking again comes to the rescue! This time, you want to track stationary objects in the frame. As the camera moves, so do these objects. The result: Your shape is moving around, locked to the background objects, and as people move through the frame they're moving through our newly relit scene. It looks completely natural. Our shape feels like it's part of the scene.

Tips on relighting:

- When selecting your tracking points, you want to select objects that are about the same distance from the camera as are the people. Otherwise, your shape will move too slowly (if you tracked distant mountains) or two quickly (if you tracked a blurry object right in front of the lens).

- Soft, rounded shapes are generally an easier sell. Unless the scene is lit with harsh lights, going soft is usually a good idea.

Just Remember: Don't Get Bogged Down

I've probably said this a few times in this book, but it's worth repeating: Don't chase rabbits down their holes. You will get stuck. And when it comes to tracking shapes onto images, this level of color grading can really slow down a session. For those moments when you decide the effort is worth the time, I suggest you glance at a clock and give yourself five minutes to determine whether tracking a face or re-lighting a scene is feasible. If you're not sure at the outset—and the client hasn't specifically asked for you to do so—inform the client that you want to spend a few minutes exploring...and then stick to the clock. Don't be afraid to call off the chase, let that rabbit go, and get back to doing the main work of the day.

—pi

Review/Discussion Questions

1. Name the three Intraframe effects that can be used for color grading.

2. Describe the characteristics that Intraframe effects have in common.

3. True or false: The Intraframe effects are found only in Symphony, not Media Composer.

4. Which tool can be used to define custom shapes, such as to outline an actor in a shot?

5. How is a vignette constructed?

6. Which Intraframe effect can be used to create a gradient?

7. What does the Magic Mask do?

8. How many trackers are needed to track a change in position on the X and Y axes? How many trackers if the object is moving toward or away from the camera?

9. What is one characteristic of a good point to be tracked?

10. Which effect(s) can be used to create vignettes?

Lesson 8 Keyboard Shortcuts

For more information, see "Effect Editor Reference for the Paint and AniMatte Effects" in Symphony's Help file.

Lesson 8 Keyboard Shortcuts

Shortcut	Result
Double-click an intraframe shape	Toggles between Selection tool and Reshape tool.
Alt-drag (Windows) or Option-drag (Mac) handle of object in Paint Effect	Rescales object from its center
Alt-click (Windows) or Option-click (Windows) the Send Backward button in the Paint tool	Sends object to the back layer
Alt-click (Windows) or Option-click (Mac) the Bring Forward button in the Paint tool	Brings object to the front layer
Option-click (Mac) or Alt-click (Windows) in the monitor while creating an Intraframe effect with the brush	Changes pointer to eyedropper to select foreground color from video image
Select Reshape, and then Alt-click (Windows) or Option-click (Mac) control point of join	Changes straight-edge join to smooth join or smooth join to straight-edge join
Select Reshape, and then Alt-click and drag (Windows) or Option-click and drag (Mac) either end of the direction bar	Allows movement of direction bar, independent of direction bar on opposite side of control point

Creating Shape-Based Secondaries

In this exercise, you will practice performing secondaries with shape-based qualifications.

Media Used:

Avid Color Grading (MC239) project > 2_Exercise Bins folder > Ex8_Intraframe Effects Exercise bin > Ex8_Spot Corrections and Vignettes sequence

Duration:

60 minutes

GOALS

- Perform spot corrections using the Paint Effect, Spot Color Effect, and AniMatte
- Track image elements
- Animate spot corrections using tracking data
- Create vignettes using the Paint Effect

Overview

The desert scene has some of the most interesting shots in the film, as well as a range of exposures and shot latitudes to deal with. In this exercise, you will use spot corrections to address specific issues on selected shots within the sequence. These have been marked with markers and have a defined goal. After completing those effects, move on to apply vignettes throughout the scene to finish grading the sequence.

As you work, here are some key points to keep in mind:

- You are free to apply any of the effects and techniques you've learned to accomplish the goal.

- Some of the shots have limited latitude. Be on the lookout for artifacts and banding.

- If using an AniMatte, you'll need to copy the clip onto a second video track yourself.

- When creating vignettes for the scene, feel free to experiment with different looks. Vignettes can be created with varying degrees of darkening and/or color around the edges. When you decide which one you like most, use it for the whole sequence.

- Above all, remember that the shots must match to create a cohesive scene.

To begin the exercise:

1. Open the project AVID COLOR GRADING (239) and the bin Ex8_INTRAFRAME EFFECTS EXERCISE.

2. Load the sequence Ex8_SPOT CORRECTIONS.

3. Move through the locators, performing spot corrections as directed.

Finishing the Grade

Many films and shows have a distinct look. Some are so stylized, they've become iconic. The final stage of the grading process is about creating the "look" of the piece. In this lesson, you will learn the various tools and techniques for doing so in Media Composer and Symphony.

Media Used: Avid Color Grading (MC239) project > 1_Lesson Bins folder > 9_Finishing the Grade bin > 9_Creating Looks sequence, 9_Keyframing Corrections sequence

Duration: 60 minutes

GOALS

- Define the term, purpose, and value of "looks"
- Explore useful tools and techniques for applying final creative corrections
- Identify common looks and how to create them
- Keyframe HSL and Curves adjustments
- Manage correction relationships across multiple sequences
- Conform the sequence to legal gamut range using the Safe Color Warnings and Safe Color Limiter

What's in a Look?

After you have established a primary grade on the scene, applied secondary corrections where needed, and achieved shot-to-shot consistency, you might want to apply a final correction or a stylistic "look" to the entire sequence or a portion of it. This involves stylizing all the shots in some way to fit the emotional tone of the scene (such as in narrative film and documentaries) or to express the artistic vision of the video (as in music videos and commercial spots). You might slightly increase saturation across the whole sequence to create richer colors, for example, or slightly darken all the shots and add a blue or green cast to enhance tension or suspense.

Especially at this juncture, you should be in close discussion with the stakeholders in the project—typically the film director or client. It is critical to understand the goal, vision, and emotional tone of the piece. In some projects, the look is expected to be largely consistent throughout. In others, it will vary from scene to scene. Understanding the role of the scene you are grading in the larger narrative will enable you to make informed creative choices to support, rather than distract from, the story arc.

With regard to the workflow, I am admittedly talking about a process that becomes quite fluid with experience. Colorists tend to simultaneously correct problems in the image and grade *toward* a look. Secondary corrections especially are often as much about achieving a look as they are about correcting problems in the image. This is particularly true in the case of vignettes, because those are often one of the last adjustments applied to the grade. For the purposes of organizing an organic process into the linear presentation of a book, however, it is helpful to examine this as a separate topic.

A look, also called a *treatment*, can be created manually or applied from preset templates. Some manufacturers of effects plug-ins specialize in creating preset looks. These can be useful during the offline edit to help you shape your vision and stimulate your creativity. They let you explore different looks for the scene very quickly to see which fits best. There are disadvantages to using them for the finished grade, however, including the following:

- Using plug-ins negates many of the workflow benefits of using Symphony's built-in color-correction tools.

- Without sufficient customization, your program looks like others that used the same plug-in.

- Using preset plug-ins can become a crutch that handicaps your own mastery of the tools.

The best way to boost your imagination and color sensitivity is to become a student of the use of color in art, photography, TV, and film. Study its use in different styles and genres; then practice re-creating the look in Symphony. Practice, practice, practice....

There are many great examples of distinct looks. Figures 9.1–9.5 show but a few.

Figure 9.1
A classic black-and-white treatment.

Figure 9.2
A gritty, urban look.

Figure 9.3
A bleach bypass treatment.

Figure 9.4
Blown-out highlights.

Figure 9.5
The *CSI: Miami* look.

Notes from the Colorist: Quickly Exploring Looks

I rarely use plug-ins for creating looks. I prefer to create them by hand. I just find it more personally satisfying. And as you break down looks, you'll come to realize they are all just manipulating the few core elements of contrast, saturation, and hue. Layer on top of them some blurred chroma or luma keys or use a transfer mode with a colored gradient, and you've just outlined the building blocks of most looks.

There is one plug-in I do like when creating looks—and I like it because it allows me to quickly iterate. This plug-in allows me to scan through dozens of variations of a bunch of basic styles of looks in just a few seconds. It allows me to quickly discount many different approaches and zero in on the look I want to pursue. I can then go in and break it apart or add more complexity to it in a very easy-to-use interface. This plug-in is Red Giant Software's Magic Bullet Looks 2. If you find yourself having to continually create looks and you work on the same computer day after day, it's a plug-in you should consider adding to your arsenal.

—pi

Techniques for Applying Looks

In the process of creating a look, you might make substantial changes to the color values of the whole sequence, to entire scenes, or to selected shots independently. You already know how to apply a correction to a single segment. Let's look at a couple options for applying a look to an entire sequence or to designated sections of the sequence.

Applying a Look as a Program Relationship

For short programs, such as a 30-second commercial spot, you may want to apply a single look to the entire sequence. In Symphony, this can be done using a program track relationship. (Options for Media Composer are discussed next.)

To apply a look to an entire sequence:

1. Load the color-corrected sequence. Enable COLOR CORRECTION mode.

2. Since this is track-based, make sure the correct top-most video track is selected and no higher video tracks are selected.

3. Set the correction relationship to PROGRAM TRACK.

4. Make adjustments to the correction tools of choice to apply the grade. The look will be applied to the entire sequence track.

5. Review the sequence to see how the look appears on the various shots.

For most programs longer than a minute or two, you will probably adjust the look of the program in multiple locations of the sequence. Rather than applying the adjustment to the entire track, you will need to be more specific in your adjustment.

To apply a look to a scene or region of the sequence:

1. Load the color-corrected sequence.

2. Enable COLOR CORRECTION mode.

3. Open the Correction settings and select the FEATURES tab.

4. Enable the USE MARKS FOR SEGMENT CORRECTION check box.

5. Set the correction relationship to PROGRAM SEGMENT.

6. Set IN and OUT marks around the scene or region to be graded, as shown in Figure 9.6.

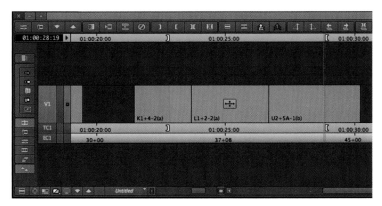

Figure 9.6
The sequence set for a program segment correction.

7. Make adjustments to the correction tools of choice to apply the grade. The grade will appear as a program segment correction—a dotted blue line at the top of the segments—on all marked segments.

Note: Even if only a portion of a segment is included within the marks, the correction will be applied to the full segment.

Applying Corrections to Filler

You can use either Media Composer or Symphony to apply a look to a sequence or portion of a sequence using a filler track. This can be a useful approach if you are grading a multilayered sequence without flattening it. The look grade can be applied to the uppermost track, encompassing all tracks below it.

To create a look for your entire sequence, you need to add a new video track to the sequence and create a Color Correction effect for the entire track. This track should be higher than the tracks you want to affect.

To apply a look to an entire sequence:

1. Load the color-corrected sequence.

2. In Source/Record mode, choose CLIP > NEW VIDEO TRACK. Or, to select a particular track number, press COMMAND+OPTION+Y (Mac) or CTRL+ALT+Y (Windows) and select the desired track number from the Add Track dialog box.

3. Select the track selector for the new track and deselect any other video track selectors. Also, deselect all audio track selectors.

4. Monitor the new track.

5. Make adjustments to the correction tools of choice to apply the grade. The look will be applied to the entire sequence track, as shown in Figure 9.7.

6. Review the sequence to see how the look appears on the various shots.

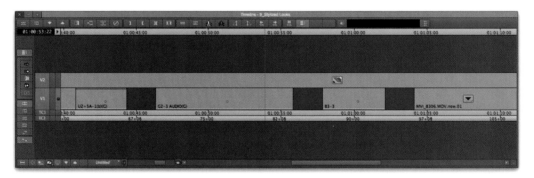

Figure 9.7
A look correction applied to the full sequence via a filler track.

Tip: The filler technique can be a great way to audition different looks. Grades can be created, then saved as templates. In the client session, replace the effect on the filler track in turn with each of the saved templates.

The same technique can be used to apply a look to a scene or section of the program. You simply need to delineate the scene or region with Add Edit before adding the effect.

Note: Add Edit is one of the few edit functions that can be used in Color Correction mode.

To apply a look to a scene or region of the sequence:

1. Follow steps 1–4 in the preceding instructions to create a new filler track.

2. Command-click (Mac) or Ctrl-click (Windows) at the edit point marking the first frame of the region to be graded. The position indicator will snap to the edit point.

3. Click the **ADD EDIT** button. A match frame edit appears in the track.

4. Command-click (Mac) or Ctrl-click (Windows) at the edit point marking the end of the region to be graded, and add another edit point.

5. Set the correction relationship to **CC EFFECT** (Symphony only).

6. Place the position indicator within the filler segment and verify that the filler track is active.

7. Make adjustments to the correction tools of choice to apply the grade. The Color Correction effect icon will appear on the region with the adjustment, as shown in Figure 9.8.

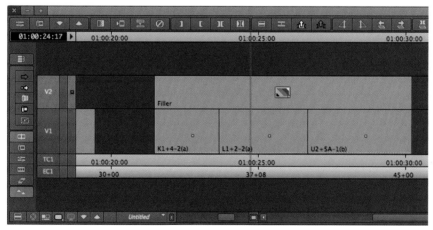

Figure 9.8
A look correction applied to a scene via a filler track.

All segments beneath the effect will be seen with the final grade when the top track is monitored. Because the effect covers multiple shots, you may wish to keyframe adjustments to the effect to change over time. The techniques for doing so are covered in the next section.

Tip: If you remove the Color Correction effect from the filler segment, the edits that define the region will be removed with the effect. You will need to add them again before adding another effect.

Keyframing Color Changes

Both Media Composer and Symphony enable you to animate most color corrections over time using keyframes in the Effect Editor. The color-correction controls that can be animated are as follows:

- HSL
- HSL Hue Offsets
- Levels Chrominance
- Levels Luma
- Levels: red, green, and blue
- Levels: master control
- Curves: red, green, and blue
- Curves: master curve
- Sec Standard Vectors
- Sec Ellipses (Custom Vectors)

Conversely, it may be helpful to think about which controls *cannot* be keyframed. They are as follows:

- HSL Luma Ranges
- Channels

Keyframing color adjustments is done in one of two ways. All parameters that contain numeric values can be adjusted in either the Effect Editor or the Color Correction tool. Curves, however, can be adjusted only in the Color Correction tool. As an example of each, we present the steps for keyframing changes to the HSL master controls and the Curves tool.

In the Avid Learning Series   **It is assumed that you are familiar with the fundamentals of working with keyframes in the Effect Editor. For additional training on working with keyframes, see the companion book in this series** *Media Composer 6: Professional Effects and Compositing.*

Keyframing HSL Adjustments

When keyframing color adjustments in HSL or secondary controls, the process is the same as keyframing any other effect: Apply a keyframe to the desired parameters or parameter groups, modify the value of the parameter at the keyframe, and Avid will automatically animate the value change between keyframes.

To keyframe a correction change in HSL:

1. Open the project **AVID COLOR GRADING (239)** and the bin **9_FINISHING**.

2. Load the sequence **9_KEYFRAMING CORRECTIONS**.

3. Enter **COLOR CORRECTION** mode.

4. Set up the Composer monitors to display the **VECTORSCOPE, YC WAVEFORM**, and **CURRENT** in the configuration of your choice.

5. Set the **VIDEO QUALITY** menu to **FULL QUALITY**.

6. Move the position indicator to the first shot, **G2-3(A)**—the now-familiar shot of the burlesque singer. Make sure V2 is active, as this is the correction effect you want to change.

   The opening of the shot has an intense red wash from the stage lights. There is already a Curves correction applied to this shot. You will keyframe an adjustment to HSL to maintain a lowered saturation at the start, then boost saturation after the red lights dim.

7. Select the **HSL > MASTER** tab (Symphony), or the **HSL > CONTROLS** tab (Media Composer).

8. Click the **EFFECTS MODE** button to open the Effect Editor. (You may wish to reposition the Effect Editor to better fit into the interface arrangement.)

9. Click the triangular openers to display the **SRC HSL > CONTROLS** parameter group, as shown in Figure 9.9. (Even if working on Media Composer, you will still see Symphony's correction groups because the base grade was done on Symphony.)

Note: If you do not see the individual keyframe tracks shown here, click the Show/ Hide Keyframe Graphs button in the bottom-right corner of the Effect Editor.

Figure 9.9
The Effect Editor displaying the Src HSL > Controls keyframe tracks.

10. Move the position indicator to the point where the red lights on the background begin to fade. Then right-click the **MASTER** keyframe track and choose **ADD KEYFRAME**.

11. Advance the position indicator to where the red lights finish fading. Add a keyframe again to the **SRC HSL > CONTROLS > MASTER** track.

12. With the second keyframe active, click the triangular opener to expand the **MASTER** group; then select the **SATURATION** slider.

13. Increase **SATURATION** to approximately **140**. To do this, you can drag the slider; alternatively, press **SHIFT+RIGHT ARROW** to increment the value by tens.

14. Play the effect. The saturation level begins at 100 with the red wash, then increases to 140 between the keyframes.

Note: To relocate a keyframe, Option-drag (Mac) or Alt-drag (PC). To delete a keyframe, simply select it then press Delete on the keyboard.

Keyframing Curves Adjustments

Keyframing changes to a curves graph is a slightly different process. Because of the unique controls enabled by the graph, there is no numerical equivalent to it in the Effect Editor. In this case, the Effect Editor is simply a tool used to add and remove keyframes. All changes to the curve graphs are made in the Color Correction tool itself and will be animated over time.

To keyframe a correction change in Curves:

1. For this section, you will use the same sequence, **9_KEYFRAMING CORRECTIONS**.

2. Move the position indicator to the second group of segments, from the rooftop scene. The director wants to exit the final shot with a luma bloom.

3. If it's not already active, switch to **COLOR CORRECTION** mode; then select **CURVES** and, if you are using Symphony, a **CC EFFECT** relationship.

4. Activate the V2 track, then open the Effect Editor. This correction effect already has HSL adjustments in place, including Clip Low Clip High. To see these, expand the HSL triangular opener. (See Figure 9.10.) You won't be working in HSL, so close up the triangular opener again for now.

Note: Color-correction keyframes are also visible in the Current monitor.

5. Place the position indicator on the frame in the last segment where our hero drops his cigarette before exiting. Then, in the Effect Editor, right-click the **CURVES** track and choose **ADD KEYFRAME**.

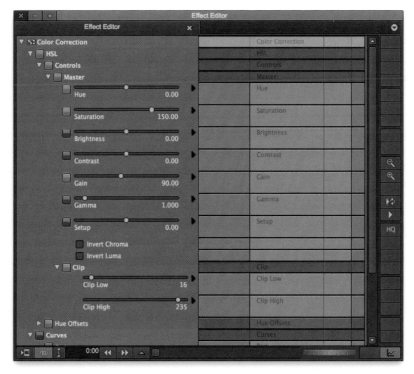

Figure 9.10
The Effect Editor, displaying the previously applied HSL adjustments.

6. Move the position indicator to the final frame. Again, right-click the **Curves** track in the Effect Editor and choose **Add Keyframe**. The Effect Editor should resemble Figure 9.11.

Figure 9.11
The Effect Editor, displaying the Curves keyframes.

7. On the master curve, add a mid-gamma control point.

8. Drag the control point up to the upper-left corner, completely whiting out the screen. (Note: If Clip Low Clip High weren't active, this would create and illegal signal!)

9. Play the effect to see the change.

Key concept: To animate changes to Curves, keyframes can be added in the Effect Editor, but all changes must be made through the Color Correction tool itself.

Creating Popular Looks

Any of the color-correction tools in Media Composer or Symphony can be used to create or shape the final look. Each can contribute to the style of the image in its own way. As such, the possibilities are endless. The only effective preparation for such work is to practice using Color Correction mode and to have a good understanding of what specific corrections will do. Here are a few ideas for getting you started creating a stylized look.

We present the curves graphs for several of the stylized looks presented in the following sections. Please note that these settings are only suggested starting points; looking at your footage and scopes will give you more information about what adjustments to make.

Keep in mind as you work on any of these styles that the instructions are meant as starting points. Often, you will need to fine-tune these adjustments. Also, these adjustments are somewhat relative; people have a different sense, for example, of what constitutes a cool or warm scene.

Monochrome Looks

From classic black and white—the *original* film look—to *film noir*, sepia tones, and more, the monochrome image is alive and well today, making regular appearances in films, music videos, commercials, and more. But there's more to a good monochrome image than just dropping the saturation to zero.

Classic Black and White

The classic black-and-white image is a medium- to high-contrast image. It has bright grays, clean whites, deep blacks, and a midrange gamma.

To create a classic black-and-white look:

1. Reduce the **Master Saturation** setting to **0**.

2. Set the master curve black point to **16, 16**. This will clip the luma at the legal limit of 16.

3. Set the master curve white point to **235, 235**. This will clip the luma at the legal limit of 235.

4. Create an S-curve on the master curve, as shown in Figure 9.12. The strength of the S-curve will depend on the shot itself.

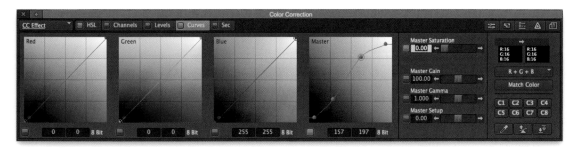

Figure 9.12
The Curves group, set to create a classic black-and-white look.

5. Adjust the upper midtone control point to set the flesh tones between **50** and **75%**.

Tip: If you're trying to create an antique look in the black-and-white treatment, lift your blacks to create a faded-film look.

Film Noir

Film noir, as implied by the name (literally *black film* in French), is characterized visually as a dark, black-and-white image. The dominant blacks and shadows reinforce the typically dark themes of the storyline.

To create a *film noir* look:

1. Reduce **Master Saturation** setting to 0.

2. Set the master curve black point to **16, 16**.

3. Set the master curve white point to **235, 235**.

4. On the master curve, add a lower gamma control point. Adjust the point to push the majority of the image below **50%**, as shown in Figure 9.13.

Figure 9.13
The Curves group, set to create a *film noir* look.

Sepia Tone

A sepia-tone image is designed to emulate an old, yellowed photographic print. It is characterized by reduced contrast, lifted blacks and a yellowish, reddish, or brownish cast. The "older" the image, the flatter is will be, and typically the stronger the color cast. Note that brighter images will require a stronger cast than darker images.

To create a sepia-tone look:

1. Reduce the **MASTER SATURATION** setting to **0**.

2. On the master curve, raise the black point at least to **20** or above, depending on the intended "age" of the film (**M: 0, 20**).

3. On the master curve, drag the white point down to **220** or below, as shown in Figure 9.14 (**M: 256, 220**).

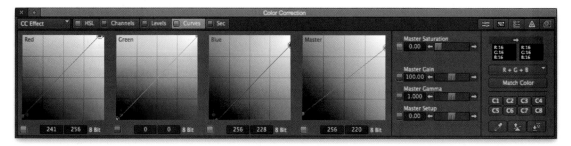

Figure 9.14
The Curves group, set to create a sepia look.

4. To create the sepia tint, start with the blue curve. Drag the black point to the right (**B:30, 0**). This will shift the blacks toward yellow.

5. On the blue curve, drag the white point downward, now pushing the highlights toward yellow, too (**B: 256, 216**). Adjust the lower midtone control point to push the majority of the image below **50%**.

6. On the red curve, create similar adjustments to shift the curve toward red. Raise the output value of both the black point (**R: 0, 12**) and white point (**R: 246, 256**). Typically, the red adjustment will be less than the blue channel adjustment, also shown in Figure 9.14. Select the **HSL > HUE OFFSETS** tab.

7. Adjust the **HIGHLIGHT** color wheel to create a yellow orange cast (refer to Figure 9.14).

8. (Optional) In Symphony, you have an alternative option of creating the tint using the Master Hue Offset wheel. You may choose to add a slight offset to the **MASTER** color wheel. This adjustment, however, will introduce a tint to the entire image, including the blacks. Depending on your goals, this may be undesirable.

Note: The reduced contrast in the master curve usually provides the latitude neces-sary to create the tint without causing illegal levels using the technique here. Clip each color channel if necessary to prevent creating an illegal signal.

Notes from the Colorist: How the Singularity Effect Can Improve Your Looks

Creating looks is a frustrating endeavor for most beginning colorists. They struggle with knowing which tools to use and how to adjust them. My solution is to teach them about the singularity effect.

In astronomy, *singularity* is another word for black hole. A black hole is a small dot in space filled with an enormous amount of mass. This mass creates a gravitational pull from which not even light can escape. The only way to detect a singularity is by looking next to it. Because light can't escape, all you see is black; you need to look elsewhere to detect it.

This natural phenomenon is a great way to think about building a convincing look. After all, 90% of the images you'll ever grade share a single constant: Somewhere in the image is black. Black is the absence of color. It's something the human mind understands at a foundational level. If something has color then it isn't black. If you want your looks to be convincing, the fastest path is by relentlessly controlling your blacks and keeping them free of tints or coloration. This isn't opinion, it's a reality of physics. Case in point: If you're going for a faded film effect, what's the first thing you do? You lift your blacks. Why? Because you're bypassing the physical world around you, in which the only time black isn't black is on old faded film stock.

—pi

High-Contrast Looks

The looks in this category boost the image contrast through the use of S-curves. They differ in the degree to which they increase contrast and in how they treat saturation.

Bleach Bypass

Bleach bypass, also called *skip bleach*, is a photochemical process for developing celluloid film in both still photography and motion pictures. The result of leaving out the bleach is a high-contrast, low-saturation image. (See Figure 9.15.)

Figure 9.15
The poker game with a bleach bypass look.

To create a bleach-bypass look:

1. Set the master curve white point to **235, 235**. This will clip the luma at the legal limit of 235.

2. Create an S-curve on the master curve with points at about **40%** and **60%**.

3. Decrease the **SATURATION** setting to approximately **50%–60%**, as shown in Figure 9.16.

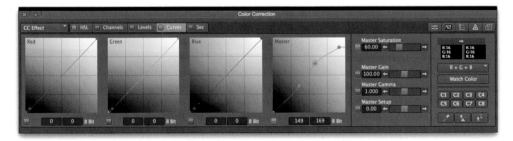

Figure 9.16
The Curves group, set to create a bleach-bypass look.

Punch

The punchy look utilizes a similar S-curve to the bleach bypass, increasing contrast without desaturating the image. With a punchy look, however, you may choose to increase contrast to make the colors pop even more. This technique gives the image a striking look, popular in commercials and promos.

To create a punchy look:

1. In the **Curves** tab, add two control points to the master curve, one in the upper gamma and another in the lower gamma.

2. Drag the lower control point down to crush the blacks slightly.

3. Drag the upper control point to crush the whites, as shown in Figure 9.17. The midtones become stretched, giving the shots dramatically more contrast and saturation.

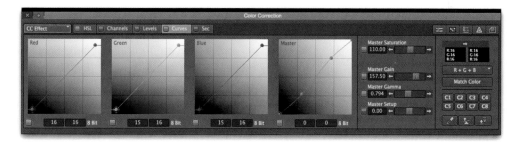

Figure 9.17
A slight S-curve on the master curve starts the punchy look.

4. You need to limit the RGB and master curves to a 16–235 range to keep the effect legal. To begin, click the black point in the red curve, type **16** in the **Input** box, and press **Return** (Mac) or **Enter** (Windows). Then type **16** in the **Output** box and press **Return** (Mac) or **Enter** (Windows).

5. Repeat step 4 for each black point in the green, blue, and master curves.

Tip: You can copy and paste the value (16 or 235) from one Input or Output box into another box. Just make sure to first select the correct control point. Press Tab to move from box to box.

6. Click the white point in the red curve, type **235** in the **Input** box, and press **Return** (Mac) or **Enter** (Windows). Then type **235** in the **Output** box and press **Return** (Mac) or **Enter** (Windows).

7. Repeat step 6 for each white point in green, blue, and master curves.

8. (Optional) Try combining this correction with the Film Grain plug-in from the Illusion effects (in the Effects Palette) to further enhance this look.

Tip: The inverse of the punchy look is a soft pastel. This can be created by raising the gamma and reducing saturation slightly.

Blown-Out Whites

This look is a high-key image, characterized by blooming and clipped whites, slightly desaturated colors, and dark blacks, as shown in Figure 9.18. This look is especially popular in advertising and music videos.

Figure 9.18
The image of Zero, with and without the blown-out look.

To create a look with blown-out highlights:

1. Set the master curve white point to **235, 235**. This will clip the luma at the legal limit of 235.

2. Set a control point at approximately **60%** and lift it up to approximately **75% (M: 130, 180)**.

3. On the **HSL > MASTER** tab, increase the master **GAIN** to make the highlights bloom to the desired level.

4. Decrease the master **GAMMA** to restore some of the midtones.
    (See Figure 9.19.)

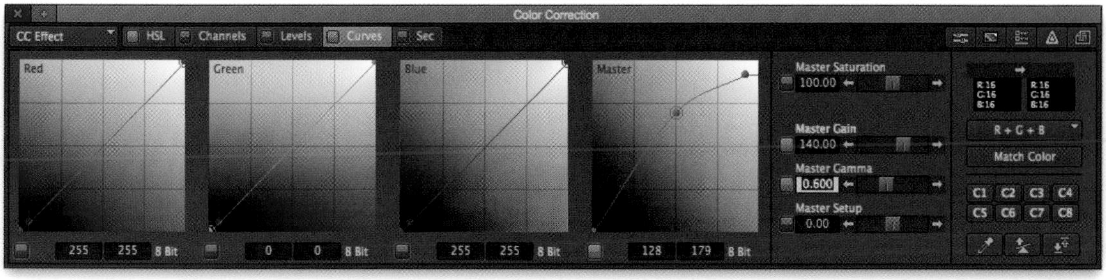

Figure 9.19
The Curves settings used to create the blown-out highlights look.

Changing the Color Temperature

An effective way of stylizing a scene is to change the color temperature of the scene. There are common conventions used to support the emotion of the scene. Cool tones—blues, greens, and grays—tend to be associated with tension, anxiety, depression, etc. Warm tones—yellows and reds—tend to be associated with joy, happiness, contentedness, etc. Saturation is an extension of this; bright, saturated colors convey happy feelings. Darker, muted colors are associated with darker feelings.

Tip: Changing the color temperature can also be used to convey location.

Warm and Saturated

A look popularized in recent years by the show *CSI: Miami* is a warm and saturated look. This look is most easily accomplished with the HSL controls, as presented here.

To create a warm and saturated look:

1. Select the **HSL > MASTER** tab.

2. Boost the **SATURATION** setting to approximately **150**.

3. Reduce the **GAIN** setting to approximately **90**.

4. Select the **HSL > HUE OFFSETS** tab.

5. Adjust the **HLT** wheel to create a strong yellow cast in the highlights.

6. Adjust the **MID** wheel to create a slight yellow cast in the shadows. Do not change the balance of the shadows. (See Figure 9.20.)

Figure 9.20
The HSL Hue Offsets and controls used to create the *CSI: Miami* look.

Urban Grit

No crime drama would be the same in pastels or bright punchy colors. To give a scene that tense, gritty feel, darken the image and push it toward blue or green.

To create an urban-grit look:

1. Select the CURVES tab.

2. On the master curve, set a control point in the mid-shadow range, at approximately **15%**.

3. Lower the control point to crush the blacks (**M: 43, 24**).

4. Set a midtone control point and elevate it to restore the midtones (**M: 140, 140**).

5. On the blue curve, drag the black control point up the left edge, increasing blue in the shadows.(**B: 0, 16**).

6. Also on the blue curve, drag the white control point left, boosting the blue gain (**B: 225, 255**).

7. Increase the gain in the green channel as well. Drag the white point left until an acceptable highlight tone is achieved (**G: 234, 255**). To see the cumulative adjustments to Curves, see Figure 9.21.

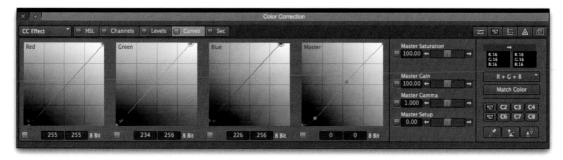

Figure 9.21
The Curves settings, to create a tense, crime-thriller look.

Day for Night

Day for night (DFN) is a popular technique due to the production conveniences of shooting during the day compared to the challenges of a full night production. To create a suitable DFN grade, you must create a dark blue desaturated image with balanced highlights.

To create a day-for-night look:

1. Select the **Curves** tab.

2. Darken the image by reducing gain on the master curve. Drag the white control point down until the image is quite dark (**M: 255,170**).

3. Add a low gamma point and lift the lower midtones to restore whatever detail is necessary.

4. On the blue curve, set a high gamma control point and lift the point dramatically to create a strong blue cast (**B: 125, 200**).

5. On the green curve, set a center gamma point and drag it quite strongly toward magenta (**G: 170, 70**). Repeat on the red curve (**R: 170, 70**).

6. (Optional) It may be necessary to lock the black levels at 16 on the red and green channels to prevent illegal black levels. Activate the black point on each curve; then set the **Input** and **Output** values to **16**. Figure 9.22 shows the full set of adjustments on the Curves tool.

7. Finish the look by desaturating the image. Lower the **Master Saturation** setting to approximately **80**.

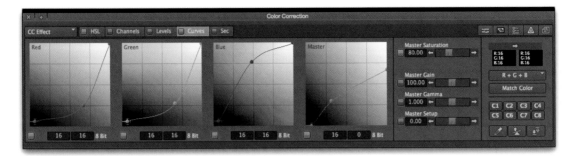

Figure 9.22
The Curves adjustments to create a day-for-night look.

Managing Multiple Grades

In the process of exploring looks for a scene, you may find that you duplicate the sequence multiple times. The challenge, then, is how to efficiently manage the grades and integrate the desired one into the final sequence.

Symphony includes a function by which you can merge and update color corrections between sequences. In post houses that produce shows with limited turnaround time, these functions are used to deliver under tight deadlines. The online editor can start grading even before the picture is locked. Once it's finished, the picture-lock version is merged with the initial grade, thereby transferring all the corrections to the final sequence. The online editor then has only a small number of additional changes to make before the final master is ready for air.

In other workflows, the ability to merge corrections between sequences opens additional creative options:

- Individual scenes can be graded in isolation, then merged with the master sequence.

- Scenes of similar locations can be graded side by side, then merged back into the final master.

- Duplicate copies of the program can be used to experiment with different looks. Whichever look is preferred can be merged with the master.

Merging and Updating Sequences

The following steps can be used, regardless of the workflow in which it is necessary to merge or update sequences.

To work with two copies of a sequence and then merge the corrections:

1. Create a first version of your sequence.

2. (Optional) Click the **COLOR CORRECTION MODE** button in the Timeline palette and make initial color adjustments to the sequence.

3. Save the sequence. Then create one or two copies of the sequence.

    How you handle copies of the sequence depends on the requirements of your workflow. You need only two versions of the sequence: the original and one copy. For example, the colorist might keep the original while the editor works on the copy. However, it might be safer to keep the original as a backup and work with two new copies.

Tip: Name your copies clearly. For example, if you create two copies and also keep the original, you might use the extensions .Editor, .Colorist, and .Original to distinguish the three versions.

4. Continue to work on the two copies independently.

5. When you are ready to merge the two copies, click the **SOURCE/RECORD** button to enter Source/Record mode.

6. Load one copy of the sequence into the Source monitor and the other into the Record monitor. (You can load a copy into either monitor. The only difference is that your Avid editing application merges into the sequence in the Record monitor unless you instruct it to create a new sequence for the merge in step 10.)

7. Enter **COLOR CORRECTION** mode.

8. Right-click in the **COLOR CORRECTION** tool and choose **MERGE CORRECTION**, as shown in Figure 9.23.

Figure 9.23
The Merge Correction options.

Note: Flatten Correction, also shown in the right-click menu in Figure 9.23, changes all corrections in a sequence to segment relationships. This enables you to safely alter a segment without affecting other segments. For more information, see the Symphony Help article, "Flattening Color-Corrected Sequences."

9. Select the source and program relationships you want your Avid editing application to use when deciding which segments to update in the merging process. By default, all available relationships are selected.

Note: Source segment corrections cannot be merged. Be aware of this, as it may influence the relationship you choose to use for initial grades.

10. Open the IN CASE OF CONFLICT menu and select an option to control how the system resolves conflicts between the two copies of the sequence:

   • **Prefer Source Sequence.** This resolves conflicts by preferring the information in the sequence you loaded into the Source monitor.
   • **Prefer Record Sequence.** This resolves conflicts by preferring the information in the sequence you loaded into the Record monitor.
   • **Prefer Latest.** This resolves conflicts by preferring the most recent information. This is the default setting.

11. Select CREATE NEW SEQUENCE if you want your Avid editing application to create a new copy of the sequence and merge into that copy. If you deselect this option, the Avid editing application merges the two copies into the sequence that is currently in the Timeline.

12. Click OK. The Avid editing application merges the two existing sequences, based on the options you have selected. The merged sequence appears in the Timeline.

Delivering Safe Colors

If you are grading a program, without exception you are responsible for the video signal on the final master tape. You must make sure that the program's signal does not exceed the broadcaster's delivery requirements at any time.

Most broadcast companies set specific limits for the composite signal and luma range. Programs that do not meet these limits are not normally accepted for broadcast. With the global transition to HD, many simply specify the RGB gamut and apply the same limits to the digital SD signal. For example, a typical set of limits for broadcast in the U.S. and Europe will limit RGB to 0% and 100% (or 0mV and 700mV), which equates to 16–235 (8-bit systems) or 64–940 (10-bit systems).

Slight variations may be permitted, whereby the signal will be hard-limited at, say, −10mV on the low end and 710mV on the high end. Some broadcast standards may be even stricter than these values.

Avid provides two ways for you to ensure that your program is in compliance with delivery specs:

■ Safe Color Warnings

■ Safe Color Limiter

Both Media Composer and Symphony enable you to set three different types of safe color limits. The values set for safe color limits determine how and when the system will warn and limit the signal. You can limit the composite signal range, the luminance range, and the RGB gamut, which refers to the intensity of each individual color channel.

Using Safe Color Warnings

Safe Color Warnings is an alert system that notifies you if adjustments to an image are creating illegal chroma or luma values. Having been alerted to the fact, you can take corrective actions, making adjustments to the grade in the Color Correction tools.

The system can warn you when any of three different types of safe color limits are exceeded: the composite signal range, the luma range, or the RGB gamut. You control the Safe Colors feature by selecting options in the Safe Color Settings dialog box.

Note: While you can set the Safe Color limits and warning levels at any time, we recommend that you set them when you begin the color-correction process.

To select Safe Color options:

1. Open the **SAFE COLORS** settings in the Project window or click the **SAFE COLORS** button in the Color Correction tool.

2. Set the desired limits according to the delivery specs.

3. Set the **ACTION** drop-down menu to **WARN**, as shown in Figure 9.24. (In the Color Correction tool, the Safe Colors button appears orange if Effect Colors or Video is selected and Limit or Warn is selected. Otherwise, the button appears black.)

Figure 9.24
The Safe Colors values affect how the system treats illegal values.

With Warn enabled, Media Composer and Symphony impose a small warning icon over the Current monitor if the system detects signals outside the Safe Color limits. As shown in Figure 9.25, you see an orange Safe Color warning triangle in the top-left corner of the image, along with warning indicators for each of the Safe Color value types that are currently set to Warn.

Figure 9.25
The Safe Color Warning indicates that luminance exceeds the high and low limits. All other values are within acceptable limits.

Warning color bars appear in one of three places in a column:

- At the top (indicating a level that is too high)
- At the bottom (indicating a level that is too low)
- In the center (indicating a level that is within limits)

Using the Safe Color Limiter Effect

In addition to using the Color Correction tool to achieve safe broadcast limits, you can use the Safe Color Limiter effect to clamp levels to safe color limits. The Safe Color Limiter effect can be used to effectively limit the voltages output in the final sequence. Depending on its configuration, you can limit luma, total composite amplitude, and the RGB color gamut. Both high and low limiting is supported.

Safe color limiting is processed in hardware and, if a color-space conversion is not required, it will run in real time and process simultaneously with any other hardware effect. By default, the Safe Color Limiter effect uses the limits set in the Safe Color settings.

To apply the Safe Color Limiter effect:

1. Press **COMMAND+Y** (Mac) or **CTRL+Y** (Windows) to create a new video track above all existing tracks. (This step can be omitted if an empty track already exists at the top of your sequence.)

2. Press **COMMAND+8** (Mac) or **CTRL+8** (Windows) to open the Effect Palette. Then select the **IMAGE** category.

3. Drag the **SAFE COLOR LIMITER** effect to the new track to apply it over the entire sequence.

4. Enter **EFFECT** mode. The Effect Editor opens, revealing the parameters for the effect.

The following parameter groups are available in this effect:

▪ Source Monitor Analysis

▪ Composite Luma Levels

▪ RGB Levels

The Source Monitor Analysis Parameter

This parameter enables you to view the colors being limited by the Safe Color Limiter effect. These are displayed as an overlay in the Source monitor. Two options are available from the pop-up menu:

▪ **Source Monitoring–Off.** This disables the overlay. The sequence is still limited as specified, and the limited image is displayed in the Effect Preview monitor.

▪ **Highlight Out of Range Colors.** This displays the limited colors using five different colored pixels, as shown in Figure 9.26.

Figure 9.26
The Source monitor analysis on a sepia-tone image. Highlighted pixels in this image are low-limited.

The colors used are are as follows:

- **Yellow.** This indicates pixels that fall outside the composite limits.
- **White.** This indicates pixels that fall outside of the luma limits.
- **Red.** This indicates pixels that fall outside the RGB gamut limits for red.
- **Green.** This indicates pixels that fall outside the RGB gamut limits for green.
- **Blue.** This indicates pixels that fall outside of the RGB gamut limits for blue.

The Composite/Luma Levels Parameter

This parameter enables you to limit the total composite amplitude and the luma component of the signal. The following options are available:

- **Enable button.** This enables composite and luma limiting. This parameter group is enabled by default.

- **Composite L.** This sets the minimum allowable composite amplitude. Unless your delivery-requirements document lists a different value, it is strongly recommended that you set this parameter to –20 IRE.

- **Composite H.** This sets the maximum allowable composite amplitude. This should be set as specified in your delivery-requirements document. If no limit is specified, the value of 110 IRE is recommended.

- **Composite Units.** This enables you to specify the unit of measure for the composite limits. Both IRE and mVolts are supported.

- **Luma L.** This sets the minimum allowable luma voltage. This parameter is usually set to 7.5 IRE or 0mV.

- **Luma H.** This sets the maximum allowable luma voltage. This parameter is usually set to 100 IRE or 700mV.

- **Luma Units.** This enables you to specify the unit of measure for the luma limits. The units IRE, mVolts, 8 bit, and % are supported. It is recommended that you set this parameter to either IRE or mVolts, as specified in your delivery-requirements document.

Note: The primary purpose of composite limiting is to limit voltage levels for a standard-definition broadcast. Therefore, composite and luma limiting is always performed in the ITU-R BT.601 color space. High-definition signals will be color-space converted from REC.709 to REC.601, limited, then converted back to REC.709.

The RGB Levels Parameter

This parameter enables you to limit the signal's RGB gamut. The following settings are available:

- **Enable Button.** This enables RGB limiting. This parameter group is enabled by default.

- **RGB Gamut L.** This sets the minimum allowable R, G, and B voltage. This is usually set to 0mV.

- **RGB Gamut H.** This sets the maximum allowable R, G, and B voltage. This parameter is usually set to 700mV.

- **RGB Units.** This enables you to specify the unit of measure for the RGB limits. The units IRE, mVolts, 8 bit, and % are supported. It is recommended that you set this parameter to mVolts.

Using the Safe Color Limiter Effect in Standard-Definition Video

If the standard-definition video delivery requirements specify composite and luma limits, you should set these four limits as specified in the delivery-requirements document. RGB limiting is increasingly being specified and should be considered if it is in your delivery spec. Conveniently, limiting the RGB gamut to 0mV and 700mV *also* automatically limits the C_R and C_B components to 0mV and 700mV. If you wish to limit the color difference signals, you should leave RGB limiting enabled. Because a color-space conversion is not required, the limiter will run in real time and will not affect or limit the real-time performance of your system.

Using the Safe Color Limiter Effect in High-Definition Video

If you are working in high-definition video, you need to first convert the color space and then limit. Any portion of your sequence that already contains an effect *or* a color correction will need to be rendered.

To apply the effect to an HD clip:

1. Apply a program correction to the entire sequence that enables only the Luma Clip parameter. (The Luma Clip parameter is located on the **HSL > Controls > Master** tab.) This should be done on every track in the sequence. It will effectively limit the luma portion of the signal as required.

2. Apply a Safe Color Limiter effect to an empty track above all existing tracks.

3. Disable the Composite/Luma limiter and set the RGB limiters to **0mV** and **700mV**. This will limit the C_R and C_B components to **0mV** and **700mV**, as is often specified in a high-definition delivery-requirements document.

Using the limiter in this manner does not add additional effects that will require rendering. You will still need to render any effects that exceed what can be processed in real time. Depending on the complexity of the sequence, it may be necessary to render the sequence to achieve real-time output. Effects rendering is covered in the next section.

Rendering Effects with ExpertRender

If your Avid editing system includes output hardware—either Avid DX hardware or third-party I/O hardware—you can preview Color Correction effects in real time. Depending on system performance, there may be instances where you need to render one or more effects, particularly with multilayered effects.

Rendering the effects also gives you the flexibility to output from other Avid systems. For instance, if grading in Symphony using relationships and Boris BCC plug-ins, both of which may be unavailable on Media Composer or Newscutter systems in the same facility, rendering the sequence would enable it to be opened, played, and output from those systems.

You will need to render in the following cases:

- Multilayered effects exceed the real-time capabilities of your system.

- The sequence will be output from another system without the same toolset.

- If you are using a software-only configuration of Avid Media Composer, you must render Color Correction effects before you output the sequence to tape or any other medium.

In the Avid Learning Series   We cover one method for rendering; you can use this for all rendering situations. Additional methods of rendering effects are covered in greater detail in the companion book in this series, *Media Composer 6: Professional Effects and Compositing*.

Media Composer and Symphony both include a function called Expert Render. Designed to make rendering easy for the editor, ExpertRender analyzes a group of effects to determine what needs rendering and what can be left as a real-time effect. Using ExpertRender, you can wait until you've color-corrected your sequence, and then render the effects in a batch while you take a break.

Tip: Save your sequence before rendering effects in a batch.

Always render at 16-bit resolution. This will extend the data range for effects processing and ensure the highest quality.

To set up the system for high-quality, 16-bit rendering:

1. Open the MEDIA CREATION settings and click the RENDER tab.

2. For EFFECTS PROCESSING, select 16-BIT.

3. Click OK to close the Media Creation settings.

4. Open the RENDER settings.

5. From the IMAGE INTERPOLATION menu, choose ADVANCED (POLYPHASE).

6. Click OK to close the Render settings.

To use ExpertRender:

1. Mark an IN and an OUT point around the effect(s) to render and select the track(s) containing the effect(s) to render in the TRACK SELECTOR panel.

2. Choose CLIP > EXPERTRENDER IN/OUT. A dialog box opens listing the number of effects to be rendered for the sequence to play and the effects ExpertRender has chosen to render are highlighted in the Timeline. See Figure 9.27.

Figure 9.27
The ExpertRender dialog box shows how many effects will be rendered.

Note: If no IN and OUT points exist, ExpertRender will only look at the effects on active tracks on which the blue position indicator is parked. The menu option will read ExpertRender at Position.

3. Choose the media volume where you want to store the rendered effect from the DRIVE pop-up menu. There are three things to note here:

- The volume with the most available space is in bold.

- Choosing the emptiest drive is not always the best solution. It is often better to designate a specific partition for specific items, such as effects, including Color Correction effects.

- The volume that contains the clip to which the effect is applied has a clip icon instead of a drive icon. This volume is called the Effect Source drive.

4. Click **OK**.

5. While the effect is rendering, press the **T** key on your keyboard to display an estimated rendering time for the effect.

Note: If you adjust color correction after rendering the effect, you must re-render the effect.

Notes from the Colorist: How To Run a Color-Correction Session

For the past couple hundred pages, you've spent a lot of time exploring how to *see* like a colorist, from setting up your room and reading waveforms to manipulating skin tones and controlling the viewer's eye. But now is a good time to write about the most difficult job you have when color correcting: running a productive color-grading session.

Color Correction: Thy Name Is Intimidation

Very few of us spend our lives discussing grayscale values, tonal ranges, hue vectors, or chrominance values. And neither do most of our clients. Yet, when our clients walk in the door, they are suddenly confronted with having to spend hours or even days communicating in this strange world, with its carefully controlled lighting and perfectly calibrated displays. They watch us commune with a screen filled with strange representations of their pictures as we mumble to ourselves about black levels, clipping, and gamma settings. They sit in our room, afraid as we pass judgment on the quality of their images or the camera they used. All this is to say our clients walk into a perfect storm of intimidation. Our first job is to relax them. This means we have to communicate with them. And our most important communication skill: listening.

Listen and Identify Stress Points

After the session starts, it shouldn't take long before you start hearing your clients' stress points. It could be overexposed scenes. Or one shot (or camera) that's completely mismatched from others. Maybe they're nervous that there's not enough time to get the job done. Whatever they start talking about first, don't dismiss it. They've been anticipating this moment for a very long time. All their concerns are valid until you can prove otherwise.

As you hear these stress points, take note. You'll want to address these concerns. I advise budgeting a short amount of time at the start of a color-grading session for bouncing around the Timeline and seeing what they want to show you. Just remember: It's too early in the session to get bogged down in any one of these concerns, so don't. Often, all you have to do is play down those areas, let the client talk, and silently decide for yourself whether it's productive (or will relax the client) to spend five minutes up front to see what kind of problem you've actually got. Just keep to the clock.

Let Clients Know When to Comment

One technique you'll use while color grading is pushing the colors and contrast beyond where you want to set them, just to see how the footage reacts and to help you settle where to place your final correction. This can confuse the heck out of your client. They'll try to comment in fits and starts as you keep passing through the range where you'll finally rest. Save them this confusion. Let them know what to expect. Teach them to give you a few moments to dial in the shot. It'll immediately help reduce their stress level and keep open lines of communication.

The Language of Color

Some clients get tongue-tied when communicating about what they want to see. They try speaking the colorist's language, but trip over themselves and get frustrated. I suggest you put them at ease by asking them to talk about how they *feel* about what they're seeing. Is it too cold or too warm? Does it feel dark or light? What is bothering them? They don't have to express themselves in hue and contrast, but in emotion and feeling.

This can be especially good advice for clients who start giving you extremely specific instructions, such as, "Can you add a point in the green curve and pull some blue out of the blacks?" Sometimes, this kind of instruction is helpful—but often it fixes one problem while destroying the overall shot. If this starts happening, recognize that they're giving you solutions. Finding solutions is your job, not theirs. Start asking what the problem they're trying to solve is. Once you understand the problem, you can usually find a better solution.

The Anatomy of a Color-Grading Session

It's also important that you know how to break down a color-grading session. It'll help you more accurately estimate the time you need to finish a job. I've found most jobs go through a few of five stages. (See Figure 9.28.) Not every job has every stage—and sometimes the distinctions between the stages get blurred. These stages start with prep and finish with the delivery of your final elements.

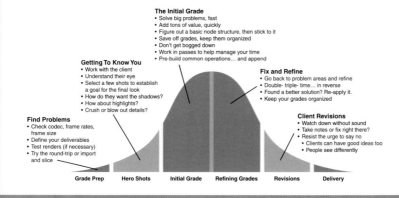

Figure 9.28
The five stages of a color-grading session.

The core of a grading session spans from the "getting to know you" stage through the "client revisions" stage. This is the time you spend actually color grading. In my experience, the bigger the budget, the more time you can spend on each of these stages and the better your final results. On some jobs, it's all one big blur as you race against the clock (and do the best job you can in a short period of time). The "find problems" stage is an important one for workflows in which the color grading is happening outside of Avid. In most sessions in Media Composer or Symphony, you won't need to deal with this chore, providing a speed advantage to Avid-based colorists.

The "delivery" stage is an interesting beast. It may take zero time for you, the colorist, as you simply hand off the project to an online editor. Or, it might take almost as long as the grading session itself if you're also handling various other duties, which can include graphics integration, audio mix layback, finalize lower thirds, and output to tape.

The Key to Estimating Time

The only way to accurately estimate time is to know your shot count. This is especially true for long-form projects, in which you have hundreds of shots to grade and match. If you don't know with certainty how quickly you actually grade, your time estimates will be consistently off—usually under. And that's bad for business and careers. To figure out your pace, keep track of shot counts (how many shots you get through in an hour or a day). Write this number down—and *keep* writing it down. Over time, you'll get to know yourself, and you'll be able to estimate how much time you need for each stage of a color-grading session.

—pi

Review/Discussion Questions

1. What is the purpose and value of applying a look?

2. Name two ways a look can be applied to a region of the Timeline, such as a scene.

3. Which method of adding a look is available in Media Composer?

4. Which parameters cannot be keyframed?

5. What is the difference between keyframing HSL and Curves adjustments?

6. Name two monochrome looks.

7. Describe the bleach-bypass effect.

8. What function enables you to apply the corrections from one sequence onto another?

9. Refer to the following illustration. What can you determine about the color levels of the image?

    a. The R, G, and B levels are too high.

    b. The luma levels exceed limits.

    c. The composite levels are too high.

    d. All levels are acceptable.

    e. None of the above.

10. On which track should you apply the Safe Color Limiter?

Lesson 9   Keyboard Shortcuts

Command/Action	Result
Command+ Y (Mac) or Ctrl +Y (Windows)	Adds a new video track
Command+Option+Y (Mac) or Ctrl+Alt+Y (Windows)	Opens the Add Track dialog box to add the video track of your choice
Add Edit*	Divides the current segment on all active tracks, including filler; useful for segmenting filler for scene-wide adjustments using the CC effect
Semicolon	By default, adds a keyframe at the current frame to all parameters
Ctrl+8	Opens the Effect Palette

* This function can be mapped to the key of your choice. For information on how to map your keyboard, see the article "Mapping User-Selectable Buttons" in the Media Composer or Symphony Help.

Creating Stylized Looks

In this exercise, you will use the techniques from the lesson to create stylized looks on the footage while ensuring they remain within safe color limits. In addition, you will merge a previous grade to the current sequence to leverage work you did earlier in the course.

Media Used:

Avid Color Grading (MC239) project > 2_Exercise Bins folder > Ex9_Creating Looks Exercise bin > Ex9_Stylized Looks sequence, Ex9_Poker Scene.Final Grade sequence

Duration:

60 minutes

GOALS

- Create different image looks
- Perform keyframe adjustments
- Merge relationships across sequences

Overview

Unlike previous exercises, your goal on this exercise is to create a wide variety of image treatments (looks) rather than working to create a consistent image across an entire sequence. This will enable you to explore the range of possibilities for this footage. In the second part of the exercise, you will merge sequences, apply the treatment of your choice to a larger scene, and ensure safe delivery levels.

As you work, here are some key points to keep in mind:

- Be on the lookout for noise and artifacts. Go gentle with your adjustments!

- The "recipes" for each lesson are *starting* points. You will want to tweak the values based on the unique tonal range in each image.

Part 1: Creating Stylized Looks

To begin the exercise:

1. Open the project AVID COLOR GRADING (239) and the bin EX9_CREATING LOOKS.

2. Load the sequence EX9_STYLIZED LOOKS. This sequence has groups of shots taken from the different scenes in the film that you've graded in other lessons. You will create a different look for each group of shots.

3. Choose TOOLS > MARKERS to open the Markers tool. The list of markers identifies the look to be created on each group of shots in the sequence.

4. Open the Correction Mode settings and enable the USE MARKS FOR SEGMENT CORRECTION option.

5. Create each look identified on the markers using a program segment relationship. As you grade, reference the "recipes" provided in the section "Creating Popular Looks."

6. For each look you create, save a template to the bin.

Part 2: Preparing a Final Sequence (Symphony Only)

In this exercise, you will merge the corrections from two sequences, using a sequence you graded in Exercise 7. Because source segment corrections cannot be merged, you may wish to alter the corrections on that sequence if you used the source segment relationship extensively. Either way, the merging process will be the same, though the results may differ significantly.

To begin the exercise:

1. Select the **SOURCE/RECORD** workspace.

2. From the **Ex9_CREATING LOOKS EXERCISE** bin, load the **Ex9_POKER GAME.FINAL GRADE** sequence. This sequence is not graded.

3. Locate and open the bin containing the sequence **Ex7_SECONDARIES_ POKER GAME**. This is the grade you completed on the poker scene with both primary and secondary corrections in place.

4. Load the **Ex7_SECONDARIES_POKER GAME** sequence into the Source window.

5. Enter **COLOR CORRECTION** mode; then merge the grades to update the current sequence.

6. Add a video track and apply the template to the sequence as a filler-based correction.

7. Examine the sequence for shots that need further adjustments.

8. Either keyframe the adjustments needed or divide the effect with add edits and tweak the grade for those shots.

Answers to
Review/Discussion Questions

Lesson 1 Answers

1. A properly calibrated viewing monitor, lighting of the correct color temperature, a neutral gray wall behind the monitor, and an external waveform/vectorscope

2. Because everything you do in color grading is based on what you see in the picture. If the monitor isn't showing you an accurate representation of the media, you may incorrectly grade the shot.

3. The wrong gamma, which means the black detail will not be correctly represented; the wrong gamut, which means the color space will not be correctly displayed, resulting in colors being either not properly saturated or shifted in tone; and the wrong color temperature, typically meaning that the grayscale is much bluer than desired

4. The answer to this question depends on the display being used by the reader or student.

5. 6,500° Kelvin, commonly written as D65

6. The wall provides an accurate frame of reference for neutral color.

7. You can manipulate more than one parameter simultaneously.

8. Setting the baseline grade, achieving shot-to-shot consistency, and achieving a final look.

9. So you can get a sense of the kinds of corrections required and plan your approach

10. So you can see the full detail of the shots you are working with

11. Click the Color Correction Mode button in the Timeline or switch to the Color Correction toolset.

12. In Media Composer they appear as Color Correction effects, while in Symphony they appear as colored horizontal lines at the bottom of the corrected clip.

Lesson 2 Answers

1. Increased contrast in any region of the image attracts the viewer's eye to that region. Increased contrast appears to sharpen the image.

2. Saturation decreases as the luminance approaches the white point or black point.

3. a

4. The RGB Parade displays the waveforms of the component red, green, and blue video signals.

5. The RGB Parade can be used to determine the balance of the black or white point by comparing the position of the traces of white or black objects in the scene. If the corresponding traces are aligned, the tone is balanced.

6. The I-line, which is at approximately the 11 o'clock position on the Avid internal Vectorscope, is a standard reference for proper skin tones. This can be used to verify or correct the skin tones such that the traces aggregate along the I-line.

7. d

8. e

9. The YC Waveform is useful for verifying that the composite luma and chroma signal falls within the limits of the delivery specification, as set in the Safe Colors setting.

10. Out-of-range values can be manually corrected or clamped by the Safe Color Limiter effect.

Lesson 3 Answers

1. Hue, Saturation, Luminance

2. The principal tonal controls are Gain, Gamma, and Setup. They are found on the Controls tab in Symphony and on the Hue Offsets tab in Media Composer.

3. The chroma controls are the Hue Offset wheels. They are on the Hue Offsets tab in both applications.

4. The recommended workflow for setting the luma range is to: 1. Set the black point using Setup; 2. Set the white point using Gain; 3. Adjust the midtones of the shot using Gamma.

5. The black point is the darkest point in the image; the white point is the brightest. These are not necessarily black and white in color.

6. The parameter adjustment that most strongly affects the mood of the shot is the midtone gamma adjustment.

7. Shadows with a blue cast would have an elevated trace group in the blue channel of the RGB Parade as compared to relatively even red and green channels.

8. To correct a blue shadow cast, drag the crosshair pointer of the Shd Hue Offset wheel toward yellow until the R, G, and B levels even out.

9. The Color Match controls can be used to get precise RGB data on any point in the image. Drag from the Input or Output color well to the object in the image; release the mouse button to sample the image.

10. Saturation should be adjusted after everything else.

Lesson 4 Answers

1. False. In the RGB color space, luma and chroma are not separate signals.

2. Increasing contrast appears to sharpen the image. It also draws the eye of the viewer.

3. Increase the angle of the master curve to increase contrast over the whole image.

4. To increase contrast within a portion of the luma range, increase the angle of the curve within that region. This is typically done through an S-curve.

5. RGB curves are processed before the master curve.

6. HSL is processed before Curves.

7. a

8. c

9. a, b, and c

10. To make fine adjustments, you can alter the input or output value. You can also Shift-drag the control point to slide it without altering its deviation value.

11. To improve sampling response, enable the Eyedropper 3×3 Averaging option.

12. When balancing a strong color cast, balance the strong and weak signal to the middle signal.

13. c

Lesson 5 Answers

1. Automatic color matching; correction templates; manual eye-matching

2. Possible reasons may include the following:

   • The correction produces unwanted results to other objects in frame because it applies to the entire image, not only to the object of interest within the frame.

   • The differences in lighting and tonal values throughout the image are too great to be matched effectively.

   • There is insufficient latitude (limited color information) in the shot being corrected.

   • A perfect match in RGB values produces a visual mismatch due to simultaneous contrast.

3. D: Manually grade the shots with the least latitude and match shots with more latitude to them.

4. The color to be corrected should be sampled as the input color.

5. The Input color swatch is the one on the left.

6. a

7. Double-click the Output color swatch.

8. NaturalMatch is available in the Curves group.

9. NaturalMatch corrects only hue and saturation, not luma. Standard color matching corrects all three.

10. A template saved to the bin is permanent. One saved to a correction bucket is saved only during the current session.

Lesson 6 Answers

1. Symphony adds subtabs to the Controls group for shadows, midtones, and highlights; a fourth Master tab; a hue offset wheel; and the Luma Ranges controls.

2. c

3. Luma Ranges controls enable you to change the values that define the highlights, midtones, and shadows in an image to customize how the other HSL controls will affect the image.

4. a, b, and d

5. Curves graphs in Levels have only one midtone control point. The graphs in the Curves group can have as many as 16 points. In Levels, each graph is on its own tab; in Curves, they are all visible concurrently.

6. Correction relationships primarily speed the grading process by allowing the grade from a single segment to be applied to many others automatically through source relationships.

7. Relationships are combined and processed into the final image.

8. Any source correction relationship except for Src Segment (for example, Src Tape) and Program Segment.

9. The Channels group is used to repair damaged or deficient video signals by borrowing from stronger component signals.

10. The advantages of grading in Symphony include the added features/functions of correction relationships; additional HSL controls for shadow, midtones, and highlights, plus luma ranges; and the Channels and Secondary groups. Together, they enable the user to grade faster, with greater control and higher image quality.

Lesson 7 Answers

1. Secondary group, HSL Luma Ranges, Paint Effect, Spot Color Effect, AniMatte

2. Qualification isolates a portion of the image for secondary correction.

3. The luma range curves can be adjusted to isolate the target values within the shadow, midtone, and highlight range.

4. Changing the luma range curves has no impact on the image until other HSL controls are changed.

5. The advantage of luma and chroma qualification is that the qualification adapts automatically to the moving image. The disadvantage is that elements within the image that share the same luma or chroma values will be included in the selection, regardless of whether they are intended for secondary correction.

6. Chroma qualification

7. 12 vectors; six standard, six custom

8. Syringe

9. c

10. d

11. Isolate Vector

12. Define the input hue using a standard or custom vector; then offset the hue using the output vector color wheel or output Hue slider.

Lesson 8 Answers

1. Spot Color Effect, Paint Effect, and AniMatte

2. Intraframe effects create an effect by altering the pixels within a user-defined shape. The drawing tools are common to all Intraframe effects, as are the built-in tracking tools.

3. False. Intraframe effects are in both Media Composer and Symphony.

4. The Poly tool

5. Using the Paint Effect, create a large rectangle that creates the effect—darken, desaturate, etc.—and a second shape inside as a hold-out mask, set to Erase.

6. The Paint Effect

7. Magic Mask limits the pixels affected within a shape by qualifying the luminance, hue, or saturation (chroma and/or luma qualification).

8. One; two tracers minimum

9. Pixels of high contrast

10. Paint, AniMatte

Lesson 9 Answers

1. To create a stylized look to distinguish the program and/or support the emotional arc through color

2. A look can be applied as a program segment correction to a marked region if the Correction setting is enabled; it can also be applied using a CC effect to a filler track.

3. The Color Correction effect method is available in Media Composer.

4. HSL Luma Ranges and Channels

5. HSL value changes can be made in the Effect Editor or the Color Correction tool. Curves adjustments can be made only in the Color Correction tool.

6. Black and white; sepia; film noir

7. Bleach bypass is a high-contrast, low-saturation effect.

8. The Merge Correction function enables you to update corrections from one sequence to another.

9. c

10. A top track that contains filler only

INDEX

<u>Notes</u>

Notes

Notes

Notes